STRAIGHT POWER CONCEPTS IN THE MIDDLE EAST

Straight Power Concepts in the Middle East

US Foreign Policy, Israel, and World History

Gregory Harms

PlutoPress
www.plutobooks.com

First published 2010 by Pluto Press
345 Archway Road, London N6 5AA and
175 Fifth Avenue, New York, NY 10010

Distributed in the United States of America exclusively by
Palgrave Macmillan, a division of St. Martin's Press LLC,
175 Fifth Avenue, New York, NY 10010

www.plutobooks.com

The right of Gregory Harms to be identified as the author of this work
has been asserted by him in accordance with the Copyright, Designs and
Patents Act 1988.

British Library Cataloguing in Publication Data
A catalogue record for this book is available from the British Library

ISBN   978 0 7453 2710 5   Hardback
ISBN   978 0 7453 2709 9   Paperback

Library of Congress Cataloging in Publication Data applied for

This book is printed on paper suitable for recycling and made from fully
managed and sustained forest sources. Logging, pulping and manufactur-
ing processes are expected to conform to the environmental standards of
the country of origin.

10 9 8 7 6 5 4 3 2 1
Designed and produced for Pluto Press by
Curran Publishing Services, Norwich

Printed and bound in the European Union by
CPI Antony Rowe, Chippenham and Eastbourne

CONTENTS

ACKNOWLEDGMENTS

Many thanks are owed to Roger van Zwanenberg for immediately supporting this project, as well as to David Castle and everyone at Pluto Press.

Regarding time spent in Israel and the West Bank in late 2005, I owe sincere gratitude to: Dr. Mohammad "Mo" Hishmeh and family, Abdallah Jibreen and family, Ammar Sameeh and family, and friends Peter Muller and Megan Clark. On other legs of the same trip that took me just into 2006, the following individuals and families are owed my thanks and appreciation: in Amman, Jordan: Nabil and Wael Makahleh and family, Hani al-Rifae and friends (Hotel Farah), Alex Ma'louf, and Devin Murphy. In Cairo and the Sinai Peninsula: Jake Wells, Abed Zant, the Iyad Essa family, and the Windsor Hotel Cairo—a warm and friendly place to hang a weary hat.

I am thankful to Walter Opello and Stephen Rosow for their reading of and suggestions for Chapter 1. Deborah Kisatsky's detailed and thoughtful evaluation of Chapter 2 strengthened it significantly. David Lesch provided an incisive critique of Chapter 4. I am indebted to Jeremy Pressman for his careful and honest review of Chapter 5. (These scholars did not always agree with my approach and/or particular interpretations and bear no responsibility for the end result of these chapters, only for improving them.) Arthur Goldschmidt, who will also not entirely agree with my analyses and renderings in this book, imparted valuable advice and has been a mentor and a friend.

To the usual suspects I owe immense appreciation for their time and dedication: Scott Darley, Steve DeBretto, Mark Eleveld, Todd Ferry, and Michael Slager. Tom Jasper is the key reason this book was started when it was, and without him it simply would not have been possible. At the same time, Givon and Madison Jasper made ideal companions in our religious weekly viewings of *Doctor Who* at 116. To Darryl Nephew I owe considerable gratitude for his friendship, support, and chess camaraderie. Much appreciation goes to the Frattini family for keeping me well fed. Many thanks and years worth of gratefulness go to my mother, Martha. To my father, Joseph, and the continued spirit of the farm I am, to say the very least, thankful. To my sister, Lauren, and her generation, you have my apologies and my faith.

Professor Tanya Reinhart (1943–2007) refereed this project's initial proposal, gave it her endorsement, but never saw the result. I can only hope it would have met with her approval.

Gregory Harms

We should dispense with the aspiration to "be liked" or to be regarded as the repository of a high-minded international altruism. We should stop putting ourselves in the position of being our brothers' keeper and refrain from offering moral and ideological advice. We should cease to talk about vague ... unreal objectives such as human rights, the raising of the living standards, and democratization. The day is not far off when we are going to have to deal in straight power concepts. The less we are then hampered by idealistic slogans, the better.

GEORGE F. KENNAN

Head of the US State Department Policy Planning Staff, 1947–49*

---

* Policy Planning Staff report PPS/23, February 24, 1948. See US Department of State, *Foreign Relations of the United States, 1948*, vol. 1, part 2: *General; The United Nations* (Washington, DC: GPO, 1976), 525.

PREFACE

My point is not that we must, in telling history, accuse, judge, condemn Columbus *in absentia*. It is too late for that; it would be a useless scholarly exercise in morality. But the easy acceptance of atrocities as a deplorable but necessary price to pay for progress ... —that is still with us. One reason these atrocities are still with us is that we have learned to bury them in a mass of other facts, as radioactive wastes are buried in containers in the earth. We have learned to give them exactly the same proportion of attention that teachers and writers often give them in the most respectable of classrooms and text-books. This learned sense of moral proportion, coming from the apparent objectivity of the scholar, is accepted more easily than when it comes from politicians at press conferences. It is therefore more deadly.[1]

Howard Zinn, *A People's History of the United States*

The title of this book is taken from a declassified document in which one of America's chief architects of Cold War policy elucidates in a top secret report how strategy should be carried out in, in this case, East Asia. The unvarnished honesty in the quote by George Kennan (on page ix) is an adequate picture of the mentality that has driven how the United States has conducted its affairs across the globe, especially in the Third World. What would commence in Korea, Vietnam, and Indochina not long after the report was filed serves as verification that this kind of thinking was both representative and taken quite seriously among planners. As one traces the basic contours of American foreign relations, George Kennan's remarks are summoned repeatedly. Given this relative consistency, the validity of the frequent argumentation and dispute over America's various foreign undertakings—past and present—is naturally called into question.

Discussion of American involvement in the Middle East, and in particular its connection with Israel, is no less the subject of debate. But as in most cases, there is an inversely proportional relation-ship between facts and opinion: where one predominates, the other plays a marginal role. While legitimate disputes can and do exist, on balance the fundamental historical record is rather clear, and if attended to can narrow the space for contention.

The purpose of this project is to provide an introduction to

US foreign policy that is connected with world history, American history, and current events. Its objective will be to link three normally isolated subjects into a single narrative. Moving from the general to the particular, the subjects are: the advent of the European nation-state, the birth and growth of the United States into a world power, and America's eventual intervention in the Middle East and its "special relationship" with Israel. Placing these histories in a cohesive chronology allows us to see patterns of how political, economic, and military power tend to be wielded in the international arena. Much of what we see in the news concerning warfare, conflict, and human rights abuses is the result of policy. But without a sense of history, each episode can be (and usually is) successfully explained away by heads of state and commentators as being exceptional, with the attendant avalanche of contemporaneous details. History allows consistency and continuity to emerge.

In other words, what plagues discussion of US foreign relations and their contact with the Middle East is lack of context. America's association with Israel, specifically, can only be understood within the when, why, and how of Washington, DC, coming to play the role it does in the region. If we proceed with that simple line of inquiry—virtually nowhere to be found in the televised discourse—US interests there raise a number of questions, including: How and why did the United States become a superpower projecting its influence across the globe? And what were the circumstances in the Middle East prior to Uncle Sam's arrival? As we trace these chronicles to their origins we arrive at the genesis of the nation-state.

In examining *foreign* policy and *international* relations, our investigation stands to benefit from surveying at least the foundations of how nations came to be and why world maps require at least four colors of ink (and one for the water). The parallel evolution of the state and the global capitalist economy is the subject of Chapter 1. Once we have a rudimentary sense of this evolution, the behaviors of particular countries should appear as a continuation of this historical process, a process that could just as well not have been initiated, and not as something that is simply given and intrinsic to humanity's needs. Countries are relatively new creations, and were forged in the fires of inconceivable European violence and destruction. They are not predetermined, indispensable, or necessarily permanent.

Our study is primarily concerned though with a specific nation-state, one that is an offshoot of the original community of modern

states (Western Europe), and one that ended up surpassing its forebears in size, power, and prestige. In Chapter 2 we examine this
trajectory, from the Founding Fathers to the Cold War. The United
States, originally a British colony in the New World, followed a
path that, in less than 150 years, delivered it to global supremacy.
In taking stock of the sweep of America's expansion, certain regu-
larities of behavior become discernible throughout its foreign policy
history. It is in these currents and courses of action that one can
begin to comprehend what the country's leadership has valued,
pursued, and avoided over the eras. By the time the United States
gets to the Middle East after World War II, rough and general
forecasts can be made with reasonable safety.

Chapter 3 sets the stage for the rest of the book, containing a
review of how the modern Middle East emerged as a geopolitical
subsystem divided into European-style nation-states, how Israel
entered the regional scene, and how the Palestine–Israel and Arab–
Israeli conflicts developed.

Chapter 4 is an account of US involvement in the Middle East,
the establishment of Washington's firm alliance with Israel, and
what these configurations have meant for the area. A continuation
of the first three chapters, this chapter looks first at US replacement
of British and French primacy in the region, American corporate oil
interests there, and the pursuit of Washington's strategic concerns
by way of the various concepts covered in Chapter 2. The US–Israeli
relationship then becomes the focus of this chapter, examining the
role the Jewish state has played as a client in the service of American
regional designs.

After tracing the background of US hegemony in the Arab
Middle East, the book continues to narrow in scope in Chapters 5
and 6 by taking two particular issues surrounding US sponsorship
of Israel which further illustrate the larger aspects of our study of
American state power. The peace process, as a view into the arena
of diplomacy, is outlined from the beginning of Israel's occupation
of the Palestinian territories (1967) to the Bush II administration.
A second outline is performed on the recent controversy over the
degree of influence the domestic pro-Israel lobby in Washington
holds over US foreign policy with respect to the Jewish state
and its Arab neighbors. Particular attention here is paid to John
Mearsheimer and Stephen Walt's work *The Israel Lobby* (2007) and
the responses it generated.

My hope is that *Straight Power Concepts* will serve as both
a map for those looking to see US–Middle Eastern relations in a

less mystified/controversial and more rational/historical light, and also as perhaps a rough method of approach for those looking to study similar subjects. The pervasive uncertainty among Americans regarding their country's foreign policy, especially as it pertains to the Middle East, is confirmation that history has been left out of the picture, despite the unremitting news coverage and commentary. We keep watching—ABC, CBS, MSNBC, CNN, FOX—but we are not being informed. Most Americans are disillusioned with the operations in Afghanistan and Iraq. However, it is a reasonable guess that if the population had been routinely shown what was happening in these places in precise detail—the kind of detail that is seldom spared when the stakes are between low and nonexistent, pick a topic—withdrawal would have been prompt. (Armed with a basic education before the fact, it is difficult to imagine deployment at all.) The same sort of principle obtains concerning the larger picture of our foreign policy. If we knew the realities, new ones would presumably take their place, in accordance with popular demands. It has been my ambition in this project to contribute to what the major news networks and commentators, either unwittingly or with the strictest discipline, are remiss in confronting.

Gregory Harms
December 2009

PART 1

HISTORY AND CONTEXT

1

FROM EMPIRE TO NATION-STATE: THE GENESIS OF MODERNITY'S 500 YEARS

In his *Politics*, Aristotle imparts sound and simple advice: "He who thus considers things in their first growth and origin, whether a state or anything else, will obtain the clearest view of them" (bk. I, ch. 2). For our investigation into the relationships between the United States, the Middle East, and Israel, the Greek philosopher's suggestion will serve as a guiding principle. Though most surveys of the alliance might start with the post-1945 period, tracing the history according to Israel's development from its birth in 1948, the approach here—which might seem peculiar at first—will instead be to begin with a world history perspective in the context of the birth of modern Europe and its contact with the New World in 1492. There is much benefit in pulling back and allowing ourselves to see patterns over long segments of time. When larger, systemic relationships can be identified over centuries, the particular topics of our study are made much easier to analyze and therefore much easier to comprehend. An historical event is far more than the sum of its parts; and while those parts are vital, so too is the whole of the total event as well as its ambient historical context.

THE WORLD-SYSTEMS FRAMEWORK

Given our goal of establishing a wide perspective in which to work, it will be beneficial to identify where we are located in the awesome expanse of world history. Therefore a framework of insight allowing for broad examination will be valuable, but one that does not impose ideological constraints. One such approach to understanding world history in its totality, established in the 1970s (though certainly working from and adding on to previously existing modes of analysis) is that of "world-systems" analysis.

Those scholars who developed this method operate from the observation that the current political and economic configuration of the world has its roots in the sixteenth century. Instead of viewing the history of global operations as a daily set of discrete national activities, world-systems analysts identify a global interdependence, one that began with Europe's conquest of the New World. According to world-systems pioneer Immanuel Wallerstein:

> World-systems analysis meant first of all the substitution of a unit of analysis called the "world system" for the standard unit of analysis, which was the national state. On the whole, historians had been analyzing national histories, economists national economies, political scientists national political structures, and sociologists national societies. World-systems analysts raised a skeptical eyebrow, questioning whether any of these objects really existed, and in any case whether they were the most useful loci of analysis. Instead of national states as the object of study, they substituted "historical systems."[1]

So what do we see when we look beyond individual national histories (for example, the story of Guatemala and its relations with its neighbors), and instead cast our view over the development of modern states and how they interact within an encompassing system (for instance, the story of why there are countries, one of which is called Guatemala, and where it stands in relation to the world-system)?

As mentioned, the temporal fulcrum that the world-systems analysts focus on is the sixteenth century, or what Wallerstein calls the "long sixteenth century" (1450–1620). Prior to Columbus's arrival in the Bahamas the world existed as a system of world-empires. Each empire was a self-contained political unit. It engaged in some trade with neighboring empires, but the essential economic operation was the farming of taxes from the rural, agrarian peasantry. Empires therefore spread to the boundary limit where they could effectively exert power and collect taxes and tribute. Unlike modern states, empires' boundaries were rather fluid and adjusted with the times. The state machinery was highly centralized, usually managed by hereditary elites, and as a result of the similitude from one empire to the next, a rough balance and equivalence in power was struck; no one empire had any significant upper hand in the areas of technology, defense, economy, and politics. This of course is not to suggest that empires did not fall and get scooped up or divided by others. In general, however, the system of world-empires was a more or less stable one existing from before recorded history to roughly the 1500s.

Western Europe at this time began to undergo economic stagnation. What is referred to as the "crisis of feudalism" (c. 1300–1450) marks for some analysts and historians the threshold between the late Middle Ages and the modern period. Brought on or accompanied by famine, peasant revolts, the Black Death, and increased competition, this stagnation spurred regional powers to begin to consider the possibilities beyond the Mediterranean Sea in search of a solution to the crisis. Europe saw fit to expand the stage so as to open broader markets, gain access to gold bullion, and acquire sources of food and raw materials. Furthermore, the technology was also available—three-masted sailing ships and firearms being key innovations—to allow for further exploration and the projection of power over less-developed cultures. It was in this transition that the global configuration shifted from a world-empires system to the modern world-system, or world economy, composed of sovereign states. Though hardly an overnight transformation, as of the sixteenth century the way Western Europe did business began to change, and the world along with it.

In the system of world-empires those who derived wealth and power were the very elites to whom the empire belonged. Farmers and craftsmen, on the other hand, produced a product, sold that product, and hoped to make enough to pay for food, taxes owed, and materials for further production. In other words, the market existed for the sake of subsistence; if anyone was coming out ahead it was the ruling class. But the changes that were occurring in the sixteenth century catalyzed a massive economic reordering that remains today. The primary catalyst was the ability and desire to seek markets on a global scale. It was in everyone's best interest, from laborers to the ruling elite, to produce for the worldwide market. Increased revenue helped the governments that were emerging out of constant conflict in Western Europe to fund such conflict, and the people involved in agriculture and the trades obviously benefited from a broader source of income. Out of this transition came forth a novel idea: Instead of generating enough income to merely subsist, global access spelled the opportunity for limitless accumulation of capital. Prior to this time surplus income was generally in the hands of the ruling class, whereas the subject class, if indeed they did make any surplus monies, usually reinvested it in their businesses. But with accrual of capital being the primary objective of the burgeoning capitalist merchant class, reinvestment became another means of creating income. Thus, the capitalist world-system began to take shape.

Two key aspects of the modern world economy, both of which are mutually dependent, are the sovereign state and capitalism. As Spain and Portugal made colonial contact with South and Central America, as well as gaining access to Asian and African markets, the powers in Western Europe began to consolidate their holdings. In neither a quick nor tidy manner, the Europe that now exists on maps began to unfold. Also, the parallel development of the state-based political structure and the capitalist world economy revealed another essential component of the modern world-system: the world division of labor.

By the mid-1500s the world-system was split roughly three ways according to "production processes." Western Europe—taken here to mean Spain (under the Spanish Habsburgs), Portugal, Britain, and France—emerged as the *core* of the world-system. The core of the world-system is composed of states that are technologically, militarily, and economically more developed, and as a result are able to dictate relational terms to the rest of the world-system. The core establishes markets in which it can sell exported manufactured goods and in return secure raw materials to maintain production in factories. Today, Western Europe still exists in the core, along with the United States and Japan.

The second economic zone is referred to as the *periphery*. The peripheral states and regions are less developed, less organized, militarily weaker, and exist solely to benefit the core. South-Central America and Eastern Europe were the original peripheral zones, but over the centuries the periphery came also to include Africa and much of Asia. Today, some parts of South America and Asia exhibit traits of both zones. World-systems analysts include a third zone in the global production processes, which consists of states producing both core-like and peripheral-like products, and that share general characteristics of both those zones. These states are classified as *semi-peripheral*. Some twenty-first-century examples of semi-peripheral states are Brazil and India.

In the following sections, we will move from the more abstract descriptions above to look at some of the historical contours with which our world-systems framework corresponds.

LAND WORLD-EMPIRES

The world of sovereign states and its correlating capitalist world-system constitute a fairly recent development in human history. It was not until the last two or three hundred years that the present interstate system fully got under way. As mentioned, preceding this modern configuration was a world loosely organized by world-empires. However, the word "empire" can take on an array of meanings as well as apply to various eras, and therefore we should be clear about its usage. In addition, the designations "ancient" and "modern" also require some clarification.

The words "empire" and "imperial" (and "imperialism") frequently crop up in our everyday usage. Talk of corporate empires, or America's imperial behavior, or British imperialism, surrounds us, but meanings can be myriad and change over time. Even among writers and scholars there exist different approaches and debates on the subject. For the purpose of describing the dominant political structure previous to that of sovereign states, our use of "empire" (from the Latin *imperium*, meaning authority or command) will edge towards the traditional and the general, specifying a vast political unit comprised of multiple territories and subject peoples, and one ruled from a highly centralized locus of power, typically an emperor. This description will also incorporate the adjective "imperial." Likewise, the ideology of imperialism (owing to its -ism suffix) will simply denote the *imperial* thoughts, desires, and philosophies behind the creation and expansion of such systems.

Similarly, the terms "ancient" and (especially) "modern" are used in a variety of meanings and contexts. In keeping with our remote look at world history, it will suffice to adhere to the periodic divisions generally agreed upon by historians when attempting to map key benchmarks in the Western world. The ancient period can basically be sectioned off between 3000 BC and 500 AD. The fall of the western half of the Roman Empire marks the beginning of the medieval (from the Latin *medium aevum*, meaning middle age) period, or Middle Ages, from 500 to 1500. The past half-millennium, beginning with Western Europe's arrival in the New World, the dawn of overseas empires, and the Reformation, encapsulates the modern period, from 1500 to the present. This tripartite division will serve as a loose frame of reference, though it should be noted that such periodizations are merely historiographic devices used by scholars to aid them in understanding their material, and are neither divisions within the history itself nor precise demarcations. Similar to the variance and disagreements with the use of empire and imperial, scholarly debate continues regarding periodization, as well as the seemingly endless subdivisions that are also employed, for example, "early modernity." Nevertheless, this rudimentary vocabulary will suit our purposes in looking at the transition between the ancient world-empire system and the modern world-system.

It is far back into the ancient period, or antiquity, that we can trace empire's roots as the predominant and most influential political structure. As early as the first civilizations inhabiting Mesopotamia (present-day Iraq) one can see the advent of such systems. Though perhaps not as vast or sophisticated as the Persian or Roman empires 2–3,000 years later, the city-states in Sumer (c. 3500–2400 BC) serve as prototypes for what we see develop later throughout the ancient world. Their narrative introduces us to powerful, semi-legendary figures such as Sargon, the Akkadian conqueror of Sumer, and the Amorite king of Babylon (a Sumerian city-state), Hammurabi—known best perhaps for his law of retaliation (*lex talionis*), or "eye for an eye." The conquering, expansionism, and subjection that characterized the early politico-military activity in Mesopotamia applies, if perhaps loosely, to our concept of empire. However, it is not until the tenth century BC that we start to see the onset of polities that fit squarely within our scheme.

In approximately 900 BC the Assyrians, a civilization that developed formidable military power after centuries of living under external forces, forged an empire that approximated their desires. With a determined, expansionist mindset the empire grew from a cluster of humble localities along the Tigris into an imperial arc stretching from Egypt up through modern Israel/Palestine, and into Syria and north-central Iraq. In efforts to control trade routes between western Asia and the eastern Mediterranean, the Assyrian Empire became what is termed a "universal" power. Proving that draconian ruthlessness achieves results (at least for a while), the Assyrian leadership ruled with a brutality considered excessive even for the time. Their empire was characterized by massive deportations, and various torture and killing techniques. But fear eventually turns to hatred, and as the empire slowed down for various reasons, the list of enemies it had accrued was ready and willing to help bring the Assyrians to their knees. After the empire fell in 612 BC, Mesopotamia returned more or less to its independent, pre-imperial way of life. The next unifying political force to sweep across the region took a less tyrannical approach and would change the Near East and Western civilization forever.

The Persians, a group that came from modern-day Iran, formed a vast empire sprawling from northern Africa to the Indus River winding through modern-day Pakistan. Their empire, which started in 539 BC under the Achaemenids, would only last 200 years, succumbing to internal conflict, corruption, and finally defeat by Alexander the Great in the Battle of Issus. However, in this relatively short period of time (roughly the duration of the United States' existence so far) the Persian Empire managed to unify much of the Middle East. Economically, politically, geographically (with the construction of highways and systems to transmit information), the empire's vast groups of subject peoples began to think regionally instead of tending exclusively to independent entities at the local level. As world historian J. M. Roberts notes, "In so far as the story of antiquity has a turning point, this is it. An independent Mesopotamian tradition going back to Sumer was over. We are at the edge of a new world."[2]

Similar developments and innovations were taking place around this time in those regions that would eventually become the modern states of China and India. Egypt in the ancient period offers much to study as a long-standing, powerful empire, yet as with China and India, it lies beyond our focus due to its relative insularity and existence outside our historical path of inquiry. It should also be mentioned that in Africa, generally speaking, there is not much in the way that adheres to our use of empire. The continent's political landscape was characterized more by individual monarchical polities and urban centers, with higher concentrations in the northwest. Likewise, this holds true for the Americas, where large-scale formations are not visible until later, with the emergence of groups like the Maya in the first millennium AD and the Aztecs and Incas in the early second. For our goal of tracing the pedigree of Western Europe's eventual supremacy, the ancient Near East is where our tale begins, for it was the social, political, and military activity in Mesopotamia that provided the matrix for Greco-Roman culture, which in turn was the crucible of Western modernity.

Roughly 4,000 years ago, the region surrounding the Aegean Sea, lying between modern-day Greece and Turkey, began to serve as host to such cultures as the Minoan and the Mycenaean civilizations. The group that would make the biggest impact, however, became the

Hellenes, centuries later referred to by the Romans as the Greeks. By the end of what is termed the Aegean or Greek Dark Age (c. 1200–800 BC), a period marking the rise of Greek prominence in the region, the beginning of what is known as classical Greece occurs. The period of 750–550 BC coincides with the Greek development of, and subdivision into, sovereign territories, as well as expansion into autonomous "colonies" that developed along the coasts of the Mediterranean and Black seas. The city-state, or *polis* (the source of our term "politics"), served as the nucleus of social and political life. Governance was participatory, but predominantly for wealthy, educated males. Nevertheless, it is in this city-state structure that the first signs of democracy (from the Greek *demos*, meaning "people") start to appear. But similar to privilege being concentrated along the lines of patriarchy and wealth, this semblance of democratic process was tempered with a system of oligarchy, placing ultimate executive power in the hands of a few (*oligos*). Despite these mitigating forces preventing too much democracy, the development is a noteworthy one, especially given the age. Of course, city-states varied as to how egalitarian or inegalitarian their political processes were—the most commonly known and sharply contrasting examples being Athens (more so) and Sparta (less so). In the main these political units functioned as a national community (save for the servant and slave classes), where people who would have merely been subjects were instead citizens playing a direct and instrumental role in their polis' overall operations.

Regardless of the orderly and relatively civilized interior political situation within the city-states, their foreign policies were nothing resembling anything orderly or civilized, and would ultimately lead to their demise. The location of the Aegean region—as a some-what protected and secluded hamlet—aided in the prevention of foreign invasion. The attrition of near-constant battling among the city-states, however, eventually led to their weakening, the most critical and well-known episode being the Peloponnesian War (431–404 BC). This internecine strife and conflict in general helped usher in hegemony by Macedonia, an adjacent territory to the north.

The Macedonian king, Philip II, planned to extend his power eastward into Asia Minor (modern-day Turkey) and Persia, a task later carried out with aplomb by his legendary son, Alexander III ("the Great"), with the aid of the Greek city-states corralled by Macedonian influence. Alexander, for a brief period, created an embryonic universal empire on the scale of what the Persians had achieved, stretching from Egypt across Mesopotamia, into Persia and Pakistan. But his notion of a single world would last only until his death (in 323 BC, at age 32). The influence and reach of Alexander's conquests inaugurated the period of what historians call Hellenism. With Greeks living and operating from the far-western Mediterranean shores to now being scattered across the Middle East, the attendant mingling of Greek and oriental* cultures had a lasting effect on the region.

In the political and economic spheres, on the other hand, regional developments were perhaps slightly less "Hellenistic." After Alexander's death, his empire fragmented into a chain of large "states," ones much larger than the average Greek city-state. Unlike the democratic/oligarchic systems found in the Aegean, these Hellenistic states, as they are called, were administered according to absolute rule by a hereditary monarchy—presumably a more efficient means of running a larger, more heavily populated geopolitical unit.

The large city, or *metropolis*, became the epicenter of civilized life and sprouted up across the Middle East, a variation on the polis theme. The enormity of these urban centers, such as Alexandria in Egypt, expanded enterprise and production, creating an economic network that spanned the entire region as far east as India. The composite attributes of the Hellenistic world would next be transmitted westward via an imperial power that would surpass all before it, and with its demise precipitate the West's odyssey into the modern age.

ANCIENT ROME: REPUBLIC, EMPIRE

The link between the system of world-empires and the initial subdivision of Europe into territorial, pre-modern states is the Roman Empire, the last and greatest of its kind in the context of Western civilization. (The imperial greatness of China, for example, runs somewhat of a parallel course to that of Rome, and indeed outlived its Western counterpart.) The expansive epoch of world-empires, spanning from early Mesopotamia to classical Greece and the subsequent period of the Hellenistic states, set the historical stage for Rome's emergence.

At almost the same time that the Greeks were settling around the Aegean Sea, an itinerant group of Indo-Europeans moved down

---

* The Orient, deriving from the Latin word for "east," is a term that refers to the whole of Asia, from the eastern Mediterranean Sea to the Pacific Ocean.

into Rome and the surrounding territory, and eventually grew into a culture referred to as Latin. Not moving into a vacuum, the Italian peninsula was something of a cultural patchwork, though the dominant Etruscans there held political sway over much of the area. After throwing off the yoke of Etruscan control around 500 BC, Rome arose free and independent. Though no longer a hegemon, Etruscan cultural influence over the Romans was profound. Another group to influence the Romans was the Greeks. The Greek colonies discussed in the previous section were established in Sicily and southern Italy, creating points of contact between the two cultures; Greek culture would remain a strong influence for the duration. As historian Fernand Braudel remarks, "Behind the Roman facade Greek civilization lived on."[3]

The study of ancient Rome is a field unto itself, but it will suffice to limit its discussion here to the basic outline of its rise and fall. Roman primacy is typically divided into two periods, the republic and the empire. Its republican phase covered the years 509/8 BC to 44 AD, from Rome's break from the Etruscans to the assassination of Julius Caesar. More than eschewing its Etruscan overlords, the Roman city-state also parted company with their system of monarchical rule. Instead, Rome retained the use of a Senate (from the Latin *senex*, meaning "old man") composed of members of the aristocratic patrician class, as an oligarchic means of governing the city-state and its citizenry. This relationship was emblematized in the Latin abbreviation *SPQR* for *Senatus Populusque Romanus*, or "the Senate and the Roman People." Yet this delicate balance was frequently disturbed by class tensions. With administrative power concentrated among elite patricians, the common people (*plebs*), or plebeians, chafed under the inequalities of oligarchy. Be that as it may, making up the majority of both the civilian and military populations, plebeians managed to win a modicum of concessions. The plebeian classes gained limited access to the consuls (the highest executive bodies, or magistrates) as well as representation through the creation of tribunes, a kind of elected representative. These rather constrained participatory structures created sufficient harmony between the two social tiers, allowing the real business at hand to continue relatively uninterrupted:

Roman civil law was not concerned with regulating the relationships between individuals but with the transference and protection of private property. With respect to indebtedness, for example, it protected the creditor far more than the debtor.

Roman civil law did not give legal and political protection to the entire population, or even to all citizens, because it was based on the idea of "absolute private property," which separated property from political and moral restrictions. As the preeminent principle of civil law, the institution of property itself never required justification.[4]

The reflex in such an endeavor to maximize profit is to expand the available opportunities. In an economy like Rome's driven predominantly by agriculture, this meant a needed increase in land, which in turn necessitated increased labor power (more plebs and slaves). In all of this the expansion and, afterwards, defense of the newly acquired territory would require an augmented martial capacity. But as we saw in the shift from the smaller Greek city-state to the larger Hellenistic states, democratic processes became a hindrance and were replaced with absolute authority.

By the middle of the third century BC, Rome had secured control of the Italian peninsula. After its defeat of Carthage (a North African empire centered in modern-day Tunisia) in a century-long conflict called the Punic Wars (264–146 BC), Rome had begun its transition from republican city-state to world imperial power. Along with its Spanish and African acquisitions from the Carthaginians, Rome had headed east into Greece and Asia Minor, and eventually northward conquering the present-day areas of Spain, France, Germany, and the Balkans. The near boundless expansion eventually altered the make-up of the military, moving it from an army of citizens (frequently farmers) to an army increasingly composed of careerist soldiers; war profiteering and warlordism were only a matter of time. Nevertheless, territorial expansion continued to siphon off Rome's labor force. The more demand there was for military service, the more the labor force dwindled and thus the republic had to depend on slave labor. By 150 BC, Italy's population was nearly one-third slaves.[5] And as farms were abandoned by farmers leaving for military duty—remaining gone for long years or not coming back at all—the small farm plots were consolidated into larger ones, called *latifundia*.

The republic was in need of reform and control: competing military warlords, corruption, and a widening gap between rich and poor signaled Rome's imminent peril. Efforts to inspire substantive reform were generally squelched, and occasionally inspired murder, as Tiberius Gracchus would learn. That the elite class found this wealthy tribune's candor unacceptable indicated its pertinence:

The men who fight and die for Italy share the air and the light, but nothing else .... They fight and perish to support others in wealth and luxury, and although they are styled the masters of the world, have not a single clod of earth that is their own.[6]

Reform and control were instead delivered by consolidated, autocratic power in the form of an emperor. The beginning of the Roman Empire is marked by the start of Octavian's rule in 27 BC.

Better known as Augustus Caesar, Octavian initiated a series of reforms that stabilized the empire and the military, inaugurating a period in the empire's history known as the *Pax Romana* (Roman Peace), ending in 180 AD. This period was followed by a time of instability and civil war, but would be redirected by two emperors, Diocletian and Constantine, whose collective rule (284–337) contains the last attempts to prevent Rome's demise. The former initiated the splitting of the empire into east–west designations to help ease executive management, while the latter began to convert the polytheistic empire into a Christian one. Yet efforts to fortify the power of the emperor's office, as well as maintain stability within the imperium itself, were no match for the expansionism the republican phase gave rise to and which the imperial phase attempted to sustain. That is not to say that there were not long periods of stability; Rome's decline occurred over a couple of centuries. However, one could make a convincing argument that the decline was in fact precipitated by the rise, that it was inherent in Rome's existence that it could not perpetuate a system hinging on expansionism, militarism, authoritarianism, reliance upon slavery, overspending, and heavy taxation.

As the empire was approaching its final moments, aspects of the socioeconomic order that would take Rome's place were already apparent. The strength of the imperial throne was waning, as was unification among the military. Those suffering unemployment and increased taxes and inflation began to look to their localities for assistance not forthcoming from the Senate and the emperor. Wealthy landowners on the one hand, and the bishops of the increasingly powerful Church on the other, as a class unto themselves began to supplant the machinery of empire. It was also at this time that the northern and western frontiers began to blur, with increased mingling and incursion from the various barbarian groups. The year 476 marks the official end of the western half of the empire when a Germanic chieftain replaced the last emperor.

The eastern half would survive as the Byzantine Empire until 1453 when it fell to the Turks, a story we will resume in Chapter 3.

WESTERN EUROPE AND THE MODERN INTERSTATE SYSTEM

The gateway between the ancient and the medieval is traversed with the fall of the Western Roman Empire and its replacement by subdivided Germanic kingdoms. By the year 500 this process, along with the conversion of the people living within the former imperium to Christianity, was well under way, if not complete. Moreover, the pagan Germanic peoples to the north began looking southward. As the boundary between the Christianized western Roman territory, or Christendom, and the pagan north dissipated, what would later become Western Europe degenerated into something of a relative hinterland.

Europe, a label that started to gain currency in the eighth and ninth centuries,[*] formed a more or less land-locked territory, one beset and besieged by all surrounding it. Frequently more sophisticated, Europe's neighbors boxed them in: The emergence of the Islamic Middle East in the 700s gave birth to an empire that claimed the Roman Empire's former holdings in that region along with the northern rim of Africa and control of much of the Mediterranean. Norsemen, or the Vikings, visited brutality upon Christendom's northern frontier, and groups of Asian pagans from the east, most notably the Magyars, kept Europe's eastern flank in check. With the largely useless Atlantic coast serving as its western border (trade and exploration were only later launched from the seaboard), the Eurasian continent's western peninsular extremity resembled something of a cage. Likewise, the tumult at the edges of this backwater bore little distinction to its interior.

The invasion of the Germanic warrior tribes divided the former Roman territories into various kingdoms. These kingdoms in turn then subdivided into counties, and further still into principalities and duchies, all the product of delegation as well as internal, dynastic disagreement after the death of a king. Two groups worthy of note in this period are the Anglo-Saxons, who established kingdoms in the former Roman territory of Britain (a large portion of which would later become the "land of the Angles," or England), and the

---

[*]   The term dates back to ancient Greece, likely used as a designation for the "mainland" between Africa and Asia. Possible etymologies trace its source to Europa of Greek mythology.

Franks, namesakes of modern France. The Frankish chieftain Clovis, of the Merovingian family, successfully unified the confederacy of Frankish tribes inhabiting the modern areas of France, Belgium, and western Germany (what comprised Gaul under the Romans). Clovis's fragile dynasty, begun in 481, lasted until 750 when the Merovingians were displaced by the Carolingians.

Also a family of Frankish nobility, the Carolingians were named after the most distinguished member of their line, Charles the Great, or Charlemagne, and chiefly through him established what resembled the Western Roman Empire, a territory that covered modern France, Germany, the Low Countries (Belgium, the Nether- lands, and Luxembourg—together known as "Benelux"), and much of Italy. Charles was even pronounced, somewhat curiously, as a Roman emperor by Pope Leo III. Nevertheless, the empire belong- ing to Charles and the Carolingians would essentially not outlast its emperor, who died in 814. The dissolution of the empire after the rule of Charles's son, Louis the Pious, ended up creating the initial basis for the modern designations of France and Germany. Louis's three sons each took a slice of the empire, creating a western king- dom for Charles the Bald; a central kingdom for Lothar, forming a strip between France and Germany and extending well into Italy; and an eastern kingdom for Louis the German. This settlement, called the Treaty of Verdun (843), initiates the very beginning of the modern map of Europe. Incidentally, it was the Carolingian Empire that also provided the first manifestation of our concept "Europe." According to historian Norman Davies,

> It was in the court of Charles the Great [Charlemagne] that the ancient term "Europe" was revived. The Carolingians needed a label to describe that section of the world which they dominated, as distinct from the pagan lands, from Byzantium, or from Christen- dom as a whole. This "first Europe", therefore, was an ephemeral Western concept which lasted no longer than Charles himself.[7]

Shifting temporarily from chronology and narrative, let us consider thematically some of the issues concerning political economy and what the above developments set in motion. As we have seen, post-Roman attempts at broad imperial consolidation were typi- cally unsuccessful. Between the instability of the different kingdoms within, and the attacks from without by Muslims, Vikings, and others, a system called feudalism began to take root, starting in France.

Organized around a plot of land called a "fief" (from *feodum* and *fee*, meaning livestock, goods, and money), feudalism was a more decentralized system where the embryonic European states became grids based on vassalage. Historian F. L. Ganshof's description is an accepted standard:

> "[F]eudalism" may be regarded as a body of institutions creating and regulating the obligations of obedience and service—mainly military service—on the part of one free man (the vassal) towards another free man (the lord), and the obligations of protection and maintenance on the part of the lord with regard to his vassal.[8]

In essence, feudalism was based on a network of land and loyalty. Though the king, or sovereign, still resided at the top of the pyramid; power within the feudal "state" was rather diffuse, being distributed among the nobility. Nobles who held fiefs subsequently divided and parceled out land to lesser nobles and knights. In turn, the vassal would do homage (pledge loyalty) to his lord, generally in the form of military service. The vassal in this scenario might in turn subdivide his fief and parcel out units to lower-ranking knights, who became vassals, and he a lord. This hierarchy created a continuum where, in the words of historian Perry Anderson, "The functions of the [feudal] State were disintegrated in a vertical allocation downwards, at each level of which political and economic relations were, on the other hand, integrated."[9] Everyone was a vassal to someone and in many cases a lord as well. At the bottom of the feudal stratification resided the peasants, or serfs, tending their plots and providing labor service to the lord of the manor in exchange for the plot itself and protection in times of trouble. Though hardly a utopia, serfdom in the feudal network was a notch up from slavery, with peasants enjoying a measure of autonomy and security.

What we call feudalism (something its participants did not) lasted basically from the tenth to the thirteenth century. This system, characterized by castles, knights, chivalry, and vassalage, plus a tripartite socioeconomic structure composed of the three "estates"—those who pray, those who fight, and those who work—was never and should never be considered as anything well-ordered and consistent throughout. Today's descriptions are generalizations that ease discussion; in practice, the medieval way of life was quite varied, heavier on exceptions than rules, and existing in slightly different forms from one territory to the next. Nonetheless, the picture we have is a reasonable approximation. But by 1200, this picture begins to change.

From its Carolingian roots to the thirteenth century, the feudal Middle Ages remained basically stable for 500 years, although by the thirteenth century, urbanization was beginning to change the face of European history. As population growth, surplus production, and merchant activity increased, towns began to take hold, eventually forming walled cities, or *bourgs*, typically nestled against a castle, monastery, or cathedral. Operating outside the feudal structure, the towns and their expanding and increasingly wealthy bourgeois class were on the whole independent entities. Charters, guilds, and corporations were developed to define, regulate, and incorporate a town into the feudal scheme of things, and in return towns paid the king. The medieval nucleus of the lord–vassal dynamic began to be superseded by the relationship between monarch and the bourgeois class. As this occurred, according to a collegiate text, "Towns began to renounce their privileges and autonomy and integrated themselves into these emerging territory-wide legal frameworks, which came to link capitalism and state power in a single political formation."[10] Until this point lacking centralized and consolidated power under feudalism, medieval kings were in the process of producing such an order. This is a critical transition in the development of the state apparatus.

In addition to economic rearrangement, technological advancement also altered the way wars were fought and armies were organized. With the introduction of gunpowder (by way of China) and the innovation of different implements of warfare—most notably the cannon and the iron cannonball—castles became a less effective means of protection. The size of armies expanded, which in turn made them more expensive to operate and more vital to organize. The feudal patchwork of independent retinues was replaced with a standing army, one composed uniformly and whose allegiance was to the throne instead of a given knight owing allegiance to a given lord. Administration of the military coupled with the conversion to an economy based on money and credit required increased tax revenue and an ever-expanding array of offices to oversee the legal and financial demands that were moving closer and closer to the sovereign center. Warfare and bureaucracy are the forebears of the modern state.

The years 1300–1500 offer a general framework when tracing the evolution of the nation-state. In fact, they contain the DNA of the global capitalist economy in which we live today. During these two centuries Europe's division into sovereign states replaced

Christendom, empire, and feudalism as the infrastructure of power and authority. Over this period, the continuing military and economic changes mentioned above were also met by newly emerging ones. Peasant uprisings in the fourteenth and fifteenth centuries ignited as a result of the financial strains of bad weather and poor crops, wars ruining farmland (for example, the Hundred Years' War), increased taxes, and general discontent. Time and again, this dissent was ruthlessly put down with military force.

Adding insult to injury was the Black Death, or bubonic plague, occurring in the mid-1300s and lasting only a few years. However, the fatality in those few years is estimated to have been between a quarter and a third of Europe's total population, or some 25 to 40 million people. Uprisings would continue after the pandemic, now occurring in an extremely dislocated European demography and economy. But resistance from beneath never cohered—quite a task given the methods of suppression—and instead continued against the ever-increasing consolidation of financial and political power.

As the feudal system dissolved, the now cash-based economies throughout Europe fostered greater opportunities for merchants and bankers to accumulate surplus capital in the realms of domestic and foreign commerce. This surplus was then reinvested, loaned at interest (usury), and processed through increasingly elaborate financial institutions designed specifically to advance the efforts of this evolving class of capitalists.[11] In a slow departure from the agrarian economy, peasants found themselves performing specialized, repetitive tasks in a growing industrial sector, referred to as the "division of labor," and doing so for fixed and often meager wages. Rent paid to a landlord (another departure from the feudal scheme) and escalating taxes also contributed to the peasantry's hardships. This early capitalist economy facilitated the establishment of ever larger and more expensive armies along with the requisite battlefield equipment. The somewhat distributive nature of feudalism gave way to a socioeconomic landscape defined by highly concentrated power, and in order to prevail politically in this new era, one's financial and martial resources were the primary factors.

At this time, while religiosity among the people remained strong, attachment to the Church did not. Popular disapproval of papal and clerical corruption increased throughout the fourteenth and fifteenth centuries. This sentiment was eventually captured in the 1500s by influential reformists like Martin Luther and John Calvin. The movement called the Reformation ended up producing different "Protestant" sects of Christianity and drastically diminishing the power of the Roman Catholic Church. Politically, monarchs and rulers stood to benefit from this diminution, with many establishing state churches and thus enjoying increased authority as a result. In many cases severing ties with Rome also meant acquiring the Church's large real-estate holdings in a given dominion. The religious aspect of the Catholic–Protestant contest, it is worth noting, merely added to the non-religious tensions within and between countries, and produced relentless warfare throughout continental Europe. What are referred to as the Wars of Religion—a somewhat misleading label given the secular core of intrigue on which they were based—is a period that ran the latter half of the 1500s and into the following century. Religious conflict, territorial expansion, commercial dominance, wars between various princes, attempts to check the expansion of competing powers, and suppression of popular revolt all contributed to a holocaust of death and destruction on a scale that would not be seen again on the European peninsula until the twentieth century.

This violence reached a crescendo with the Thirty Years War (1618–48), which occurred predominantly within the boundaries of the Holy Roman Empire (essentially modern-day Germany), but involved almost the entirety of Europe. The international conflict ground to a stalemate as the economic strains of warfare began to discourage its continuation. The wars were formally concluded at a series of conferences that produced treaties known as the Peace of Westphalia, signed in 1648. This settlement instituted the concept of state sovereignty, closing the chapter of imperial and papal authority in Western Europe, and ordained the modern state system in which we currently live.

Even in this general review of the history, it becomes apparent that Europe's largest exports—the nation-state and capitalism—were formed over hundreds of years of cataclysmic human suffering. For the common people alone, the wars spelled "murder, burning, plundering, torture and beating," with cities left "a heap of ashes and stones."[12] We might, and perhaps should, ask why all this was done. Charles Tilly, a leading specialist on state formation, offers a simple and chilling answer:

> The central tragic fact is simple: coercion *works*; those who apply substantial force to their fellows get compliance, and from that compliance draw the multiple advantages of money, goods, deference, access to pleasures denied to less powerful people.[13]

It is safe to make inferences about the disposition and character of the sovereign state on the basis of these issues, which are clearly visible in the manner in which they were built, and the motives which initiated and sustained their development. The character of the Westphalian system is defined by the index of power, evident in its creation and subsequent conduct for roughly 350 years. This was later summarized by prominent American statesman Henry Cabot Lodge: "For the unfit among nations, there is no pity in the relentless world-forces which shape the destinies of mankind."[14]

During the events of the late fifteenth century Europe was making its way westward via transoceanic expeditions. Starting with Christopher Columbus's arrival in the opposing hemisphere, the West began expanding across this newly available briny frontier. In other words, Europe was transitioning from being a region ruled by empire to one ruling by empire. A byproduct of this venture was British overseas settlement and the birth of the United States of America.

2

THE RISE OF AMERICAN POWER: FROM COLUMBUS TO THE COLD WAR

As stated in a standard collegiate survey of Western civilization, Europe's "overseas penetration triggered the expansion of capitalism into a worldwide system. The fact is that after 1500, the world became a treasure house for the West."[1] North America, initially a mere addition to the treasure house, would become a European outpost from which it administrated its Western Hemispheric affairs, eventually evolving into the core's central office, one of unparalleled power as of the post-World War II era. The United States can be viewed as a footnote and heir to this turn in European history—what historian Hugh Seton-Watson describes as a "tremendous outburst of navigating skill, commercial greed and military aggression."[2]

INDEPENDENCE: "THE PROPER GUARDIANS OF THE PUBLIC WEAL"

The history of American foreign relations can roughly be segmented into three phases: independence, continental expansion, and globalization. And while it is the last item that concerns us most, the first two very much inform how and why the United States took the historic path it did, one on which it continues.

The themes revolving around Christopher Columbus's venture set a precedent for Europe's involvement with the New World, namely, westward expansion, hopes for penetration of Asian markets, and the question of a native population. With the original desire for access to markets in China put on hold, having miscalculated and run into the Caribbean along the way, the Spanish busied themselves with gold, ushering Western Europe, in philosopher and historian

Tzvetan Todorov's words, into the "transitional period between a Middle Ages dominated by religion and a modern period that places material goods at the top of its scale of values." "Certainly the desire for riches is nothing new, the passion for gold has nothing specifically modern about it. What is new is the subordination of all other values to this one.... This homogenization of values by money is a new phenomenon and it heralds the modern mentality."[3]

Subsumed within this phenomenon of subordinating values to the wealth principle were the native inhabitants, who either served as slave labor (South America) or perturbed expansionist intentions (North America). The point here is not simply to highlight that the American Indians were treated with brutality, but to indicate the general view of "Third World"* (peripheral) people from the imperial/colonial (core) perspective; Columbus's sentiments regarding the indigenous peoples are recurrent throughout the history of European–US foreign involvements. The "bestial men" who lack "letters [and] long-standing memories," and who cannot discern island from mainland, at the very least "make good and industrious servants," because after all, "They are fit to be ruled."[4] The attendant bloodshed, however, is a slightly different matter. Despite a native's presumed inferiority—and accompanying utility—he or she is ultimately in the way. Colonizers do not proceed with the direct intent to commit genocide or ethnic cleansing; they proceed with the simple desire to increase their wealth. As the Spanish priest Bartolomé de las Casas observed in the sixteenth century of his fellow countrypeople in their New World dealings with the natives: "I do not say that they want to kill them directly, from the hate they

---

* The term "Third World" dates back to the early Cold War era, which we will discuss in this chapter and again in Chapter 4. In 1955 a conference was held in Bandung, Indonesia, attended by those countries that would later (1961) form the Non-Aligned Movement (NAM). These countries, from Latin America, Africa, and Asia, mostly former colonies, attempted to create a tripolar world system based on their longing to pursue self-determination, outside the bipolar US–USSR contest and foreign intervention altogether. The Western (capitalist) and Eastern (communist) blocs came to be known as the First and Second Worlds respectively, though these terms are rarely used. Today, Third World countries are considered collectively in their hemispheric concentration as the "global South," and are generally described as "developing" according to evaluations published by the UN Human Development Index (http://hdr.undp.org/en). While the NAM is still active, Third World solidarity and cooperation tends to remain regional.

bear them; they kill them because they want to be rich and have much gold, which is their whole aim."[5]

About a century later, Great Britain entered the game thus far dominated by Spain and Portugal. The English settlers at Jamestown, Virginia, in 1607 were more or less on a similar mission and presented with the same native presence. The new arrivals were initially looking for a passage to China, something they and others eventually abandoned given the geographical realities. Finding crops and goods to export instead, the settler population dug in, grew in number, and expanded in search of more land on which to live, farm, and hunt. French, and to a degree Spanish, colonials pursued similar ends. The presence of three major imperial powers spelled almost continual warfare, especially between Britain and France. The years 1689–1763 mark this period of conflict, ending with the Seven Years War (or the French and Indian War). By the end of nearly a century of off-and-on fighting, Great Britain gained total control of North America from the Atlantic Ocean to the Mississippi River (minus Florida and New Orleans), including large portions of Canada. In an ironic twist, the way for future revolution had been paved. As Thomas Paine commented in his highly influential 1776 pamphlet, *Common Sense*, "In no instance hath nature made the satellite larger than its primary planet."

British America and its 13 colonial provinces were coming into their own. It was now time, according to the colonial legislatures, to change status, but not necessarily the underlying order. In other words, they sought independence from London, and preservation of the domestic status quo. The benefits of throwing off the bonds of British economic control, especially for the landed and commercial classes, were clear and obvious. But the population in general was not looking for such drastic change, especially if it meant war. With significant effort and coercion, the revolutionary leadership was able to encourage a largely uninterested populace to join the national struggle for independence. Contemporary estimates suggest perhaps 20 percent were in favor, with even the future second president, John Adams, guessing that opposition, support, and neutrality throughout the colonies broke more or less evenly into thirds.[6] In spite of popular lack of enthusiasm, over time the people were sufficiently aroused, with increasing protest, disobedience, and acts of sabotage against the British (for instance, the Boston Tea Party) coming to a head in 1775. The American Revolutionary War began on April 19, 1775, and over the course of six years—with significant French support—the Continental Army emerged victorious.

Formally claiming independence in 1776, the 13 colonies received international recognition of their sovereignty in 1783 under the Treaty of Paris, stating that "His Britannic Majesty acknowledges the said United States."

Four years after recognized independence, establishment of a constitution began in Philadelphia, a central focus of which was foreign policy concerns.[7] The framers felt the colonies should be bound in a tighter union by a strong, centralized government as opposed to the looser one codified under the Articles of Confederation, the Constitution's predecessor. While state rights would not disappear, they would be sharply curtailed, with taxation, commerce, and warfare placed in the charge of the "federal" government. On balance the plan was, for the time, a progressive development in the history of governance. But despite its rough approximation of classical liberal principles—improved after the states demanded more clearly enumerated civil liberties and protections, later enshrined in the Bill of Rights—the authors of the Constitution had successfully forged a document in their own image, as they saw fit.

During the contentious ratification process, three of the key architects anonymously published a series of 85 essays entitled *The Federalist*.[8] In them Alexander Hamilton, James Madison, and John Jay made an elaborate defense of the Union as imagined in the new charter, "examining the advantages of that Union, the certain evils, and the probable dangers, to which every State will be exposed from its dissolution" (*Federalist* 1). As an early American statement of political economy and a window into the thoughts and concerns of its authors—and the classes they represented—the collection of papers written under the pen name "Publius" is of inestimable value. A brief survey of *Federalist* 10, one of the better known of the series, provides ample insight.

In this essay, Madison discusses economic regulation, particularly in the face of domestic instability, or "factions." These factions are groups, minority or majority, "who are united by some common impulse ... adverse to the rights of other citizens, or to the permanent and aggregate interests of the community." Owing to the "diversity in the faculties of men, from which the rights of property originate," Madison concludes that "[t]he latent causes of faction are thus sown in the nature of man." In other words, the diversities among men produce a "propensity of mankind to fall into mutual animosities." He continues: "the common and most durable source of factions has been the various and unequal distribution of property," with the haves and have-nots forming "distinct interests."

Therefore, regulating these interests "forms the principal task of modern legislation."

In short, Madison's encouragement of his readers to support ratification was based on the preservation of the "unequal distribution of property." In his view, the Constitution and the strong centralized Union it would create would mitigate against a latent majority imposing undue pressure on the commercial and landed classes. As he summarizes:

> To secure the public good and private rights against the danger of such a [potential majority] faction, and at the same time to preserve the spirit and the form of popular government, is then the great object to which our inquiries are directed.

The solution: a large republic. Larger numbers, in Madison's analysis, allow for a greater variety of "parties and interests," thus

> mak[ing] it less probable that a majority of the whole will have a common motive to invade the rights of other citizens; or if such common motive exists, it will be more difficult for all who feel it to discover their own strength and to act in unison with each other.

And choosing the format of a republic over that of a "pure democracy" simply reduces the amount of democracy by "refin[ing] and enlarg[ing] the public views by passing them through the medium of a chosen body of citizens, whose wisdom may best discern the true interest of their country." These "proper guardians of the public weal," with their "enlightened views and virtuous sentiments," will protect against the "rage for ... an equal division of property, or any other improper or wicked project."[9]

Madison's thinking on the subject makes clear his interests, and we can safely assume the principal interests of those in support of ratification. In Charles A. Beard's landmark 1913 study, *An Economic Interpretation of the Constitution*, in which he considers the backgrounds and financial interests of those participating at Philadelphia, the noted historian observes:

> Inasmuch as the primary object of a government, beyond the mere repression of physical violence, is the making of the rules which determine the property relations of members of society, the dominant classes whose rights are thus to be determined must perforce obtain from the government such rules as are consonant

with the larger interests necessary to the continuance of their economic processes, or they must themselves control the organs of government.[10]

Power tends toward pragmatism in its methods. To ensure the government protects the interests of the elite, it is best for the elite to handle legislation. Alexander Hamilton's candid remarks at the convention provide reasonable support for Beard's analysis:

> All communities divide themselves into the few and the many. The first are the rich and well born, the other the mass of people. The voice of the people has been said to be the voice of God; and however generally this maxim has been quoted and believed, it is not true in fact. The people are turbulent and changing; they seldom judge or determine right. Give therefore to the first class a distinct, permanent share in the government. Can a democratic assembly who annually revolve in the mass of the people, be supposed steadily to pursue the public good? Nothing but a permanent body can check the imprudence of democracy.... It is admitted that you cannot have a good executive upon a democratic plan.[11]

Similar points of view were expressed by Gouverneur Morris, another member of the convention and author of the Constitution, amid social unrest in 1774 among propertyless "tradesmen, etc.": "The mob begin to think and reason. Poor reptiles! ... [T]hey bask in the sun, and ere noon they will bite, depend on it. The gentry begin to fear this."[12]

`In the summer of 1787 in Philadelphia, the Continental Congress, in heated and secret debate, replaced the Articles of Confederation with the Constitution. With ratification, and therefore the establishment of a centralized Union, the United States finally and formally set up shop in North America. From revolution to ratification, economic power among the colonies (now states) had been consolidated, concentrated, and protected within a federal structure. What remained on the agenda—an intention revealed in the tenth *Federalist* essay—was expansion: To "extend the sphere."

CONTINENTAL EXPANSION: "OUR PROPER DOMINION"

The years 1815 to 1860, roughly between the War of 1812 (America's conflict with Great Britain along the US–Canada border) and the Civil War, enclosed the period of continental expansion. The guiding principle of this era came to be called Manifest Destiny, an expansionist ideology undergirded by the religious assumption that God's chosen people were doing God's will on God's land; the western frontier was destiny made manifest, and existed solely for the sake of white settlement. The phrase appeared in a political journal of the time, called the *Democratic Review*, in an article discussing the annexation of Texas and "the fulfillment of our manifest destiny to overspread the continent allotted by Providence for the free development of our yearly multiplying millions."[13] The desire and quest for increased territory, of course, did not begin in 1815. As historian Walter LaFeber points out, expansion had been "the central theme of the American experience since 1607."[14] The years that gave rise to Manifest Destiny were merely a very focused period of this tendency, and mostly so in the 1840s.

By varying means of purchase, coercion, annexation, and war the national territory grew dramatically throughout the first half of the mid-nineteenth century. From the Louisiana Purchase (1803) to the acquisitions of Florida (1819), Texas (1845), Oregon (1846), the Southwest and California (1848), to the final adjustment of the southern boundaries of Arizona and New Mexico with the Gadsden Purchase (1853), the territory now comprising the contiguous 48 states was in place. (Alaska was purchased in 1867 but did not become a state until 1959, along with Hawaii which is discussed later.)

When John Quincy Adams, as secretary of state, opined that "the continent of North America" was "our proper dominion," the tacit assertion was that those already living there were improperly occupying said dominion.[15] The prevailing hierarchies according to race, gender, and class were key determinants in the configuration of the domestic social and political spheres. Slaves, indentured servants, women, and the propertyless classes were not seen as fit to wander outside their narrow roles. These groups, the best of whom—"our countrymen"—possessing "all the folly of the ass and all the passiveness of the sheep" (Alexander Hamilton),[16] played a necessary role in the national scheme of things as a labor force. Those physically in the way of the march of progress, however, did not rate quite as highly.

As Theodore Roosevelt lamented in his multi-volume study *The Winning of the West,* published shortly before he became president, "Their presence has caused the process of settlement to go on at unequal rates of speed." And while he regretted the instances where the "weaker race" occasionally "suffered terrible injustices," on the whole within America's policy towards the natives "there has been little wilful wrong-doing." "The claims and desires of the two parties [Americans and Indians] were irreconcilable," and for even an American to get in the way of the "course of conquest" indicated a "warped, perverse, and silly morality." Furthermore, he advised that:

> All men of sane and wholesome thought must dismiss with impatient contempt the plea that these continents should be reserved for the use of scattered savage tribes, whose life was but a few degrees less meaningless, squalid, and ferocious than that of the wild beasts with whom they held joint ownership.[17]

Dispossession was therefore the order of the day, for, according to War Secretary Lewis Cass years earlier (1830), "barbarous people ... cannot live in contact with a civilized community." It is from this point of view that figures such as General William T. Sherman elucidated the seemingly obvious and practical solution (1868): "The more we can kill this year, the less will have to be killed the next war, for the more I see of these Indians the more convinced I am that all have to be killed or be maintained as a pauper species." Regarding the latter scenario, there were routine agreements between the Americans and the natives prior to the latter's displacement, which were described by a governor of Georgia as "expedients by which ignorant, intractable, and savage people were induced without bloodshed to yield up what civilized peoples had a right to possess."

So we come full circle to Roosevelt's advice above, the essence of which Andrew Jackson floridly captured over two decades earlier:

> What good man would prefer a country covered with forests and ranged by a few thousand savages to our extensive Republic, studded with cities, towns, and prosperous farms ... occupied by more than 12,000,000 happy people, and filled with all the blessings of liberty, civilization, and religion?[18]

Like Roosevelt and his acknowledgement of the "terrible injustices," Jackson similarly lamented the price of progress: "Circumstances that cannot be controlled and which are beyond the reach of human laws render it impossible that you can flourish in the midst of a civilized community."[19] We don't make the world, we just live in it.

This view of the other and the concomitant language used to express it are not difficult to find in the historical record. Though one might surmise that judgments like these are aberrant, they are in fact closer to standard, and are rife throughout even sympathetic accounts. And while this truism concerning how the Founding Fathers and subsequent architects and planners perceived those unlike themselves deserves serious attention, overstating the point can skew the larger picture. The westward advance across the continent was not in and of itself an expression of contempt and hatred for the indigenous population—recall Las Casas's comments in the preceding section. The move west was by design, with the natives creating an obstruction. (Historian Thomas Hietala uses the phrase "manifest design" in his book of the same title, suggesting a more deliberate, conscious mindset among policymakers.[20]) Better the land devoid of obstacles, but given the realities on the ground the appropriate mindset was necessary—and ready at hand. The example of the war with Mexico (1846–48) serves as a suitable case study, being the first instance where the various concerns regarding expansion—territory, destiny, racism, avoidance of formal imperialism—converged.

The war was initiated in the interest of moving the southern boundary to the Rio Grande, though the United States was militarily in a position to go much farther. Still, the land acquired in the Treaty of Guadalupe Hidalgo vastly increased the national territory and so reduced the size of Mexico. But despite the immense transfer of land to American possession, few Mexican citizens were inherited along with the territorial spoils: Land without population was much preferred. As one senator whose party (Whig) was hesitant about the affair, but who decided to vote in support of the treaty, reasoned, "it is less evil, to have ... a most sparsely settled part of Mexico, than the whole with its mixed breed of Spaniards, Indians, and negroes."[21] In other words, displacing native inhabitants required effort, but including them within the democratic arrangement was out of the question. Furthermore, ruling over them as colonials was also out of the question on account of this style of direct imperial rule being—as it always would be—something the United States wanted to avoid. A tactic like ethnic cleansing required force but was a temporary measure; direct European-style colonial control required constant policing. All in all, racism merely greased the wheels of practical power politics.

Over the course of the period defined by Manifest Destiny, the ultimate project was clear: a coast-to-coast national entity, by hook or by crook. What was still being worked out was America's approach to foreign relations beyond those pertaining to territorial expansion. Roughly a decade into this period, two related developments inspired the United States to further augment and announce its in-progress foreign policy.

In the early nineteenth century, Spain's 300-year-old Latin American empire disintegrated, with revolutionary wars of independence converting the various colonial viceroyalties into republics. By 1822, the maps of Central and South America were beginning to take their modern form. Also during this time, across the Atlantic Ocean leaders in Europe were attempting to suppress among their populations the liberal spirit created by the French Revolution (1789) by imposing conservative counterrevolutionary measures. The main European powers, except for Great Britain, formed the Holy Alliance (1815) and set to putting out these fires wherever they started, as in Spain, Italy, and Greece. Some in Washington, DC, feared that the revolutions in Latin America might become a target of this repression and the thought of allied European military power arriving in the Western Hemisphere was unsettling. In addition, there was the lingering issue of British and Russian presence on North America's northwest coast. This was all too close for comfort. The time had come for President James Monroe and his secretary of state, John Quincy Adams, to declare their concerns.

In his seventh annual address to Congress (December 1823), Monroe expounded on the three points mentioned above—Latin American independence, the conservative European agenda, and the Anglo-Russian presence on the Pacific Northwest—with three corresponding principles: non-colonization, hemispheric division, and "hands-off," as historians have termed it. The pertinent excerpts from the executive message, in order, are as follows:

- [T]he American continents, by the free and independent condition which they have assumed and maintain, are henceforth not to be considered as subjects for future colonization by any European powers ...
- In the wars of the European powers in matters relating to themselves we have never taken any part, nor does it comport with our policy to do so.
- [W]e should consider any attempt on their [Europe's] part to extend their system to any portion of this hemisphere as dangerous to our peace and safety.... [W]e could not view any

interposition for the purpose of oppressing them [Latin America], or controlling in any other manner their destiny, by any European power in any other light than as the manifestation of an unfriendly disposition toward the United States.[22]

This came to be called the Monroe Doctrine. In it the United States had declared itself a world power by claiming the Western Hemisphere for itself. For all the protective language of the doctrine, its primary author "cast a very conservative view of the South American question," in that Adams "was swayed by no theoretical devotion to republicanism."[23] As for his confidence in the new regional states, his comments reveal it to be scant: "They are not likely to promote the spirit either of freedom or order by their example. They have not the elements of good or free government. Arbitrary power, military and ecclesiastical, was stamped upon all their institutions."[24] Even Thomas Jefferson's assessments ran parallel to the secretary's, claiming that Latinos were "immersed in the darkest ignorance," and naturally were "as incapable of self-government as children."[25] While indeed there was a degree of well-wishing, even from Adams and Jefferson, dubiousness was a steady undercurrent. Right idea, wrong people.

To the point, Europe was steadily being sent back across the Atlantic where the United States felt it belonged. And while fears did exist both among the leadership and the populace over the possibility of European military power aiding Spain in reconquering its Latin American colonies, and of this effort perchance moving northward, the secretary of state was under no such illusions. Adams remained sober and analytical, seeing a very slim chance of European intervention. Irrespective, however, of where one stood on the Latin American question, the vision of two global spheres of influence divided by the Atlantic was shared by elites in general. This thinking, after all, was "indigenous to the soil," "in the air," and "in the utterances of many different figures of the age."[26]

As for inter-American relations, there would be no hemispheric fraternal alliance, as Adams made clear: "As to an American system, we have it; we constitute the whole of it; there is no community of interests or principles between North and South America."[27] The preeminent power in the Americas declared its authority, while viewing its neighbors as maybe well-intended incompetents. The inference is therefore readily available as to how American foreign relations might play out over the next 150 years.

GLOBALIZATION: "A CLEAR PREPONDERANCE OF INTEREST"

As mentioned, Manifest Destiny is generally confined to the concentrated period of territorial expansion leading up to the Civil War. It hit its peak in the 1840s, lulled in the 1850s, and was (temporarily) interrupted by savage internal conflict in the 1860s. In the postwar period, however, the country continued apace along ideological lines similar to those of the antebellum period. Yet new factors influenced the method and style with which the United States would follow its path to becoming a competing global actor and eventual superpower. With the borders of the national territory established, the country politically unified, and the business sector undergoing industrialization, the era after the Civil War marked America's entrance into world power status.

A number of issues affecting this turning point came into play. With there no longer being a frontier into which expansionist energies could be poured, a look inward began to occur. At the same time, agriculture and industry were producing well beyond what the domestic market could absorb, creating a surplus, or "glut." Moreover, economic depressions in the 1870s and 1890s contributed to class conflict and labor movements, which were already being provoked by the consolidation of corporate enterprise—and the poor working conditions and low wages that went with it—and industry's increasing influence on government and policy.

There also existed a wish to preempt European economic power, as the United States was now in a position to do so. Political and private power desired continued expansion; the Monroe Doctrine and Manifest Destiny were the established principles and were not about to be discontinued. In addition to the glut, depressions, domestic labor strife, and international competition, territorial intrigue outside the national homeland was deepened by the assumptions common among the top political and business strata: suspicion of the lower classes, dismissal of foreign people and nations as childlike, and the general senses of national, religious, and racial superiority and righteousness. And while these inclinations of the late-nineteenth-century American leadership were anything but new, they did align uniquely in accordance with the social, political, and economic circumstances, establishing an orientation that would remain in place for the next century. In his classic survey, *A People's History of the United States*, historian Howard Zinn makes the observation that the government of the United States was behaving almost exactly as Karl Marx described a capitalist state: pretending neutrality to maintain order, but serving the interests of the rich. Not that the rich agreed among themselves; they had disputes over policies. But the purpose of the state was to settle upper-class disputes peacefully, control lower-class rebellion, and adopt policies that would further the long-range stability of the system.[28]

The long-range stability of the system, according to those in power and elite opinion, lay in overseas markets, raw materials, and labor.

Such opinion was ubiquitous among the political, military, and intellectual classes—groups with plenty of overlap and intersection, it should be noted. In 1890, Captain Alfred Thayer Mahan, a preeminent naval strategist who had the undivided attention of heads of state, made his case time and again for oceanic supremacy. In an article entitled "The United States Looking Outward," he argued that "beyond the broad seas, there are the markets of the world, that can be entered and controlled only by a vigorous contest, to which the habit of trusting to protection by statute [international law] does not conduce." This "vigorous contest" necessitates well-defended coasts "as to leave the navy free to strike where it will," thus allowing the country to "maintain our rights; not merely the rights which international law concedes ... but also those equally real rights which, though not conferred by law, depend upon a clear preponderance of interest." "The motto seen on so many ancient cannon, Ultima ratio regum [the last judgment of kings], is not without its message to republics.[29]

In the academic world of the late nineteenth century, especially in the work of historian Frederick Jackson Turner, similar arguments were being made. Turner predicted that because the westward movement had "come to a check," the "energies of expansion" demanded a "vigorous foreign policy, for an interoceanic canal ... a revival of our power upon the seas, and ... the extension of American influence to outlying islands and adjoining countries." As he observed, "The free lands are gone, the continent is crossed, and all this push and energy is turning into channels of agitation," which "is demanding an extension of governmental activity in its behalf." Simply put: "a drastic assertion of national government and imperial expansion under a popular hero."[30]

While strategic and tactical issues were debated back and forth among politicians and captains of industry, the overall doctrines propounded by Mahan, Turner, and many others reflected the national interest—from the perspective of power, also known in international relations as the "reason of state" (*raison d'état*). Foreign military venture, it rates mention, was hardly a novel concept in the United States. According to a continually updated Congressional Research Service bulletin, roughly 50 counts of foreign US military activity are noted in the 1800–50 period.[31] However, this activity never amounted to long-term hegemony in a given area or region. The "vigorous contest" did not become an endeavor in earnest until the turn of the century.

Though the assortment of factors, forces, and opinions that moved the country in the direction of overseas expansion do inform the issue, we might invoke what students of philosophy know as Occam's Razor: the principle that plurality should not be posited without necessity. In other words, simplicity in explanation tends to take precedence over multiplicity. While human (individual and group) decision making is a complex subject, from its inception the national agenda was forged by small groups of mostly like-minded individuals in places of power and privilege. As Thomas Hietala plainly says about the events of the 1840s in the preface of his revised edition of *Manifest Design*:

> What mainly propelled United States expansion? I still think the evidence points to the fears and ambitions of a small corps of American political figures, not to threats from abroad or demands from pioneers. This perspective rankles because it is inconsistent with American exceptionalism—the belief that the nation's politics and diplomacy have been uniquely altruistic, open, and therefore beyond reproach.[32]

Historian William Appleman Williams also draws the appropriately simple conclusions based on the historical evidence in his influential analysis, *The Tragedy of American Diplomacy*. In it he summarizes that, on balance and given the different forces at work on the country's foreign-policy trajectory, the United States made its choices toward global hegemony based on "a general outlook which externalized the opportunity and the responsibility for America's domestic welfare."[33] Turner's "vigorous foreign policy" reestablished a virtual frontier beyond which lay the world. On the question of the debates that took place between "imperialists" and "anti-imperialists" around the preferred kind and degree of expansionism the country should pursue, Williams locates the center

of gravity of America's political economy, to where it had indeed
shifted by the 1890s:

> It is far more accurate and illuminating ... to view it as a three-
> cornered fight. The third group was a coalition of businessmen,
> intellectuals, and politicians who opposed traditional colonialism
> and advocated instead a policy of an open door through which
> America's preponderant economic strength would enter and
> dominate all underdeveloped areas of the world. This coalition
> won the debate, and the Open Door Policy became the strategy
> of American foreign policy for the next half-century.[34]

No different from the authors of the Constitution in reflexively
protecting the interests of the echelon to which they belonged, the
politico-industrial class, with amenable rhetorical support from
intellectuals and the press, and not without occasional disagreement, decided to maintain course—one from which they would
benefit, and one which had its roots in 1607, 1776, 1787, and
1815–60. The year 1898 would become the inaugural year for this
move beyond the frontier of contiguous territorial aggrandizement
to an overseas reach.

Like Christopher Columbus 400 years earlier, the much sought-after
markets of China and the assumption that that country's hundreds
of millions of people would offer a nearly bottomless consumerist
pit for American goods remained highly influential for entrepre-
neurs and policymakers. This failed to work out for explorers, and
had not become a reality in the late nineteenth century, nor would
it. Nevertheless, the notion of creating and sustaining an open door
remained a potent one. The Open Door Policy was initially a means
of America obtaining uninterrupted (by foreign powers operating
there) commercial access to China, but led to a global concept
whereby the United States could project economic power—unload
exports, demand resources, dictate terms—in areas where it lacked
direct authority; the open door broadened the economic dimension
of Manifest Destiny. As a result, the Pacific Ocean was envisioned
as just as much of a sphere of influence (to serve as a threshold
to the open door) as Latin America and the Gulf-Caribbean were.
The Spanish–American War, or what we will call the War of 1898,
was the first step into that sphere.[35] Briefly stated, the United
States went to war with Spain over Cuba on account of Spanish
inability to maintain order against anti-colonial resistance on the

Caribbean island. Revolution and the possible threat of independence endangered American property and investments there, and needed to be prevented. The war effort also spread to the Philippines, much coveted by American strategists. From April to August, the United States gained control of the Spanish colonies of Cuba, the Philippines, Puerto Rico, and Guam. Likewise, the William McKinley administration (1897–1901) formally annexed Hawaii, whose queen the United States had dethroned in a bloodless coup in 1893.

While August concluded the war, events turned course in the Philippines early the following year with an insurrection against American occupation, and the declaration of the Philippine Republic by rebel forces led by Amilio Aguinaldo. America's counter-revolutionary war there called over 120,000 troops to the islands, claimed the lives of roughly 200,000 Filipinos (mostly civilians), and finally defeated the insurgency three years later.[36] As influential congressman Albert Beveridge dismissively remarked, "the turbulent children know not what they do."[37] Yet, special care was taken to smooth over the harsh realities by asserting the exact opposite. Thomas Schoonover, a leading scholar in this period of American history, comments on the linguistic legerdemain employed, and that remains standard to this day:

> Inventive use of language obscured U.S. conduct. Captain [Alfred Thayer] Mahan adopted a form of modern-speak or political speak to address U.S. imperialism. He preferred "outward impulses" to "imperialism," "liberate" as a code for "occupy," and "pacify" for "conquer." Many others in the press or government used similar language. The U.S. military introduced the Filipinos to modern war—burning, looting, the scorched-earth, rape, pillage, and the water torture. These troops took few prisoners and kept few records. To carry out a "near-genocidal policy," U.S. troops had to dehumanize the opponents with language and images—the enemy were "niggers," "googoos," "Kodiak ladrones," or "gooks." The human psyche required subhumans for extermination. General Jacob ("Hell Roaring Jake" or "Howling Wilderness") Smith, who encouraged combat savagery, was court-martialed and "admonished." Incredibly, it appears that his real error was not savagery, but reducing his orders to writing. By 1901, the U.S. military used concentration camps, curfews, and kill-and-burn policies to "civilize" the Filipinos.[38]

At the dawn of the twentieth century the Philippines learned—and in turn a clear message had been sent to underdeveloped countries in general—that failure to cooperate under American control would result in disciplinary action. Put differently, independence and self-determination outside the parameters of US political and economic interests would not be tolerated. Subsequent examples are in abundance, a recurrent theme that we will revisit.[39]

The lead-up to the late 1890s set the country's foreign-policy course. The coming century of international affairs would feature minor alterations along the way, but there would never be anything other than variations on established themes. The two major guiding tenets of Manifest Destiny and the Monroe Doctrine, in their global application, remain anchor points to this day and largely explain US possession of over 800 globally positioned military installations as of 2007.[40]

Around the turn of the century, two policies were appended to their precursors, one more general in character, one more particular. The former was enshrined in the Open Door Notes, issued by President William McKinley's secretary of state, John Hay. As mentioned, the policy of the open door was a non-colonial option to expand American economic interests through a corporate-industrial model of Manifest Destiny. Initially the policy was geared toward East Asia, in an effort to prevent Western Europe, Russia, and Japan from dividing China into exclusive economic spheres of influence. Instead, a situation of cooperative exploitation was created to keep China open to all. Somewhat predictably, this foreign presence and manipulation had destabilizing effects and inspired the Boxer Rebellion (1900), which endeavored to drive out this unwanted external interference. The United States sent a few thousand troops in contribution to the international military effort to put down the uprising.

The focus on China notwithstanding, the open door was simply a way for the United States to diversify its economic opportunities around the world without, as we have noted as a constant American hesitation, having to deal with the expense of direct control of local populations. Aside from instances of formal imperialism as was carried out in Hawaii and the Philippines, the desire was global, remote, unimpeded commercial access, especially to the peripheral regions. For this system to run smoothly, two key requisites had to be maintained: First, Europe, Russia, and Japan would have to keep out of the way and not obstruct American entrance, and second, revolutions in the Third World would have to be judged and handled on a case-by-case basis. By and large, they would not be looked upon with favor. While it did not practice imperialism in the traditional sense, the nature of Washington's economic relationships could safely be construed as such. As pointed out by William Appleman Williams,

> When an advanced industrial nation plays, or tries to play, a controlling and one-sided role in the development of a weaker economy, then the policy of the more powerful country can with accuracy and candor only be described as imperial.[41]

The second policy exemplifies this realistic, if self-evident, observation.

Closer to home, Theodore Roosevelt's administration (1901–09) was attempting to smooth out economic disagreements between Europe and various Gulf-Caribbean states, and issued what became known as the Roosevelt Corollary (to the Monroe Doctrine). Not only were Britain, Germany, and others reminded of the previously existing Latin American doctrine, but Roosevelt's 1904 message to the United States' southern neighbors—"every country washed by the Caribbean Sea"—was both supplemental and rather unambiguous:

> Chronic wrongdoing, or an impotence which results in a general loosening of the ties of civilized society, may in America, as elsewhere, ultimately require intervention by some civilized nation, and in the Western Hemisphere the adherence of the United States to the Monroe Doctrine may force the United States, however reluctantly, in flagrant cases of such wrongdoing or impotence, to the exercise of an international police power.[42]

Foreign economic intervention frequently disrupted a weaker country's political stability. But the muscle that the president affixed to Monroe's message made it clear that orderly compliance was expected, while ferment and revolution would force America's hand as a "police power." The Corollary had indeed added much heft to the 1823 original. "Roosevelt justified such intervention as only an exercise of 'police' power, but that term actually allowed U.S. presidents to intervene according to any criteria they were imaginative enough to devise," Walter LaFeber points out in his standard account of US involvement in Central America. "In the end they could talk about 'civilization,' and 'self-determination,' but their military and economic power was its own justification."[43] Over the course of Roosevelt's presidency, as well as the subsequent administrations of William Taft (1909–13) and Woodrow Wilson (1913–21), Cuba, Panama (Colombia), the Dominican Republic, Haiti, Nicaragua, and Mexico all felt the pressure of US political, economic, and military coercion, some repeatedly and for decades to come. Though a treatment typically reserved for smaller, more vulnerable peripheral states, Russia, much like China during its vulnerable phases, would receive comparable handling, until (like China) it developed in a way that would transform its relationship with Uncle Sam.

Though it is commonly assumed that the end of World War II dramatically ushered in the Cold War, the pieces were in place well before 1945. Tensions between the United States and Russia (later the Soviet Union) developed in the 1890s over Moscow's undertaking to gain exclusive control over Manchuria (northeast China), an instance of czarist expansion that the United States felt hindered its open door access. This course of action, however, was temporarily interrupted with the rise of the Bolsheviks in the revolution of 1917, the leaders of which, most notably V. I. Lenin and Leon Trotsky, maintained a position of anti-imperialism and anti-capitalism. Withdrawing early from World War I and signing a treaty with the Germans (Brest–Litovsk), the communists set to securing their power, allocating land for the peasantry, and rebuilding their war-torn country. This perceived challenge to America's desire to exert near-total control over postwar affairs raised Woodrow Wilson's ire. In response, the president sent 10,000 troops into Russia and tens of millions of dollars to support the counter-revolutionary White Army in what was now the Soviet Union, in a failed campaign to check the "Red Menace." While American military presence on Soviet territory lasted from 1918 to 1920, Russian memory of this intervention lasted much longer.

By the end of World War I, the United States had moved beyond being a contender in the international community to a position of preeminence. According to the *Cambridge History of American Foreign Relations*: "the twentieth century, as the century in which the United States emerged as the principal world power, may be said to have begun in 1917."[44] Throughout the interwar period (1918–39), Washington and Wall Street worked in concert using their new-found financial leverage to order the postwar situation. With this leverage, in addition to various treaties, coalitions, and organizations such as the League of Nations, the United States hoped to realize an international system by which Western Europe, Japan, and Russia cooperated, avoided warfare, and engendered and maintained a stability that was conducive to America's state-corporate aspirations—namely, the open door in the context of Manifest Destiny, the Monroe Doctrine, and its Rooseveltian reassessment. Part of this stability necessitated a world devoid of armed conflict.

International accords such as the Kellogg–Briand Pact (1928) were a step toward "condemn[ing] recourse to war for the solution of international controversies," and settling disputes "by pacific means."[45] Part of this stability also required, according to the Wilson administration and its successors, preservation of a non-revolutionary status quo. The 1920s were a time where revolution, nationalism, and anti-colonialism amplified throughout the regions of Asia, Africa, Latin America, and the Middle East. While Wilson's talk of "self-determinism" and making "the world safe for democracy" was enticing and suggested the best of intentions,[46] as witnessed in Latin America the principle of self-determination meant self-determination within parameters set by Washington.

The president's highly interventionist methods belied his rhetoric and indicated a fear of what would later be labeled the rotten apple theory, or the domino theory. As described in the specialist literature,

> the domino theory's nightmare scenario [is] a vision of a chain of events that begins with a localized and seemingly insignificant incident which then mushrooms into a decisive global struggle on whose outcome hinges the survival of America's liberal institutions.

Paraphrasing Wilson, the global "ideological disease pool" containing revolutionary tendencies would have to be controlled for risk of the United States becoming "infected by [these] contagions from abroad."[47] Though we will pick up this subject below, it is worth noting that the metaphorical falling domino is not strictly a Cold War concept, but in point of fact has its roots in Wilsonian internationalism, not to mention *Federalist* 10 and the Roosevelt Corollary.

In a spirit similar to Kellogg–Briand, the United States over time shifted to "the policy of the good neighbor," a phrase popularized by Franklin D. Roosevelt in his first inaugural address (1933).[48] This policy, where "the neighbor who resolutely respects himself and, because he does so, respects the rights of others," moved US hegemony in Latin America to a less military mode of dominance. Yet, much like Wilson's exalted language, the Good Neighbor Policy was a mere streamlining of its informal imperialism in the region— more remote, same control. The procedure "employed economic penetration, political subversion, non-recognition, support for dictators who kept order, arbitration treaties, Pan Americanism, financial supervision, Export–Import Bank loans, and the training of national guards."[49] In sum, this neighborly arrangement tightened the screws on the Caribbean, protecting American business interests in the region and leading to wrenching poverty and dictatorial regimes such as existed in Nicaragua under Anastasio Somoza and the Dominican Republic under Rafael Trujillo, with lasting effects. As historian David Schmitz summarizes, "This emphasis on order came to permeate policymaking in Washington, and the United States found strong-arm rule, the maintenance of stability, anticommunism, and protection of investments sufficient reasons to support nondemocratic rulers."[50]

After this examination of early American foreign relations, especially those in the Western Hemisphere, by the time World War II comes and goes, the period known as the Cold War should appear less mythical and more business as usual. The touch-and-go nature of Soviet–American relations between the world wars was merely suspended by World War II, when the Soviet Union was allied with Great Britain and the United States, forming the Allies, or the "Big Three." The conflict with the Axis powers of Nazi Germany, Italy, and Japan ended in an Allied victory, with much of the war's belligerents left in utter ruin irrespective of what side they were on. The United States, on the other hand, suffered nary a scratch on the homeland (Pearl Harbor not being a homeland attack) and found itself in a global position even superior to the one it found itself in after World War I. This time, the United States was unrivaled in its economic and military strength, including a monopoly on atomic capabilities.

By "business as usual" what is meant is a continuation of the doctrines that had been driving American foreign policy since independence, with the domino theory growing out of prior suppositions that the self-interested actions of colonized peoples almost always contradict those of Washington and its interlocutors in the dominant classes. Although it was still in possession of a sizable military, Russia had suffered profound devastation in its conflict with Germany;[51] in the Cold War "superpower" bipolarity between Washington and Moscow, the latter was in second place by a healthy margin. Given the massive reconstruction facing the Kremlin (the seat of executive power in Russia), the likelihood of Soviet aggression was quite low, as was noted by the State Department even at the time, when it stated that the Russians "are not too greatly concerned about developments in Western Europe so long as the Western European countries do not show signs of ganging up on them."[52] Among Soviet leader Joseph Stalin's primary postwar concerns were mending a damaged Mother Russia and securing her boundaries. World War II had not been the only event in history where Russia had experienced invasion and all the adversity that goes with it, and Stalin looked to Eastern Europe (mainly Poland) as a sphere of influence from which Moscow could reap the benefits of resources for reconstruction, as well as a physical buffer in the event of further European instability. Despite Stalin's barbarous and inhumane policies within his country, the Kremlin's postwar conduct was in the main characterized by relative moderation; beyond recovery, the chief Soviet importance as of 1945 was security, within a defensive mindset.

Washington's aspirations were more managerial in disposition. With its superlative power and the attendant opportunities that such a position affords, the United States desired to essentially create a worldwide open door to protect its interests, from Western Europe to East Asia, and all the peripheral regions connected one way or another to these areas. The two primary industrial powers in Eurasia—Germany and Japan—were now out of commission and their redevelopment would have to be closely monitored. With Britain and France enfeebled, the seeds of Third World revolution further germinated as these two powers began to lose their grip on their colonial possessions. Even in areas throughout Europe, people began turning to the left politically in search of a solution to what they felt were the egregious failures of capitalist greed and conservatism. As noted by Dean Acheson, Harry S. Truman's fourth secretary of state (under-secretary to the previous three) and chief architect during the Cold War years:

> They have suffered so much ... and they believe so deeply that governments can take some action which will alleviate their sufferings, that they will demand that the whole business of state control and state interference shall be pushed further and further.[53]

This was a central Cold War fear among planners in Washington. Much like the US preference for "stability" in Latin America, the threat of radical or dissident appeal anywhere, in the core or the periphery, could inherently perturb the global corporate-industrial vision the United States aimed to achieve after 1945.[54]

With anticommunist sentiment having been cultivated within the United States during the interwar years, the inclination toward "leftist" concepts like reform, welfare, and increased popular participation in government was associated with Soviet-Stalinist ideology. Regardless of whether the various revolutionary movements were Marxist or not, the word "Soviet" was indeed a bad one, and came with the word "Marxism" attached. It should be noted, however, that the Bolshevik-Leninist system had little to do with Marxism (despite its stated communist ideology), as the writings of Karl Marx constitute an analytical assessment of capitalism and are not a blueprint for the creation of a utopia—a gross and common misunderstanding in America to this day. Nonetheless, in order for policymakers to forge ahead with molding postwar Europe, requiring massive amounts of capital, Congress and the public would have to be brought over to this way of thinking.

The proper mindset was captured by another principal author of Cold War policy, George F. Kennan, who at the time was an employee of the embassy in Moscow and in 1947 was appointed to be director of the State Department's Policy Planning Staff. During his embassy years he penned an internal State Department telegram that was eventually published in the *Foreign Affairs* journal as "The Sources of Soviet Conduct." In the article, Kennan outlined the strategy of containment: "containment of Russian expansive tendencies" by means of "adroit and vigilant application of counter-force" to Moscow's intended "duel of infinite duration."[55] This was the program the Truman administration would follow; everything it would set about—the Truman Doctrine and the Marshall Plan being the larger initiatives—would be in the name of containing the Soviet threat. But with little evidence of the Kremlin's "expansive tendencies" or the envisioned "duel," a certain measure of hysteria had to be established in Congress and among Americans if funding for the Truman–Marshall proposals was to be acquired.[56] However, achieving executive influence over Congress (especially a Republican one, oppositional to the Democratic White House) in peacetime posed a greater challenge. The expedient amounted to propaganda.

According to foreign policy scholar Warren I. Cohen in *The Cambridge History of American Foreign Relations*,

The tactics applied by the Truman administration in 1947 were designed to create an atmosphere, in Washington at least, in the country as a whole if necessary, that would enable the executive to dominate the legislative agenda much as it would in time of war. If misleading Congress and the people about the nature and immediacy of the Soviet threat to American interests was necessary to gain congressional and public support, it seemed a small price to pay.[57]

As Kennan asserted during a speech at the National War College in 1949, communism was not the disease but a complication, and the United States should not "get too violently indignant over the fact that such a complication exists. As one of my associates recently said: 'If it had never existed, we would have had to invent it, to create the sense of urgency we need to bring us to the point of decisive action.'"[58] Hence the sense of urgency was spelled out by Truman addressing a joint session of Congress to gain financial support for the Communist uprising in Greece, as well as aid for Turkey.

Greece was embroiled in a civil conflict between right-wing, pro-monarchy forces and the People's Liberation Army (ELAS), which had played a key role in driving Nazi forces from the country during the war. Referred to at the time as "those gallant guerillas" by Britain's prime minister, Winston Churchill, London began to support the right-wing forces, elements of which had collaborated with the Germans, and among whom were over 200 ex-members of the Nazi Security Battalions.[59] But the British could no longer foot the bill for combating the resistance, and appealed to Washington to take over. Truman approached Congress in March 1947; condemning the "terrorist activities" of the "Communists who defy the government's authority," while asserting that "Greece must have assistance if it is to become a self-supporting and self-respecting democracy."[60] This was to be attained by sending hundreds of millions of dollars and hundreds of advisers to help crush a popular uprising and reinstall an oppressive regime that would remain dutifully in line with Anglo-American interests. Yet three points are worth noting:

1. Regarding Greece's value as a country, Truman himself in the speech described it as "not a rich country," one lacking "sufficient natural resources." So the interest was clearly not physical.
2. The USSR, by Churchill's own admission (and Truman's tacit

acknowledgment), did not start, support, encourage, or interfere in any way in the Greek Resistance, the problems being internal to Greece and political in nature.[61] So the standard Cold War fears failed to apply. Even the US ambassador to Greece conceded that "the best men" in the country "are the heads of the Communist movement .... That is the sad part of it."[62]

3. Intervention could not be chalked up to a charitable impulse to help the Greek state, as the United Nations, which was designed specifically to help resolve such conflicts, was never involved, with Truman assuring Congress that the United Nations was "not in a position to extend help of the kind that is required." The kind of "help" that was required, if actions speak louder than words, featured: support for and/or advisement of assassinations, executions, massive arrests, the outlawing of strikes (punishable by death), martial law, the jailing of newspaper editors, tens of thousands sent to island-based detention camps, and the displacement of peasant populations in an evacuation program (accelerated by American advisers) which created approximately 700,000 refugees.[63] And with such methods, the resistance was put to rest.

Unable to attribute this intervention to a natural-resources impulse, containment of Soviet objectives, or legitimate resolution of the conflict through peace-keeping missions and negotiations, we are left with what had become procedural in Latin America, specifically, prevention of revolution and popular uprising. Acheson in his memoirs makes the following description:

> Like apples in a barrel infected by one rotten one, the corruption of Greece would infect Iran and all to the east. It would also carry infection to Africa through Asia Minor and Egypt, and to Europe through Italy and France, already threatened by the strongest domestic Communist parties in Western Europe. The Soviet Union was playing one of the greatest gambles in history at minimal cost. It did not need to win all the possibilities. Even one or two offered immense gains. We and we alone were in a position to break up the play.[64]

Judging by the historical evidence, the rotten apple threatening the infection of its neighbors was any small and poor country steering an independent, progressive course of any kind, communist or otherwise, that might not fully defer to external expectations. And if Country A was successful, Country B might become similarly inspired with the idea of improving the lives of its population, and thus another domino would fall. By contrast, in 1949, China's internal friction resulted in the defeat of Western-favored Kuomintang leader Chiang Kai-shek and the emergence of communist rule under Mao Zedong (or Tse-tung), all to barely detectable disappointment in Washington. Yet curiously, Greece threatened the world with "infection." As Charles Evans Hughes, secretary of state under presidents Harding and Coolidge, reflected after his time in office, "It is easy to point to places of chronic unrest among the smaller nations."[65] The pattern established in the Caribbean and duplicated in Greece would be repeated over and over again: in Iran six years later, with its progressive, popular leadership overthrown in a CIA-engineered coup, and in Vietnam less than two decades later, to cite just two examples.

Regardless of the continued rhetoric—of the Kremlin's efforts toward "domination of the Eurasian land mass," a conflict "which has been imposed upon us" by the "amoral," "opportunistic" Soviet "monolith" perched ready "to do its evil work" while "animated by a new fanatic faith" as it "seeks to impose its absolute authority over the rest of the world"[66]—American penetration of the Third World beyond the Western Hemisphere was just beginning to intensify. As Great Britain found itself unable to bear the costs of maintaining its imperial pursuits in the Middle East, a vacuum was forming that Washington abhorred. After a look in Chapter 3 at how that region came to be the "modern" Middle East, we will see in Chapter 4 how and why the United States drew upon its long prior history of imperialism and expansionism to play the central role that it does there today.

PART 2

DOMINION AND SUPREMACY

3

THE MODERN MIDDLE EAST AND ISRAEL: A SUMMARY

An examination of how the Ottoman Middle East was divided into nation-states between the two world wars will help maintain our historical thread and set the stage for the entrance of the United States, picked up in the following chapter.

FROM IMPERIAL TO PERIPHERAL

Today's map of the Middle East is a relatively new development in world history, with the first of its lines not being drawn until after World War I. The appellation itself, "Middle East," is also a somewhat recent convention, popularized by Alfred Thayer Mahan (whom we met in the previous chapter) as well as Western journalists and geographers at the turn of the century; if the saying that to name a thing is to own or control that thing has any validity, it would seem to apply reasonably in this instance. As will be discussed, those who guided the cartographers' pens were European powers, when they decided that they could—and should—take virtual possession of the area. But the region's modern overlords are only the latest in a long line of external forces that have imposed pressure and dominance on the Middle East.

Before the petroleum era, the Middle East had long been a coveted crossroads, sitting abreast the eastern rim of the Mediterranean Sea, connecting Africa, Europe, and Asia, and serving as a passageway to a valuable list of seas, straits, and gulfs. For this reason, imperial and military influence came from all around, and had done so for millennia. For present purposes we must fast-forward to the period following the European aggression known as the Crusades (1095–1291) and the brief yet brutal Mongolian invasion that took place in the mid-thirteenth century: specifically, the era of the Ottoman Empire.

The Ottomans were a Turkish group in northwest Anatolia (modern-day Turkey), who came as nomads from Central Asia, converted to Islam (the predominant religion as of the Arab Empire's establishment in the seventh century), and created principalities in Asia Minor at around the time the Mongols were finishing their scourge and the Crusades were winding down. One principality, led by Osman I, and subsequently his son Orhan, began to grow in martial prowess and reputation, and size as a result. In an effort to expand the territory of Islam and gain access to land and resources, Osman and his frontier warriors (*ghazis*) pushed against the Byzantine boundary, where Turkey and the Balkans meet, in near-constant raiding and warfare. The Ottomans (named after Osman) made short work of consolidating their dominion: In 1299 Osman declared his nascent kingdom independent; in 1326 his son secured their first capital city at Bursa; decades later much of the Balkans had been conquered; in 1453 the Ottomans captured the Byzantine capital, Constantinople; and throughout the sixteenth century the growing empire reached its zenith. Geographically, Ottoman rule would eventually blanket the northern rim of Africa, Egypt, the Balkans, Anatolia, the Arab areas that would later become Lebanon, Syria, Palestine, Jordan, and Iraq; the southern portion of Ukraine, and much of western Persia.

Generally speaking, by the mid-sixteenth century (and in particular the death of Suleyman the Magnificent in 1566, considered the last of the great Ottoman sultans) the empire began its decline. While not a sharp or jarring descent by any means, the Ottoman Empire was gradually slipping in rank as a world power.[1]

At about this time, Western Europe was embarking on the age of overseas exploration and colonization, undergoing the Reformation, the Thirty Years' War, and its overall savage conversion and ascendancy to the seat of global power. The Ottomans were able to sustain their strength throughout this period, with business carrying on as it had since the empire's emergence. While warfare and conflict were certainly part of this business, there was also a great deal of economic, diplomatic, and cultural activity between Christian Europe and its Turko-Islamic neighbor. But commercial exchange would fatefully end up playing a key role in Ottoman dislocation and entry into peripheral status within the larger world economy.

Though the empire's incorporation into the expanding capitalist world economy occurred mainly during the period 1750–1815,[2] the beginning had its roots in the late 1500s. As transatlantic commerce increased, the Middle East became less of an actor as the Mediterranean economy became a subordinate market. In addition, South American silver, mined by the Spanish (with local slave labor), made its way back to Europe, flooding markets, depreciating in value, and producing inflation that was especially damaging to the Ottomans.

Inflationary trends were also exacerbated by Ottoman merchants exporting increased amounts of raw materials and in turn importing European manufactures. As a result, fewer raw materials were available for domestic consumption, which raised prices, adversely affected the domestic economy, and displaced people working in the agricultural sector—the majority of a population that was growing significantly—into urban centers where poverty and unemployment awaited them. These currents also took their toll on state revenues, and therefore the military and the level of corruption throughout.

In an effort to create a counterbalance, the Ottomans instituted what were called "capitulations." These agreements were unilateral on the part of the empire and allowed merchants from a given European country legal and tax immunity while operating in Ottoman territory; a merchant would instead remain under the jurisdiction of the state of which he was a citizen. The capitulations were initially as much a diplomatic instrument as they were an effort to increase commerce. (The first capitulatory treaty was with France in 1569, but England, Holland, and Russia were eventually extended the same offer.) As time marched on, the Ottomans were no longer operating from the position they once enjoyed, and over the course of the next two centuries the empire diminished in strength, with foreign merchants fully penetrating its economy via these immunities. The number of merchants granted capitulations was small at first, but as it increased, and as Ottoman prestige decreased, the European powers used the capitulations as a method of intrusion which afforded them extended, damaging influence in Ottoman lands. Taken in aggregate, the causes and effects of Ottoman decline began to change the political landscape in that part of the world, especially for Europe and Russia. The ongoing question of how to contend with a powerful Ottoman Empire was slowly superseded by the question of what to do with an ailing one.

Largely owing to economic woes, the Ottomans began to slip in their military performance, with a number of setbacks and defeats occurring in the late 1600s and carrying into the late 1700s. This century-long experience indicated and precipitated a change in the empire's history. Territory was temporarily withdrawn from and permanently lost in repeated warfare with mainly the Austrian Habsburgs and Russia. It should be noted that, similar to the other aspects of Ottoman decline, this period of contraction was not absolute; the empire still chalked up scattered victories and successful counter-offensives. Nevertheless, when it lost Hungary (as well as Transylvania, Croatia, and Slovenia) to the Habsburgs in 1699, this was a first. However, permanent losses became intermittent and remained so up until Napoleon Bonaparte's temporary occupation of Egypt in 1798, resulting in Ottoman loss of that territory as well.

Over the course of the eighteenth and nineteenth centuries, a number of developments slowly converged to create two concepts historians refer to regularly when examining this era: the "Eastern Question" and the "Great Game." As the Ottoman Empire lost territory little by little, exhibited decreases in military competence, and shifted to an overall defensive posture, the European states of Britain, France, Habsburg Austria, along with czarist Russia, became known as the Great Powers. The Great Powers all took increased interest of one kind or another in the state of the Ottoman Empire—the Eastern Question.

Russia, in its drive to expand its empire, desired warm-water ports for trade and access to the Mediterranean, which it lacked. Through a series of wars with the Ottomans, Moscow gained limited command of the Black Sea and now wished fully to realize its goal by gaining control of the Dardanelles and Bosporus straits, both still lying within Ottoman domain. Given the opportunity the Russian czars likely considered moving past the straits for a larger piece of the Ottoman Empire, but Western Europe remained vigilant to this possibility, possessing similar designs (something about the commonality of great minds).

Great Britain, with its acquisition of India in the mid-1700s (taken from France), became protective of this new possession and all routes to it. Russian movement southward into Central Asia aroused British anxiety, thus initiating the Great Game, the contest between these two powers for influence from the Middle East to China. Rivalries between Paris and London also arose, with each becoming preoccupied with preventing the other from getting too far ahead, and instead maintaining a general European balance of power.

France, having lost India and other colonial holdings to the British (especially in the Seven Years War), and lacking dominance on the Atlantic, decided to take advantage of what it could in its Mediterranean backyard. In addition to colonial claims in North Africa, Napoleon, as mentioned, invaded Egypt in 1798, despite the record of relatively warm Franco–Ottoman relations. The French presence in Egypt—"harsh, heavy-handed, and hated"[3]—was soon reversed by British and Ottoman military cooperation. After French withdrawal, however, Muhammad (Mehmet) Ali rose to power and established a dynasty that lay outside Ottoman administration. It remained in power until 1952 and the era of Nasser (more on him in Chapter 4). Napoleon's occupation of Egypt was the first direct European intervention in the Middle East of the modern era.

Habsburg Austria, our fourth Great Power consideration, comes mostly into play at the fulcrum on which the Eastern Question tended to teeter most: the Balkan Peninsula. As of the nineteenth century, a sense of nationalism began to take root in southeastern Europe. Throughout the 1800s these Ottoman lands were the site of revolt, quests for independence, European influence, warfare, and diplomatic efforts by Western states to prevent Great Power conflict with a fragmenting Ottoman Empire. Greece achieved its independence first (in 1829), with countries such as Serbia, Romania, and Bulgaria following suit. Though it is tempting to assume that these movements signaled broad Balkan interest in tearing away from Ottoman rule, this was not the case. For the empire's duration, administrative flexibility and tolerance created a general sense of contentment among the populations. While not a paradise by any means, the empire was a stable and relatively well-ordered system. Donald Quataert, a distinguished scholar of Ottoman history, offers valuable comment on this matter:

> Was the empire destroyed from within by separatist or national-ist forces or from without, by imperial powers? ... In my own view, external rather than internal factors played the key role. The overwhelming majority of Ottoman subjects were not seek-ing separation or withdrawal. Rather, they would have remained within an Ottoman state framework had that political entity continued to exist into the 1920s and 1930s. The formation of independent states derived not from groundswell movements, but rather the actions of certain groups in the societies who sought economic and/or political privilege that they believed they could not obtain under Ottoman domination.... In the Balkan lands, Russia, Austria-Hungary, Britain, and/or France supported these aspirations since they believed (usually correctly) that the new states were likely to fall under their own respective influence.[4]

The nineteenth century was a major period for European imperial activity in foreign lands, the Balkans being an epicenter, generating effects that ignited World War I and changed the course of human history. In general, the Great Powers managed to avoid military conflict among themselves (with exceptions, such as the Crimean

War, 1853–56), endeavoring through many instances of diplomacy (for instance, the Concert of Europe, the Treaty of Berlin, 1878) to prevent other conflicts—or as historian William Cleveland phrases it, "to find a more peaceful method of dismantling the Ottoman Empire."[5] But with the unification of Germany (1871, previously Prussia), the delicate balance was further strained, adding another major European power to the mix of imperial global intrigue. An illustration of the degree of intrigue can be found in Africa, a continent that up until the 1880s was more or less independent, but over the next few decades leading up to World War I was devoured completely (apart from Ethiopia) by only seven European states: Belgium, France, Germany, Great Britain, Italy, Portugal, and Spain. Historian Rashid Khalidi notes the incongruity in Europe's behavior, one that can easily be found in American behavior during this era and thereafter:

> This is one of the enduring ironies of the colonial legacy of the democratic West European powers ... that dominated the lion's share of the globe by the first half of the twentieth century. Beacons of freedom and constitutional democracy, and constantly removing barriers to suffrage and expanding the rights of the individual at home, these same states conquered and ruled over the peoples of much of the earth without the slightest reference to the liberal principles that animated their own systems of government.[6]

Between increased competition, Germany's introduction to the balance, and continuing tensions in and around the Balkans, it was only a matter of time before Europe would return to its old ways of barbarity conducted internally, regardless of its efforts to keep operations in foreign locales. The spark was a conflict between the Habsburgs and Serbia which divided the Great Powers into two major alliances, and catalyzed four years of warfare that would bring about the demise of the Ottoman Empire and the birth of the modern Middle East.

THE MANDATE AND THE ARAB STATES

World War I was a conflict between the Triple Entente, or Triple Alliance, and the Central Powers, the former composed of Great Britain, France, and Russia (and the United States as of 1917), and the latter an alliance between Austria-Hungary and Germany. While initially maintaining a position of neutrality, the Ottoman Empire decided to throw in its lot with the Central Powers, for several reasons including the fact that this was the anti-Russian side. As fate would have it, Russia never finished the war and the Central Powers ended up vanquished. It is difficult to speculate how things might have gone for the Ottomans had they maintained neutrality or sided with the Entente countries—the historical record of the late nineteenth century suggests perhaps not well. This kind of conjecture notwithstanding, the outcome of the war and the European machinations conducted *during* its course had definite consequences for the Middle East.

As we saw in Quataert's remarks on the nationalist movements in the Balkans, those Ottoman subjects living in the southeastern European territories were not altogether eager to break from Turkish rule. This was a process put in motion by a small group of domestic and foreign elites, creating a movement that caught on after the fact (there are parallels to the lead-up to the American Revolution, see p. 24). The empire's Arab territories underwent a similar conversion during the war. The domestic and foreign influences this time were born of British interest in sowing disunity within the Ottoman Empire, largely as a device to undermine the Ottoman leadership and gain military advantages on the one hand, and on the other to have a ready-at-hand loyal insurgent leadership once the time came to divide up the spoils between London and Paris.

In the prewar period, British consideration of the Ottoman Empire was more remote than, say, that of Austria and Russia. Within the context of the Eastern Question, London's motivation was simply to ensure that no power's gains (from Ottoman losses) became incommensurate with any other's. Britain was protective of its colonial possessions at the time, and advocated Ottoman integrity for the practical purposes of maintaining a buffer between India and feared Russian encroachment. Just the same, when the war commenced, London's concerns for Ottoman stability were moderated by postwar aims in the likely event the empire would be carved up and divided among the victors. As evidenced in a letter from the British ambassador in Constantinople to the British foreign secretary, sent just before the war, "all the powers including ourselves are trying hard to get what they can out of Turkey. They all profess to the maintenance of Turkey's integrity but no one ever thinks of this in practice."[7] At the same time, certain elite Arab elements in the Arabian Peninsula (present-day Saudi Arabia) began entertaining notions of postwar Arab independence in Arabia, and perhaps in Greater Syria and Mesopotamia.

Britain found its client in Sharif Hussein, the amir of Mecca, a prominent religious position in the Arab world. The relationship was cemented through an exchange of letters between Hussein and the British high commissioner in Cairo, Sir Henry McMahon. The reason for McMahon's location, it might be added, was that Britain had occupied Egypt in 1882, declaring it a protectorate by wartime. The pretext at the time for British intervention there was the usual rationale we still commonly hear today, namely, regional stability, maintaining order, and so on. However, as noted Oxford historian Albert Hourani elucidates, "The real reason was that instinct for power which states have in a period of expansion, reinforced by the spokesmen of European financial interests."[8] But we digress.

The so-called Hussein–McMahon Correspondence, conducted from mid-1915 to early 1916, was essentially a quid pro quo between the two parties.[9] Hussein would aid the British by conducting an Arab revolt against the Ottomans, and in return would be granted a postwar independent state roughly comprised of the Arabian Peninsula, Greater Syria (encompassing the modern designations of Syria, Lebanon, Jordan, and Palestine), and Iraq. The correspondence, however, was nothing so clear, and the vagaries on McMahon's side remain something of a mystery among scholars. He designated certain areas not to be included in an Arab state or that would remain to some degree under British administration. The main portion not to be included was most of Lebanon, which was earmarked for France. The boundaries defining this coastal exemption are where the bulk of the controversy lies. McMahon's wording was deliberately nebulous for the sake of dealing with the French (allies and friends being two different things),[10] and was later used to justify British exclusion of Palestine—never mentioned in the correspondence—from independence. Nevertheless, the agreement was struck for a revolt to create a state, with some matters deferred for postwar settlement.

French and British negotiations were also being conducted around the same time the Hussein–McMahon Correspondence was underway. These secret discussions, later enshrined in the Sykes–Picot Agreement (named after each representative), created plans for a postwar order in the Middle East among the Allies, mainly France and England. As McMahon was making pledges to the sharif about Arab independence, London and Paris were arbitrating on the portions of the region over which each would exercise direct or indirect control. Ratified in 1916 but not published until after the war, Sykes–Picot gave Britain direct control over an area that cut from roughly Baghdad to the Persian Gulf. Its area of indirect control would be a swath from the Sinai Peninsula through the modern states of Jordan and Iraq, and well into Iran. France would gain direct control over the areas of modern Lebanon, coastal Syria, and a chunk of southeastern Turkey. Its indirect influence would encompass a good amount of Syria and northern Iraq. Much of what later became Palestine (and then Israel) was placed under international administration.

The language in Sykes–Picot can also be obscure, describing indirect influence as each signatory "hav[ing] priority of right of enterprise and local loans" and "supply[ing] advisers or foreign functionaries at the request of the Arab state or confederation of Arab states." Direct rule, however, is less vague, and grants that Britain and France are "allowed to establish such direct or indirect administration or control as they desire."[11] Regardless, what is clear is that the two allied powers were helping themselves to the Middle East, and that this division of the region into spheres of influence did not exactly jibe with the promises made to Hussein. Still and all, as a British general clarified upon examining English pledges to the sharif: "If the embryonic Arab state comes to nothing all our promises [to Hussein] vanish and we are absolved from them—if the Arab state becomes a reality we have quite sufficient safeguards to control it."[12]

As noted, most Ottoman subjects remained loyal to the empire during wartime, with uprisings and Arab movements being sparse. Hussein nevertheless cobbled together a tribal army in Arabia to be led by one of his sons, Faisal, and advised by British officers such as T. E. Lawrence ("Lawrence of Arabia"). The Arab Revolt commenced in June 1916. With provisional funding and arms from London, Faisal and company moved northward from western Arabia (the Hijaz), taking various towns on the way, disrupting Ottoman communication and transportation, fighting alongside British troops out of Egypt, and two years later taking Damascus with ample British support. The Ottomans shortly afterwards signed an armistice with the Entente powers, concluding Turkish involvement in the Great War.

With the Ottomans out of the war, and Russian withdrawal in 1917 because of the revolution there that brought to power the anti-imperialist Bolsheviks, "the war to end all wars" came to a close in November 1918. The Paris Peace Conference in January 1919 concluded the war on paper, but the establishment of a Middle Eastern arrangement continued for the next few years. At the Paris conference, along with the creation of various treaties, President Woodrow Wilson promoted the foundation of the League of Nations (precursor to the United Nations), an international organ that would attempt to prevent further conflicts through negotiation and diplomacy. Although the United States never became a member as a result of domestic American politics, Wilson's influence as its chief architect remained steadfast. His vision for the organization was based on self-determination, which included—much to the chagrin of Britain and France—the former Ottoman provinces of the central Middle East.

Among establishing its basic principles and rules, the League's charter, called the Covenant, spelled the future of the Middle East. According to Article 22 of the Covenant, the region's people were "not yet able to stand by themselves under the strenuous conditions of the modern world," and thus required "tutelage," which "should be entrusted to advanced nations." "This tutelage should be exercised by them as Mandatories on behalf of the League," in the capacity of providing "administrative advice and assistance ... until such time as they [the mandate territories] are able to stand alone."[13] Selection of the mandatories was supposed to take into account the wishes of the regional communities. These wishes had been investigated by an American delegation called the King–Crane Commission, which determined that the people of the region desired the creation of an independent Greater Syria with Faisal as its leader, and preferred the United States as its mandatory. This raises a point that cannot be overemphasized: *America as of this time had not the interventionist reputation it later developed, and was looked on rather favorably by many of the region's inhabitants.* However, the results of King–Crane were not published. With Wilson intent on trying to gain US Senate approval for League membership, as well as his failing health, the commission's report found its way onto a shelf, with Britain and France preferring to handle the matter as they saw fit. It is interesting to reflect on what might have been and how the Middle East would be different, had its desires been given consideration instead of the indifference they received.

At the San Remo Conference (April 1920) the mandates were distributed, placing Syria and Lebanon under French charge, and Iraq and Palestine under British charge. Shortly thereafter, another subdivision in the region was created, that of Transjordan (considered eastern Palestine at the time),* also sponsored by London. This

---

* The cis- and trans- prefixes come from Latin, meaning "this side of"

haphazard partitioning and/or grouping of these former Ottoman provinces into five new Arab nation-states, ratified by the League in 1922, initiated the map of the modern Middle East. But the system of tutelage was more one of vassalage, the effects of which carry into the present. As William Cleveland remarks, "the mandate system was little more than nineteenth-century imperialism repackaged to give the appearance of self-determination."[14] If evidence of this fact was not plainly available from even the wording of the mandate, discontent among the various populations made it clear. Resistance and revolt were ignited throughout the region in the 1920s, especially in Egypt, Iraq, Syria, and Palestine. Suppression of disturbance was generally meted out with harsh military force including aerial bombardment. We might recall Senator Beveridge's words (see page 37) about the "turbulent children" being unaware of their actions.

The mandates basically lasted until after World War II, a time when most of Europe's colonial holdings were becoming independent, and in many cases inheriting new sets of political and social difficulties, frequently part of the "postcolonial" experience. Of the five new Arab states created by the mandate—Palestine, Transjordan, Iraq, Lebanon, and Syria—all eventually achieved independence with the exception of Palestine, and all remaining subordinate to European power just the same. Three other Arab states not created by the mandate—Egypt, Saudi Arabia, and Yemen—emerged independent but were similarly positioned with regards to Europe; the British protectorates in the Persian Gulf, namely, Kuwait, Bahrain, Qatar, the United Arab Emirates, and Oman, remained as such but were granted independence much later. Two non-Arab states were created, Turkey and Iran, and they also followed the general pattern.

The Middle Eastern states were never designed to be progressive democracies based on the models evolving in the West. They were simply created to be peripheral to the West. Britain and France wanted open access to their economies, open access to the region's natural resources, and veto power in their policymaking. To ensure the stability of this dominance, the leadership in the various countries would have to satisfy the criteria of maintaining domestic order while remaining dutiful to their Western sponsors. This kind of linkage with Western

---

and "across," respectively. Palestine at this time could also be viewed or referred to as Cisjordan.

power destined the region for what has been highly visible for the last 60 years. Some countries in the Middle East have retained the original dynastic leadership, such as Transjordan (later Jordan) and Saudi Arabia. Some states and territories remain unstable owing predominantly to how they were formed, Lebanon and Israel/Palestine being examples of such volatility. Coups and overthrows plagued some, especially Syria and Iraq. Attempts to steer an independent course have generally resulted in punishment, as occurred in Egypt and Iran.

The current tumult in the Middle East is, in effect, a corollary of World War I and the postwar settlement of the mandatory system. As predicted by Colonel Edward House, presidential aide to Wilson, the European powers were creating "a breeding place for future war," which it indeed became.[15]

PALESTINE AND THE JEWISH STATE

A mandate country like the others, Palestine's interwar experience was markedly different from its peers. In addition to the Hussein–McMahon Correspondence and the Sykes–Picot Agreement, the British also worked out an accord with European Jews looking to realize their Zionist goal of creating a Jewish state in Palestine. In an effort to influence Russian Jews to help keep Moscow in World War I, and to influence American Jews to help guide the United States into the war on the Allied side, London decided to make a supportive pronouncement about Palestine, the entity that Hussein–McMahon neglected and Sykes–Picot internationalized. The pronouncement came in the form of a letter from the British foreign secretary, Arthur Balfour, to Lord Walter Rothschild, a leading British Zionist, stating that "His Majesty's Government view with favor the establishment in Palestine of a national home for the Jewish people." Interpretation of the so-called Balfour Declaration varied. Did a national home in Palestine mean a state in all of Palestine, or a sanctuary located within it? For the Zionists, it meant the former.

The ancient land of Canaan was home to a diversity of cultures and kingdoms, one of which was the Hebrew kingdom of Israel, existing in its unified form from 1000–925 BC and later splitting into Judah in the south and Israel in the north. Return to the Land of Israel, or "Zion," has remained a theological aspiration in Judaism for the roughly 1,900 years since most of the Jews were sent into exile from Palestine by the Romans in the second century AD.* However, in the late nineteenth century this aspiration turned political.

Over the centuries, the Jews had spread across the map, with the vast majority settling in Eastern Europe and Russia. While Western Jews still faced periodic anti-Semitism, they suffered less discrimination than their brethren to the east. The French Revolution's emphasis on Enlightenment concepts such as equality and human rights helped in this regard, allowing Jews the option to assimilate into the surrounding European culture. The situation in Poland and Russia was far more intolerant and repressive. Frequently made scapegoats, placed in ghettos such as the Pale of Settlement, and attacked by mobs (pogroms), some Jews desired to flee their circumstances and emigrate to Western Europe or the United States. By the late 1800s, the theological notion of returning to Zion took root as a literal option in the form of a nationalist ideology to create a safe-haven state.

While not a pioneer of political Zionism, Theodor Herzl gave coherence and clarity to the already swirling concept of Zionism with the publication of *The Jewish State* in 1896. An assimilated Hungarian Jew who lived most of his life in Vienna, Herzl was politically awakened by a resurgence in Western anti-Semitism, embodied particularly in the Dreyfus Affair (1894). When Captain Alfred Dreyfus, a French Jew, was wrongfully accused of treason, anti-Semitic sentiment swept through France, arousing in Herzl a desire to articulate a solution. That solution, elucidated and formalized in *The Jewish State*, was a Jewish return to Palestine.

Shortly after Herzl's manifesto was published, the World Zionist Organization was formed and the First Zionist Congress was held in Basel, Switzerland, where a Zionist declaration of principles known as the Basel Declaration was penned. By this time, however, Jews had already begun to immigrate into Palestine in waves known as *aliyah*. The First Aliyah (1882–1903) numbered around 25,000 immigrants, but these probably could not be considered altogether

---

* The name "Palestine" was originally applied by the ancient Greeks to designate the land of the Philistines, or Philistia, which was a kingdom of Aegean peoples who settled on the south Canaan coast, around Gaza. The label Syria Palaestina was later reintroduced to designate southern Syria by the Romans and subsequently used by the Ottomans. Native Palestinians are essentially a composite of original Canaanite stock and Arab bloodlines introduced after the Arabs entered the area in the seventh century AD.

Zionist in their intentions. They were Jews simply trying to escape the hardships of life in Russia and its territories. Those involved in subsequent aliyah became more ideologically driven. It is informative that large percentages of the immigrants eventually left Palestine out of surprise and disappointment. The Zionist slogan "A land without a people for a people without a land" fostered the broad assumption that Palestine was basically empty and awaiting Jewish arrival to fill it. Upon reaching their destination, the immigrants were alarmed to find the land inhabited and mostly cultivated by indigenous people. As more Jews poured into Palestine, acquisition of land became a forefront issue, one captured in the phrase "conquest of labor."

Before the First Aliyah, the population of Palestine comprised 400,000 Muslims, 43,000 Christians, and 15,000 Jews.[16] The Jewish population, accounting for 3.5 percent of the whole, was a mixture of Oriental (Sephardic) Jews, whose ancestors were among the region's original inhabitants, and European (Ashkenazic) Jews, who were for the most part devoutly religious and lived in Palestine for spiritual purposes.[*] This community, called the Old Yishuv, coexisted with the Arab population on relatively civil terms; Jews generally found Arab-Ottoman lands to be far more hospitable than Christian-European ones. The immigrant New Yishuv, in its efforts to forge a state under such circumstances, needed control of the arable land currently worked by the native Arab peasantry, or *fellahin*. Through purchase from absentee landlords (wealthy urban notables living in Palestine and Beirut), the Zionists gained such control. Initially allowing the fellahin to continue working as tenant farmers, Zionist policy later moved toward discontinuing this practice in favor of making the settlements inalienably Jewish.

Concern and suspicion began to grow among the Palestinians. The developing trend of Zionist purchases rendering peasant farmers landless and jobless engendered animosity. The farms they had worked for generations in communal ownership were now being sold out from underneath them. Palestinian fears of dispossession were well founded. Though at this time the shifting land-holding patterns were the only evidence, further evidence later emerged in the form of letters, journals, and documentation. At no point did the Zionist leadership entertain the idea of a *modus vivendi* with the

---

[*] The term Mizrahi (plural Mizrahim), meaning "Eastern," is gaining currency and is used to describe Jews from Arab and Asian regions. The label Sephardic technically refers to Jews from Spain.

Arabs; living among and with the native inhabitants in some kind of harmony was not the intention. As in North America, the indigenes were in the way. As Israeli historian Benny Morris states:

> For decades the Zionists tried to camouflage their real aspirations, for fear of angering the authorities and the Arabs. They were, however, certain of their aims and of the means needed to achieve them. Internal correspondence among the *olim* [New Yishuv] from the very beginning of the Zionist enterprise leaves little room for doubt.[17]

Even Herzl felt "the process of expropriation and the removal of the poor must be carried out discreetly and circumspectly."[18] Chaim Weizmann (Zionist forefather and first president of Israel) felt transfer would be "a courageous and statesmanlike attempt to grapple with a problem that had been tackled hitherto half-heartedly."[19] Abba Eban (a prominent Israeli diplomat and former foreign minister) observed that:

> To assert that thousands of years of Jewish connection totally eliminated thirteen centuries of later Arab-Muslim history would be to apply a discriminatory standard to historic experience.... If they had submitted to Zionism with docility they would have been the first people in history to have voluntarily renounced their majority status.[20]

As David Ben-Gurion, the state of Israel's first prime minister, said in conversation with the president of the World Jewish Congress in 1956:

> If I was an Arab leader I would never make terms with Israel. That is natural: we have taken their country. Sure, God promised it to us, but what does that matter to them? Our God is not theirs. We come from Israel, it's true, but two thousand years ago, and what is that to them? There has been anti-semitism, the Nazis, Hitler, Auschwitz, but was that their fault? They only see one thing: we have come here and stolen their country. Why should they accept that?[21]

Rhetoric to this end is abundant in the scholarly literature.

To the mounting Arab agitation over increasing Jewish immigration and Zionist land practices, the Balfour Declaration added a

whole new dimension. With London taking the place of the Ottoman Empire in mandatory Palestine, a confluence of three irreconcilable programs was formed: Palestinian desire for independence and
statehood (like the other mandate countries), Zionist desire to create
a Jewish state in Palestine, and British desire to sustain its colonial
control there. Clearly, this was an untenable situation, one destined
for violent conflict.

Throughout the 1920s and 1930s Palestinian apprehension
turned to protest and uprising. Especially feverish at the end of
each decade, the Arabs instituted boycotts and strikes, and commit
ted violence against Jews, British soldiers, and in some cases Arabs
accused of collusion. The British government sent delegations and
conducted investigations into the causes of the unrest. Half a dozen
commissions were set up and white papers issued throughout the
1930s, all of which reported similar findings. The recurrently cited
motivations of Arab rebellion were: Zionist labor policies, inalienable Jewish landholding, Arab dispossession, Jewish immigration,
Arab distrust of the British, Jewish–British cooperation, and so
forth. As Ben-Gurion soberly clarified: "politically we are the
aggressors and they defend themselves."[22]

One of the deputations during this period was the Peel Commission (1937), which along with reporting the underlying causes
of the revolts, suggested that Palestine should be partitioned into
Jewish and Arab areas, with a corridor from Jerusalem to the
Mediterranean placed under international mandate. The British
pledged devotion to both parties and their struggles, asserting that,
in all fairness, "The answer to the question which of them in the
end will govern Palestine must be Neither."[23] Of course, along with
offering "a chance of ultimate peace," this scenario also offered a
chance of ultimate British presence. Though mildly disappointing
to the Jewish population, news of the Zionists being offered 20
percent of mandatory Palestine and the remainder possibly being
united with Transjordan reignited revolts, some of the most violent
of the period. With London growing more concerned about the
gathering likelihood of a second world war, it opted to appease the
Arab population in Palestine. In a last-minute endeavor to strike
a balance, it diluted its claims in the Peel Commission, giving the
Zionists less and paying lip-service to Arab concerns. The Arabs
remained as angry and the Zionists grew more so. By the end of the
1930s Palestine was in chaos. Arab resistance and violence was met
with reprisal acts by Jewish militia (Haganah) and terrorist groups
(Irgun, Lehi). Despite British and Zionist cooperation against the

Arabs, Jewish groups began to fight against British troops. Further attempts to assuage Arab indignation by backing off slightly on offers to the Zionists again had similar consequences: Arab *and* Zionist ire. But as the revolt slowed down, World War II became the focus for Britain and the reason for its efforts, however dubious, at achieving tranquility in Palestine.

As a result of London's softened stance on how much land the Zionists would be granted and how much Jewish immigration would be authorized, Anglo–Zionist relations rested on tenter-hooks, where they stayed. Regardless of the support provided by thousands of Zionist Jews fighting alongside British troops in the war, back in Palestine relations between the two iced over. With news of the Holocaust atrocities perpetrated against European Jews, among others, inroads were made in gaining the support of many American Jews. This relationship was cemented at the Biltmore Conference (1942) in New York City, which helped create a base of support in America (where ironically, the State Department and the Franklin D. Roosevelt administration maintained rigid immigra-tion quotas, locking out thousands of Jewish refugees fleeing Nazi persecution).[24] The publicity campaign that ensued, bolstered by news of the Holocaust, took root especially in Washington, DC, and eventually the Truman White House. The United States, during and after the war, emerged as a world superpower and the Zionists viewed this as an opportunity to move away from the British.

In the early postwar period, the world had entered a new phase of global power politics, one configured along the lines of a bipolar Cold War between the US and Soviet superpowers. With the onset of the Cold War, and European potency significantly diminished, American interest in the Middle East became increas-ingly pronounced. In the interests of maintaining warm relations with Washington, the British were open to including the United States in a solution to the ever-deepening issue of Jewish immigra-tion into Palestine and refugee placement. Within this atmosphere two committees of inquiry were sent to the region in an effort to decide a course of action for Palestine's future. Meeting resistance from all involved parties—the Americans, the British, the Arabs, and the Zionists—the solutions, including partition, non-partition, restrictions on Zionist labor and land policies, and continuance of Britain's mandatory role, were rejected by some or all. London, now in an economic predicament as a result of the war, decided to hand the Palestine question to the United Nations, which replaced the League of Nations in 1945.

The United Nations created the ad hoc UN Special Committee on Palestine (UNSCOP), placing eleven member states in charge of brokering a proposal on how to resolve the conflict. The committee, after spending over a month in Palestine, returned a majority report and a minority report. The former suggested the creation of two separate states, while the latter recommended a single federated state composed of separate Arab and Jewish states. The UN General Assembly voted on November 29, 1947, endorsing the UNSCOP majority report and passing Resolution 181, with the United States and the USSR voting in approval. The resolution allocated 56 percent of mandatory Palestine to the Zionists, with Jerusalem and Bethlehem designated as a "*corpus separatum*" to be administered internationally. The Arab response was nothing short of rage and rejection, while the Zionist side, now 30 percent of the total population,[25] mostly looked on with jubilant favor. Menachem Begin, commander of the Irgun and future prime minister of the state of Israel (1977–83), however, voiced feelings commensurate with much of the Zionist leadership:

> The partition of Palestine is illegal. It will never be recognized.... Jerusalem was and will for ever be our capital. Eretz Israel [the Land of Israel] will be restored to the people of Israel. All of it. And for ever.[26]

What followed was a two-phase conflict in Palestine. The civil phase featured a guerilla war between the Palestinian Arabs and the Zionists, with the Arabs fighting on the offensive for the first portion, and the Jews eventually turning the tide. At the end of the civil phase, the Zionist leadership declared on May 14, 1948, an independent state of Israel on the UN-designated territory. The second major phase was international, and included advances by the surrounding Arab states, mainly Egypt, Syria, Iraq, and Jordan. The collective troop strengths of the Arab invasion were outnumbered by Israeli forces, owing to the complexities surrounding their manifold involvements. Given the domestic instability in their own countries and the regional concern about Jordanian designs on annexing the Arab territories of Palestine (plans discussed with Israel in then-secret meetings during the prewar run-up), the war was as much to prevent Jordan and its king, Abdullah (a son of Sharif Hussein who remained a British client) from helping themselves to a portion of Palestine as it was a battle against Israel. Over the course of the conflict, the Israelis were able to gain a decisive victory, expanding their domain from 56 to 78 percent. The ability to achieve such aggrandizement was provided by the flight of Arab villagers and townspeople, eventually exacerbated by the direct expulsion of Arabs and occupation and/or destruction of villages by Zionist–Israeli forces in general accordance with a March 1948 stratagem called Plan Dalet.[27] In sum, an exodus of 700,000 Palestinian Arabs created refugee populations in the surrounding Arab states and the now attenuated—and non-contiguous—Palestinian territories of the West Bank and Gaza. This matter has yet to be resolved.

Throughout the first half of 1949 an armistice was mediated, merely securing a ceasefire, allowing a state of war to persist, and freezing the boundaries created by Israel's victory. To the decades-long Palestine–Israel conflict, a new Arab–Israeli one had been added to the region's gathering list of burdens.

4

THE UNITED STATES AND ISRAEL: THE SPECIAL RELATIONSHIP FROM TRUMAN TO REAGAN

So far we have looked at the development of the modern nation-state, how Europe became the global epicenter of economic and military state power, and how this phenomenon gave birth to an offshoot called the United States. We have also sketched how the United States grew from a colonial outpost to a world power of unprecedented influence. This chapter begins where Chapters 2 and 3 converge, at the end of World War II, with the United States for the first time looking toward the Middle East as a zone of economic and strategic interest—what the State Department deemed "one of the greatest material prizes in world history."[1] In addition to this turn in world affairs, the Middle East, as of the mid-1940s, had been a region divided into states for only two decades and was now entering a new era of relative autonomy. Also during this period the state of Israel was added to the list of players in that part of the world in 1948, having a profound effect on the regional dynamic. These three changes in the prevailing order of the Middle East— American intrigue, fledgling Arab independence, and the emergence of the Jewish state—triangulate in this chapter.

OIL AND DOMINOES: THE UNITED STATES ENTERS THE MIDDLE EAST

In interviews and lectures concerning the US invasion and occupation of Iraq (2003–present), veteran Middle East correspondent for London's *Independent* newspaper Robert Fisk has repeatedly asked a fundamental, if rhetorical, question: "Do you really think that if the national export of Iraq was asparagus or carrots the 82nd Airborne would be in Mosul?"[2] While the question basically answers itself, it also invites inquiry regarding American superpower presence in the region. It should be kept in mind that the subject of US–Israeli relations, while the focus of this chapter, is ultimately an ancillary issue to the primary one of American foreign objectives. The evolution of Washington's alliance with Tel Aviv* would probably not have occurred, or would perhaps have done so under very different circumstances, had the United States not included the Middle East in its portfolio of global interests. Starting off with this rudiment gives the "special relationship," as it came to be known, a proper frame of reference.

Fisk's question is acute in its choice of Mosul, it being a city in Iraq rich in oil fields that attracted the desires of the British in the early twentieth century. Roughly a century later Middle Eastern oil is no less popular with powerful foreign entities. The US government's interest and subsequent direct influence there did not begin to take shape until after World War II. Yet, consistent with established policy, when the time came to look beyond the Western Hemisphere, America's approach brought to bear three themes dominant and recurrent in its foreign-relations history: the Open Door Policy (the goal), security (the pretext), and the domino theory (the method). The first of these three was and remains the principal consideration, with the other two being only procedurally relevant. First, the American corporate and state sectors each desired unimpeded access to the immense energy resources available in the Middle East. Second, the declared fear of communist expansion would provide the security-based rationale for conducting an aggressive program of gaining access to, and more to the point control of, those resources in the name of deterrence and national interest; which necessarily would entail, third, exercising management over the region in such a way as to ensure political consistency and reliability among its leaderships.

Up until the Cold War, the predominant power in the Middle East, as we covered in Chapter 3, was Great Britain. Of its colonial interests, it was not until the eve of World War I that oil became an issue of strategic importance, with the Royal Navy converting its larger ships over to oil power from coal in 1912. The enthusiasm

---

* While Israel, since 1950, has held to the position that its capital is in Jerusalem, Tel Aviv is internationally recognized (including by the United States) as the Israeli seat of government, with all foreign embassies located there. Since the Israeli assertion of Jerusalem is bound up in matters concerning its occupation of the Palestinian territories, this book will observe the international consensus.

over Middle Eastern resources was captured at the time by Winston Churchill, who described the oil beneath Iran as "a prize from fairy-land beyond our wildest dreams."[3] American oil companies moved into the picture shortly thereafter, centering their attention mostly on Saudi Arabia, and gaining what is called a "concession"—a tract of land granted typically by a weaker state to a more power-ful one for use and profit—from the kingdom's monarch, Ibn Saud, in 1933. The relationship with Saudi Arabia would be the United States' first special relationship in the region, and it is one that remains firmly in place.

Despite the early entry of private industry, Washington's interest in petroleum in that part of the world was only later aroused. Oil was already becoming increasingly important, but it was not until after World War I that it started to play an essential role in various aspects of human activity, especially warfare. Up until this time, the United States produced more than enough domestic crude for its own consumption, as well as supplying over half of the world's petroleum needs; at this point the Middle East was only just becom-ing a hotspot, producing less than 5 percent of the world's supply as late as 1940.[4] The concept of foreign oil lay outside American strategic interests, with President Franklin D. Roosevelt declining involvement with affairs concerning business between King Saud and American oilmen operating in the Arabian peninsula, saying the matter was "a little far afield for us."[5]

By the early 1940s, with World War II in full swing, the role that oil would inevitably play in the postwar order began to undergo a reversal, summarized then by Everette Lee DeGolyer, a geophysicist and central figure in the birth of the modern American oil industry:

> The center of gravity of world oil production is shifting from the Gulf-Caribbean area to the Middle East—to the Persian Gulf area ... and is likely to continue to shift until it is firmly established in that area.[6]

As foreign oil captured Washington's attention, cooperation between the public and private sectors naturally increased. Officers from the major oil companies became members on governmental advisory boards, with "their lobbying efforts play[ing] an important role in educating policymakers to the political and strategic significance" of the region's deposits, according to historian David Painter. In his words, the petroleum corporations became "vehicles of the national interest."[7]

US entrance into Middle Eastern affairs, with this state-corporate linkage in tow, went from half-hearted to earnest in the early post-war period, aspiring to secure the region in the spirit of the Monroe Doctrine; the shifting "center of gravity" aroused American determination. For instance, the cheap petroleum available in the region was used for the reconstruction of Europe, where 20 percent of the Marshall Plan aid (from the United States) for European reconstruction was spent on oil and oil equipment, roughly half of which was produced by American companies. In 1946, Western Europe received 77 percent of its petroleum from the Western Hemisphere, whereas by 1951, 70–80 percent of it came from the Middle East.[8] (Not only was the oil cheaper as a result of the concessions under which it was drilled, but it was easy to access and closer for shipment to Europe, thus reducing overhead while easing consumption of North American resources.) It was developments such as these that renewed foreign designs on the Middle East, which became comparable to those of the preceding millennia. The titanic riches contained there became progressively one of the focal points of US foreign policy, ushering in a new era in the external interference long familiar to the region.

As American diplomats working there avowed, "Oil is the most important single factor in the United States' relations with the area."[9] By the early 1950s, the Middle East was becoming Washington's sphere of influence, and as British (and French) mastery there sharply waned, a "vacuum" was being created. (Without the presence of a "civilized" power, the Third World as a whole was generally perceived as being empty.) American power and profit were superseding Western Europe and would define the new phase of external influence in the Middle East. The resolve in this endeavor was conveyed during World War II by Max Weston Thornburg (oil executive and petroleum adviser to the State Department) to Dean Acheson, then-assistant secretary of state: "Nothing essential to such a program [of state-corporate collaboration in the acquisition of foreign oil] is impossible nor incompatible with our historical ideas as to the functions of government or the nature of private enterprise."[10] Consideration of the historical record indicates that Thornburg was not alone in his thinking.

As the open door drove industrial and political ambitions, impediments were a natural concern and called for vigilance. The postwar period witnessed increasing nationalism within the Third World, when the former colonies were relinquished as a result of the imperial powers' inability to control their holdings. In addition, the threat of a vacuum was folded into Washington's stated Cold War misgivings regarding Soviet opportunism. The Kremlin's meddling in places like Azerbaijan (north of Iran) and Turkey was proof enough for American planners that a defensive posture was vital for national security. Whether these fears of Soviet aggression were real, contrived, or a mixture of both, American intrigue in the Middle East was unequivocal and probably had little to do with Moscow. Even if the Soviet Union had not existed, it is easy to imagine US appetites in the region being just as voracious. As pointed out by historian Warren I. Cohen:

> Even as they [US policymakers] contemplated projecting American power more than five thousand miles from their shores, substituting it for declining British power in the proximity of Soviet borders, they perceived Soviet behavior in the area as threatening, American actions as defensive.[11]

Regardless of how those in Washington perceived Moscow, the ostensible reason for the United States replacing Britain was the Cold War and the preemption of Soviet penetration from the Middle East all the way to the Mediterranean Sea. As a consequence, regional instability presented the dual threat of first, perturbing the wish-fulfillment of the American oil industry, and second, creating circumstances vulnerable to the Kremlin's "drive" and desire to "subvert by infiltration and intimidation" (this being its "preferred technique)."[12] Along with the virtual extension of the Monroe Doctrine, the Roosevelt Corollary was also being updated. Its call for a "police power" in the case of "wrongdoing" or "impotence" (see page 39) was echoed by the above-mentioned diplomats in the Middle East, who suggested more forceful "police controls" as a solution to internal communist activity or instability.[13]

Because their goals ran parallel, the tactical concerns of the oil corporations and Washington largely corresponded, although there were occasional disagreements. The two, according to David Painter, "produced a symbiosis," and

> Thus to maintain an international environment in which companies could operate with security and profit, the U.S. government became actively involved in maintaining the stability of the Middle East, in containing economic nationalism, and in sanctioning and supporting private arrangements for controlling the world's oil.[14]

Nationalism threatened interruption of profits for the corporate sector, and for the state could simply create an atmosphere non-conducive to "stability" (generally a euphemism for compliance, as witnessed in US relations with Latin America, the Gulf-Caribbean, the Philippines, and so on).

In 1938, Mexico set a precedent of nationalizing its oil industry by invoking its 1917 constitution and asserting that the subsoil—and therefore the petroleum reservoirs contained therein—belonged to the state of Mexico. Owing to political anxieties on the eve of World War II, the Roosevelt administration proceeded in the spirit of the Good Neighbor Policy; however, in the future, this was the kind of development that was best prevented. Though Bolivia had done the same the year before, Mexico was the first major player in the petroleum world to initiate such a move. Similarly, Iran, also one of the principal oil countries, caused a flare-up in 1932 when its leader, Reza Shah Pahlavi, threatened to nationalize the oil supply and cancel its concession to the British oil firm Anglo-Persian. Only after intense negotiations was the concession preserved, with Iran receiving a significant increase in what Anglo-Persian had to provide as payment for its operations there—much to British indignation.

Along with nationalization, the concept of the fifty-fifty agreement also became a consideration. A system where revenues get divided between company and host state, Venezuela adopted the policy in 1943 for its American and British tenants, with Saudi Arabia following suit in 1950 regarding the US corporation Arabian-American Oil Company, or Aramco. While not ideal from the perspective of major oil, it was better than full nationalization and still allowed for abundant profits. In Iran, however, the situation relating to its oil industry led to events that continue to echo in the twenty-first century.

British hegemony in Iran, especially with respect to its oil firm, the Anglo-Iranian Oil Company (AIOC), inspired the shah to establish relations with Nazi Germany. Despite Tehran's pledges of neutrality during the war, London and Moscow wanted to safeguard supply routes and therefore occupied the country as insurance. In 1941, Reza Shah abdicated his throne under British and Soviet occupation. The shah's son, Muhammad Reza Pahlavi, was installed by Britain in his father's stead, but with reduced authority. By 1946 these foreign powers had withdrawn, and in the following year tense negotiations began between the AIOC and Tehran over the oil concession, which had remained unchanged for over a decade and therefore generated less income for Iran as a result of inflation. Last-minute discussion of a fifty-fifty agreement was however squelched by advocacy—political and popular—for nationalization. From within the Iranian parliament, called the *Majlis*, support for this idea intensified, gathering under Muhammad Mossadeq, a Majlis member known for his opposition to the country's Western-sponsored royal autocracy.

Mossadeq eventually became prime minister and oriented his office toward not only nationalizing Iran's oil, but limiting the young shah's power, enforcing the constitution, instituting land redistribution, as well as reforming the military. "In both Britain and the United States," Iran scholar Nikki Keddie comments,

> Mosaddeq was pictured increasingly but inaccurately as a dangerous fanatic, likely to deliver Iran to the Soviets. In fact he was an anti-imperialist nationalist who intended to keep Iran from being controlled by any foreign country or company.[15]

In the wave of Mossadeq's popularity, the shah fled to Rome. Nevertheless, under a worldwide boycott initiated by the British and the United States, the prime minister's various policy goals began to strain under economic burden. Because of the outside economic and political divisiveness on the part of London and Washington, along with increasing internal factional division, Mossadeq's power and stature became threatened, producing the opportune moment to bring him down. In August 1953, the Central Intelligence Agency (CIA), with support from Britain's foreign intelligence service, MI6, initiated Operation Ajax and engineered the overthrow of the prime minister in a coup. Mossadeq was arrested, spent three years in prison, and lived the rest of his life under house arrest. In turn, the young shah was reinstalled, where he remained in power as a US client until the Iranian Revolution in 1979.[16]

The 1953 coup in Iran was a policing action in the mode of the domino theory. The Soviets did not feature, but Mossadeq's disregard for core–periphery rules of conduct most certainly did. The Iranian was guilty of wrongdoing. Removing him from power served the purposes of replacing him with a more cooperative leader while simultaneously establishing "credibility" in the eyes of others who might be considering Mossadeq's path. Former *New York Times* correspondent Stephen Kinzer, in his book *Overthrow*, highlights the increasing role corporations have played in US foreign policy, and the penalties brought to bear for Third World insubordination:

[The firms] have become the vanguard of American power, and defying them has become tantamount to defying the United States. When Americans depose a foreign leader who dares such defiance, they not only assert their rights in one country but also send a clear message to others.[17]

The coup was a perfect example of keeping the open door open, on the grounds of preventing the spread of similar "security" threats; it is this kind of unimpeded projection of state power that forms the substructure of the United States' relationship with Israel.

THE ORIGIN OF US–ISRAELI RELATIONS, 1947–56

As the United States maneuvered into the Middle East to secure a power position and replace the British and their waning leverage there, the developments in Palestine could probably also be described as "a little far afield" for any deep interest on America's part. By the time the 1947 partition of mandatory Palestine became an issue of international importance, many in Washington were still cool on the idea of a Jewish state taking hold in the heart of the region, and felt that supporting such a development would only jeopardize US national interests. While the State Department is most commonly known for opposing partition, former CIA analyst Kathleen Christison notes that:

Indeed, State was not alone in opposing partition; the Department of Defense, the Joint Chiefs of Staff, the National Security Council staff, and the newly established Central Intelligence Agency were united with State in fearing that partition might lead to warfare in the Middle East, force the United States to intervene militarily, enhance the Soviet position in the area, and endanger U.S. interests in the Arab world.[18]

Even the Harry S. Truman White House (1945–53) before partition was less than keen about getting behind the Zionists, as expressed by the president in a mid-1946 cabinet meeting: "If Jesus Christ couldn't satisfy them here on earth, how the hell am I supposed to?" adding that "I have no use for them and I don't care what happens to them."[19] Truman eventually moved in the direction of supporting the Jewish-Zionist enterprise, but was prone to waffling, depending on who was trying to influence him at a particular moment. In the main the president, though sympathetic to the plight of Europe's Jews, approached the issue more strategically than he is generally characterized as having done.[20]

The degree of support for Zionism in the White House and the various governmental departments and agencies notwithstanding, by the time the new state of Israel had demonstrated its martial competence in 1948, most disputes in Washington over the subject found general, increasing accord. Israel declared independence between the two phases of the war and came out on the winning side, with the United States being the first to issue de facto recognition of the new state. The Jewish state's resourcefulness and its ability and willingness to project power gained attention in Washington. Political scientist Steven Spiegel points out, "the key factor in U.S. decision making had been external events—mainly Israeli military victories."[21] Decisions were soon based on the convenience and usefulness Israel could provide in the region. As a declassified Defense Department memorandum sent to the National Security Council in 1949 revealed, "air installations [in Israel] would be most useful" in protecting Middle East oil resources from the Soviets, while Israel's armed forces could potentially be used "for the defense of the Cairo-Suez area and for land operations to defend or to recapture the Middle East oil facilities."[22] Israel had become a fact, and Washington moved toward fitting Tel Aviv into its regional scheme of things.

While the United States had its designs on the Jewish state, Israel likewise was looking to America for support in a variety of forms, most notably weapons and financial assistance. At first Washington moved cautiously in this regard. In the course of the 1948 war the Truman administration imposed a weapons embargo on the Middle East, hoping to prevent an arms race in Palestine and the surrounding states. This in turn moved Israel toward the USSR to satisfy its wants and needs. But despite receiving matériel, or military equipment, during the war from Czechoslovakia (with Soviet oversight), Israel wanted to keep its global options open by declaring a position of "nonidentification": that is, professing no sole alliance with the East (Moscow) or West (Washington). Just the same, Israel knew that a successful future involved a Western orientation, and that carefully negotiating the Cold War balance was one way it was going to continue gaining US patronage, or "how to keep milking the [American] cow," as stated by Israeli leadership.[23] According to Israeli international relations scholar Uri Bialer, "Aid vital for the maintenance of Israel's existence would continue to come from the

West, and in particular from the United States, only 'if the impression is created that we are friends,'" quoting Moshe Sharrett, then foreign minister and eventual prime minister.[24]

Desiring to fend off Soviet involvement in the region, the United States, Great Britain, and France issued the Tripartite Declaration (May 1950), allowing "applications for arms" from the Arab states and Israel "for the purposes of assuring their internal security and their legitimate self-defense and to permit them to play their part in the defense of the area as a whole."[25] The United States wanted to continue its avoidance of escalation in the region, but if arms were going to flow into the Middle East, better they be Western ones. Regardless of this change in policy, Washington remained partially steadfast on its decision not to sell heavy armaments to Israel, and did not do so throughout the 1950s—although Israel received shipments and weapons technology from France and Canada, with US knowledge and therefore tacit consent.[26]

The beginning of the Korean War in June 1950 marked a watershed in Israeli positioning, as the United States took a roll call of all nations allied and faithful. Tel Aviv abandoned its nonidentification policy and turned westward; Soviet support was valuable, but American money—governmental and private—was the ticket to Israel's future.[27] The early 1950s saw the Jewish state pledge allegiance to the United States and begin to reap the benefits. "By then," according to historian Howard M. Sachar, "even Israel's most committed Socialists recognized which side of the ocean their bread was buttered on."[28] The role and stature Israel envisioned for itself was going to require robust foreign support.

The historical record reveals that the Zionist project never accentuated living in harmony with its Arab neighbors, starting with the Palestinians. In a changing Middle East, Israel in the 1950s was positioning itself to advance as the region's preeminent power. During this period, significant political turmoil was astir. Egypt's king was overthrown in 1952 and replaced by a military leadership, two years later ushering in the era of Colonel Gamal Abdul Nasser. Also in 1952, Jordan's King Hussein replaced his grandfather, Abdullah, after the monarch was assassinated the previous year. During this time, similar instability had profound effects on Lebanon and Syria, with coups and civil conflicts occurring repeatedly. For the Western powers, this shuffling of the deck was a source of consternation. For Israel, if it was going to play a dominant role in the area, it was time.

Among the Jewish state's central intentions was expansion of its borders, hoping to acquire Gaza and maybe the Sinai Peninsula (from Egypt), the West Bank along with the rest of Jerusalem (from Jordan), and portions of the demilitarized zone along the border with Syria, established after the 1948 war. Essentially, the aim was to "occupy the rest of Western Eretz Israel [all the land between the Jordan River and the Mediterranean]," as Moshe Sharett recorded in his diary (1953), suspecting the military of these maximal intentions.[29] (Recall Menachem Begin's comment on page 68.) Israel's eventual realization of these intentions will be further discussed below. For now, we will concentrate on another of Tel Aviv's aspirations: preemption of Nasser's eminence in Egypt, as it pertains to the larger picture of American foreign policy.

Dwight Eisenhower's presidency (1953–61) took an increased and active role in the Middle East, training its attention on maintenance of the regional status quo. The foremost concern was to preserve the Western alignment of the various Arab leaderships as well as to discourage local "radical nationalism," or independent self-determination. Concurrently, the rhetoric of Cold War apprehensions persisted and deepened. As Eisenhower's secretary of state, John Foster Dulles, remarked on the subject of possible US military activity in the Middle East:

> we had always played down the American oil interests, and it would certainly not be popular if the impression should be given that we were risking military action to protect investments of American oil companies. Unless, therefore, military preparations were represented in their proper light—of reacting to a Soviet threat.[30]

An issue taken far more seriously, as the administration demonstrated in its first year with the coup in Iran, was seeing to it that Arab leaders observed US–Western authority.

Of the Middle Eastern political disturbances of the early 1950s mentioned above, the leader to emerge from them who made the biggest impact, and caused the most Western concern, was Nasser. The charismatic Egyptian president sought to guide the Middle East along the way of pan-Arabism. This ideology affirmed that Arabs, in the face of having been divided into European-style nation-states, still constituted a people, or nation, and that the region should therefore function collectively. Along this line of thinking, Nasser expressed abhorrence of, and espoused resistance to, Western imperialism and what he viewed as its latest manifestation: Zionism.

He felt it was these two factors along with inter-Arab disputes that were the Middle East's primary obstacles—not threat of Soviet intervention.

While Nasser's popular appeal was broad among Arab societies, his place in the spotlight rankled with some Arab leaders. But nowhere did it aggravate more than in Western Europe, the United States, and Israel. Nasser threatened the existing order. He cheered on the resistance in Algeria against French colonialism, and posed competition to Tel Aviv's desired supremacy. The British prime minister, Anthony Eden, said of him, "I want him destroyed" (he may have used the word "murdered"), as Nasser was "the incarnation of all the evils of Arabia," and he perturbed those in Washington with his refusal to cooperate in the East–West Cold War contest.[31] He was routinely compared to Adolf Hitler by European and American policymakers. Nasser was indeed a sizable rotten apple.

Nevertheless the United States thought it could pacify the Egyptian leader, and one effort in this direction was the brokering of an agreement (1954) between Cairo and London regarding Britain's remaining military presence in Egypt, especially around the Suez Canal zone. Another possibility, one tepidly pursued, was a settlement of the Arab–Israeli conflict. And while Nasser remained more or less flexible and open to pursuing peace with Israel,[32] the latter wanted peace on its terms, preferring to continue its work toward hegemony.* As then-prime minister David Ben-Gurion summarized in internal discussion, "we have to remember that there are limits to our desire for peace with the Arabs. This is one of our vital interests, but it is not the first and all-determining interest."[33]

A settlement between the Arab states and Israel would as a matter of course include the United States, and thus possibly move Washington closer to the Arabs, something Israel sought to forestall or prevent. Livia Rokach, in her analysis of Sharett's *Personal Diary*, makes an observation of this phase in Israel's history that speaks to much of the state's subsequent relations with its Arab neighbors and merits full quotation:

To prevent an alliance between the West and the Arab world, especially with the most important Arab country—Egypt—was

---

* Israeli prime minister Moshe Sharett, who moderately differed from his colleagues in the defense establishment regarding his approaches to statecraft, shared Nasser's flexibility, with the two engaging in secret talks through representatives in late 1954.

(and was to remain) Israel's main goal. This had nothing to do with Israel's security. On the contrary, Ben-Gurion's policy was directed at preventing guarantees from being imposed on the Zionist state by the U.S. Such guarantees would necessarily imply the achievement of a minimum agreement between Israel and the Arab world (definition of borders, a "face-saving" solution for the Palestinian refugees). The basic motivation was also clearly stated: the use of force was "the only way" for Israel to become a hegemonic power in the region, possibly in alliance with the West. Nasser had to be eliminated not because his regime constituted a danger for Israel, but because an alliance between the West and his prestigious leadership in the third world, and in the Middle East, would inevitably lead to a peace agreement which in turn would cause the Zionist state to be relativized as just one of the region's national societies.[34]

Evidence of this inclination is manifest.

The key episodes of this period—the Lavon Affair, the Gaza raid, and the Suez crisis—sufficiently exhibit Tel Aviv's desired position. The Lavon Affair was a response to an agreement of British withdrawal from Egypt. Israel hatched a scheme to undermine Western faith in Nasser by having Egyptian-Jewish spies in Cairo attempt to plant bombs in the American and British embassies. The summer 1954 operation failed, as one of the saboteurs was caught, exposing the network and Israel's involvement.[*]

The second, the Gaza raid in winter 1955, was in reaction to Palestinian acts of infiltration and sabotage on the Gaza–Israel border, sometimes claiming Israeli lives. The Israeli Defense Forces (IDF) launched an attack on an Egyptian military camp, killing roughly 40. While there is much to say about these border phenomena—refugee infiltration and Israeli retaliation—two specifics should be pointed out. First, the vast majority of Palestinians entering Israel during this time were doing so to tend crops, livestock, and gather personal belongings they had possessed before displacement. According to Israeli historian Benny Morris, who has done significant work on the subject, "Most of the infiltrators were unarmed individuals, though it appears that the proportion who came armed and in groups steadily increased

---

[*] The fallout from the Lavon Affair, and Egypt's subsequent execution of two of the saboteurs, caused the cancellation of the Nasser–Sharett talks, with the latter discontinuing them.

after 1950, largely in reaction to the IDF's violent measures."
Morris's research reveals that over 90 percent of infiltrators
crossed the border without violent intentions.[35] Second, the IDF
attack was launched, according to Egyptian and Israeli documents, "during a period of relative calm in that area and in
the wake of major efforts on the part of the Egyptian regime
to stop infiltrations in the Gaza Strip."[36]

Following the Gaza raid Nasser made vigorous efforts to
acquire arms. He first approached the United States, but his
request for a deal was essentially dismissed by Washington,
which attached conditions the Egyptian president was sure to
reject.* Predictably, Cairo then looked to the Kremlin, with
which an arms agreement was made (via Czechoslovakia). The
United States attempted to move Egypt closer by offering an
aid program to finance the enormous Aswan Dam project on
the Nile River, but because of difficulties in the negotiations—
specifically, Nasser's refusal of Secretary Dulles's deliberately
preventive conditions**—and Egypt's recognition of Communist
China, the financing plan was pulled. In a move similar to
what we have seen with regard to Third World oil supplies,
Nasser responded by nationalizing the Suez Canal, making
it Egyptian property (his legal right) and disenfranchising its
previous British and French owners, with compensation.

This move brought on the third incident. The 1956 Suez crisis
featured a coordinated invasion of the Sinai Peninsula and the
canal zone by Britain, France, and Israel, leaving the Jewish state
in possession of the peninsula and Gaza. The US response was
negative—according to Eisenhower, "they chose a bad time and
incident on which to launch corrective measures"[37]—denouncing
all three collaborators and imposing withdrawal of Israel from
its territorial gains. Though out of the loop regarding the planning of the offensive, Washington had predicted in a Pentagon
analysis a "short, blitzkrieg type of war" by Israel against Nasser
to "gain territorial objectives" and "effect a forced relocation of

---

* Part of Nasser's difficulties with the Americans was his refusal to join
  the anti-Soviet Baghdad Pact (1955), which was a regional alliance
  between Britain, the United States (observer), Turkey, Iran, Pakistan, and
  Iraq, the only Arab member. Upon Iraq's departure from the alliance, the
  pact was renamed the Central Treaty Organization, or CENTO.
** Dulles's view of Nasser darkened over this period, with upcoming elections and lobbying pressure from various groups adding to the souring
  dialogue, thus producing a change of heart.

nearby refugee camps." A day before the invasion, the Israeli ambassador, Abba Eban, attempted to convince Dulles that Nasser was positioned for attack, with the secretary electing not to notify the ambassador that the United States possessed aerial reconnaissance confirming the opposite.[38]

The Suez crisis signified a turning point in Washington's approach to the Middle East as a whole, and its relationship with Tel Aviv in particular. The "tripartite aggression," as it is sometimes called, was a last hurrah for Britain and France, a last-ditch effort by two powers desperately doing their utmost to spend what little clout they had left. The United States was now the preeminent hegemon in the Middle East. Until this point, Eisenhower and Dulles had attempted something of a balancing act in the region: trying to minimize the tensions of the Arab–Israeli conflict, attempting (and failing) to organize multilateral anti-Soviet defense alliances within the region, and generally striving to maintain Arab relations while supporting Israel, albeit to a relatively restrained degree. Washington's goals were stability and Western orientation, running both through the Cold War filter, yet as we have noted the causes of instability were not connected with the USSR. Western intervention and Arab–Israeli strife were among the central issues, which in turn gave rise to phenomena like Nasserism.

From independence to 1956, Israel had frequently been a strategic liability in American efforts to maintain calm, or at least consistency, on the Arab front. But given Israel's performance in the Sinai, the Jewish state was starting to look more useful. Between the destabilizing factors of Nasserism and Zionism, the United States and its corporate oil interests viewed the former as a far greater threat. Israeli political scientist Abraham Ben-Zvi notes the shift in overall approach during this period: "the perception of Israel as a potential strategic asset to the United States came to increasingly permeate the cognitive map of Washington's policymakers." "It was in this revised context that Israel—which had demonstrated impressive military capabilities during the Sinai campaign—came to be gradually viewed as a power that could contribute ... toward the accomplishment of [American] objectives." In its bid to preserve the existence of the Middle East's "pro-Western regimes," Ben-Zvi continues, "the administration could not remain oblivious to the potential value of Israel as a counterbalance to the forces of radical Arab nationalism."[39] Eisenhower's second term is where we see the United States begin to look on Israel as a true asset to its Middle Eastern ambitions.

THE FORGING OF THE SPECIAL RELATIONSHIP, 1957–67

While the administration did not make an abrupt revision of how it handled Israel, the spirit of the relationship significantly warmed from Eisenhower's first four years to the post-Suez period. In the second term, the president and his secretary of state would approach the Middle East focusing almost solely on Arab and/or radical nationalism—the lookout for rotten apples and falling dominoes would be sharp. By 1957 the Middle East was largely composed of leaderships acquiescent toward Washington. (It is critical to note that the populations did not necessarily share this orientation, with even Eisenhower remarking that "the problem is that we have a campaign of hatred against us, not by the governments but by the people," who happen to be "on Nasser's side." This evokes the italicized comment on page 60.)[40] The countries of Lebanon, Israel, Jordan, Iraq, and Saudi Arabia, along with the non-Arab states of Turkey and Iran, were pro-Western clients the United States was keen on keeping that way. Egypt under Nasser was a question mark that riled Eisenhower and Dulles, though the Pentagon and the CIA less so. Syria, a state that was anything but communist, drew closer to the USSR for aid, while elements within the government in Damascus found increasing common cause with Nasser. The proclaimed fear in the American government was Soviet domination, but much of the actual apprehension was Arab groups—social and political—posing a threat to the political order Washington counted on for cooperation. The solution was contained in what became known as the Eisenhower Doctrine.

In a message delivered before a joint session of Congress (January 1957), the president made a proposal containing three main features. The plan would authorize:

- The United States to aid in "the development of economic strength" of "any nation or group of nations in the general area of the Middle East."
- "[T]he Executive to undertake in the same region programs of military assistance and cooperation with any nation or group of nations which desires such aid."
- "[T]he employment of the armed forces of the United States to secure and protect the territorial integrity and political independence of such nations, requesting such aid, against overt armed aggression from any nation controlled by International Communism."[41]

In summary, financial assistance, military assistance, and direct armed support were the envisioned methods that would keep Nasser and others, like Syria, in check. While the president's congressional address repeatedly invoked uneasiness about "international communism," it was clear enough where the initiative was aimed. As observed by foreign policy scholar Gabriel Kolko, for American interests in the Middle East "the stakes were economic rather than strategic, for the Soviet Union in no way threatened the area, the materialist foundations of Washington's policy were revealed in a quite incontrovertible manner." Kolko continues:

> When pressed, the State Department had to admit that no state in the region was under "international communist" domination, nor was there any imminent danger of a Communist coup. There was, nonetheless, Dulles warned, now "the most serious threat that we have faced over the past 10 years." Nasser and Arab nationalism, the Administration's principal concerns, were the real objectives of the new doctrine and the main obstacles to the consolidation of U.S. power.[42]

Over the course of 1957 and 1958, the Middle East experienced near-constant crisis, in which Eisenhower and Dulles road-tested their doctrine and Israel would, albeit discreetly, begin its service role. The results were mixed, if mostly negative, as the Eisenhower Doctrine attempted to force a template couched in Cold War terms on the region. Likewise, American intervention was a key source of revolutionary upheaval in the Middle East. The doctrine was trying to minimize the largely popular concepts Nasser represented: freedom, independence, self-determination, and aversion to foreign dominance—values hardly alien to the United States and Western Europe. As historian Salim Yaqub notes, "In the court of Arab public opinion, the Nasserists decisively won the argument."[43] The "conservative" (pro-Western; today described as "moderate") Arab regimes became increasingly unpopular with local opposition groups growing rebellious toward their respective leaderships' collaboration with Western power.

The crises over these two years featured repeated attempts by radical political movements to occasion the desired changes in their governments. At least seven notable incidents mark this period:

1. In April 1957, Jordan's King Hussein invokes the Eisenhower Doctrine out of fear of being dethroned by domestic opposition.

The United States responds with a show of strength by moving its Sixth Fleet into the eastern Mediterranean. Hussein tightens his grip and maintains rule.

2. Late summer and autumn, shifts in Syria's leadership (Baath party) cause concern in Washington, prompting again the movement of the Sixth Fleet, along with arms shipments to Iraq and Jordan, while Turkish troops mass along the Syrian border. Tensions rise between the United States and the USSR. Crisis subsides by November.

3. In October, during incident 2 above, Nasser expresses solidarity with Damascus, sending Egyptian troops to Syria.

4. February 1958, Cairo and Damascus form a unified state, thus creating the United Arab Republic (UAR). The UAR lasts until September 1961.

5. On July 14, a bloody coup in Iraq overthrows the pro-Western royalty, claiming the life of King Faisal II among others, and occasions a military dictatorship. Baghdad becomes allied with Egypt and Syria, though Iraq does not join the UAR.

6. The following day, political unrest and civil war in Lebanon owing to Arab nationalist pressure reacting against the pro-Western leadership there prompt the Lebanese president, Camille Chamoun, to request support from Washington. The United States, fearing Lebanon will be the next domino, sends 14,000 Marines to the beaches of Beirut, where, some historians lightly remark, ice cream and soda pop sales improve as a result—little else happens. Chamoun, desiring another term (against Lebanese law), finishes his time in office and is succeeded by a military officer who begins to smooth out tensions within the country. This is the first US military operation in the Middle East.

7. That same July, Jordan's King Hussein is again confronted with domestic opposition, and requests American and British military assistance. The United States, while hesitant about increasing its martial presence in the region past Lebanon, consents to British paratroopers landing in Amman to help protect the status quo. In doing so, Israel allows Britain use of its airspace, keeping in contact with Washington all the while. Once again, Hussein's throne is preserved.

After the tumultuous 1957–58 period, the Middle East became less of a preoccupation for the Eisenhower administration. Aside from benefiting King Hussein, the doctrine had accomplished little, and as mentioned probably did more to encourage the very developments it was trying to curtail. However, beyond matters of Arab–Nasserist resistance and Cold War politics, the United States' natural resource interests remained secure throughout. As noted by Steven Spiegel, "If any group of Americans involved in the Middle East was satisfied by the end of the Eisenhower administration, it was the oil company leadership." "Eisenhower and Dulles's policies pleased them more than any single group. This convergence of perspective occurred because of a similar world view and overlapping concerns." [11]

Washington's view of Israel warmed considerably during Eisenhower's second term, with this two-year stretch more or less sealing the relationship. And while Tel Aviv made no great showing, it did respectfully remain still, stay in contact with the Americans, and allow use of its airspace (especially when Saudi Arabia would not), much to Soviet resentment—further pleasing DC. These factors, inasmuch as they were scant, inspired the president and Dulles to look on Israel in a new light. Perhaps the clearest statement to this effect was contained in a memorandum presented to the National Security Council (August 1958; declassified in 1981), stating, "if we choose to combat radical Arab nationalism and to hold Persian Gulf oil by force if necessary, a logical corollary would be to support Israel as the only strong pro-West power left in the Near East." [45]

Though it is commonly assumed that the John F. Kennedy administration (1961–63) locked Israel into the United States' strategic orbit, Tel Aviv was already most of the way there by the end of Eisenhower's tenure. Though the Middle East was less a priority for the United States between 1958 and 1967, especially with Vietnam and Southeast Asia becoming an increasing priority for policymakers over that period, Kennedy did move Israel closer in word and deed. Unlike Eisenhower's preference for fighting shy of a regional arms race, taking a circumspect approach to arming Israel (lightly and often indirectly), Kennedy granted Tel Aviv's request to purchase anti-aircraft Hawk missiles, a momentous first US-Israeli arms deal. The young president also stepped up the public and private rhetoric, expressing for the first time that the United States and Israel shared a "special relationship."

Part of the Hawk deal was, according to the CIA's former Tel Aviv station chief, an "inducement" for Israel to "go easy on the bomb." [46] After Kennedy's election, but prior to his entering the White House, an American U-2 spy plane confirmed what had been suspected by Washington throughout 1960. Pursuing a plan it had entertained since statehood, Israel began research and development on a nuclear program in the late 1940s, eventually forming a cooperative agreement with France in 1953 on the matter. Shortly thereafter, Tel Aviv with French assistance commenced building a 24-megawatt reactor in 1957 at the Dimona installation in the Negev Desert. Israel had taken a signal step in its longstanding goal of regional superiority.

The revelation of Israel's pursuits at Dimona was less than shocking to the United States. The Eisenhower administration had played a significant role in Israel's initial nuclear efforts, providing financing and research assistance, with US Air Force and Navy involvement. Moreover, Washington was well aware from 1957 onward that Israel's programs were being administered by its Ministry of Defense. According to author Stephen Green, who was among the first to research and uncover much of this history, "From the beginning ... the Eisenhower administration was involved."[47] Nonetheless, the United States was outside of the Israeli–French enterprise, left to guess about what was brewing in the Negev, having been told by David Ben-Gurion that the Dimona site was a "textile plant," and then a "pumping station," while Kennedy was told, again by Ben-Gurion, that it was "a scientific institute for research in problems of arid zones and desert flora and fauna."[48] By this time, however, the cat was out of the bag, and the United States (as of 1964, when Dimona went critical) now had a nuclear client in the Middle East. Meetings were held, the Hawk missiles were provided, and superficial US inspections of Dimona were agreed to as a mere formality. For administrations to come the subject of Israel's nuclear weapons program would remain a discouraged subject between the intelligence community and the White House; the White House's reasoning was that if Washington did not officially know, it would not officially have to do anything. As investigative journalist Seymour Hersh states in his account entitled *The Samson Option*, "Dimona became a nonplace and the Israeli bomb a nonbomb."[49]

Kennedy's presidency was cut short when he was assassinated in November 1963. His vice president and successor, Lyndon B. Johnson, would continue the trend established by his two predecessors with commitment.

It was during Johnson's time in the Oval Office (1963–69) that Israel was drawn in the closest it had been. The president's chosen team of advisers for foreign policy made manifest his orientation, with his staff and unofficial "kitchen cabinet" taking on a decisively pro-Israeli character.[50] Johnson on the whole followed in Kennedy's footsteps regarding arms, carrying the issue further with deals providing Israel with tanks, submarines, and Skyhawk bombers. However, he opted to return to Eisenhower's strong opposition to Arab nationalism, something JFK had softened slightly in his attempt to take a different tack by warming relations with Nasser (with whom he developed a correspondence). Johnson, becoming ever more deeply preoccupied with operations in Vietnam, viewed other foreign-relations issues through this prism.

To the president's way of thinking, problematic elements such as the leaders in Cairo, Damascus, and Baghdad were comparable to the Vietnamese revolutionary leader Ho Chi Minh and the guerilla Vietcong, whereas Israel and the United States were "nations in search of a dream," sharing a "heritage" of "the principles of morality, of social justice, and of universal peace." The Alamo, too, was a symbol alluded to by Johnson and his staff, with the Israelis seen as defending themselves against the aggression of the Mexican troops of General Santa Anna.[51] History renders these comparisons backwards. Ho Chi Minh's Vietminh movement, Nasserism, and Arab nationalism in general (and for that matter Santa Anna's campaign) were *responses* to Western pressure. Ho and the Vietminh wanted to rid Vietnam of the French, the Japanese, and the United States. Likewise, Nasserism and Arab radicalism were expressions of a region-wide desire to rid the Middle East of the French, the British, and the United States. Southeast Asia and the Middle East, it could be said, were composed of populations indeed "in search of a dream," one entailing liberation from European and American state coercion.

This trend of decolonization and revolution occurring throughout the Third World was also joined by Palestinian resistance. The refugees of 1948 had seen no settlement of the issue, receiving no compensation and being denied return to their towns and villages. Johnson's predecessors made limited attempts at settlement, but the problem was essentially sidelined. Israel felt it was for the Arab world to worry about, and fearing allowance of return would jeopardize the Jewishness of the state, was not about to budge on the matter. (Resolution of the refugee problem remains elusive to this day.) Out of this displaced population grew a national liberation campaign. In the late 1950s a Palestinian guerilla organization called Fatah formed, and by the mid-1960s was carrying out cross-border raids into Israel. Led by Yasser Arafat and inspired by the resistance movements in Algeria and Vietnam as well as the writings of Frantz Fanon,* Fatah saw the path to national self-determination paved with armed struggle; politics and pan-Arab unity could only *follow* Palestinian independence. This development would contribute considerably to the chain of events that led to the June 1967 Six-Day War.

The June war was a decisive moment for all those involved, and was no less so for US–Israeli relations. In fact, an argument could be made that 1967 was *the* decisive moment in the post-1948 Middle East. While the details of the conflict itself lie beyond our study, the circumstances leading up to the war are pertinent. The three factors that are generally taken as the war's underlying causes, ones cited by Israel as threats to its existence, were:

- Tensions on the Israel–Syria border.
- Nasser's removal of the UN Emergency Forces (UNEF) placed in the Sinai after the Suez crisis, and replacement of them with Egyptian troop concentrations.
- Nasser's closing of the Strait of Tiran (between the southern tip of the Sinai Peninsula and Saudi Arabia) to Israeli ships, which Tel Aviv deemed a cause for war. The first point basically gave rise to the subsequent two.

Fatah, among other similar groups, carried out raids and planted explosives from Lebanon, Syria, and Jordan, stealing across the borders, all to the discomfort of the governments in those countries. Fear of Israeli reprisal for the raids prompted the Arab leaderships to aim at prevention of them. In 1964, Egypt sponsored the creation of the Palestine Liberation Organization (PLO), which would serve as an umbrella organization for the Palestinians, but Cairo's agenda was, as historian Mark Tessler describes, "to co-opt and restrain the Palestinian resistance movement, in order to prevent existing guerilla organizations from drawing the Arab states into a war with Israel."[52] Arab leaders may have talked a good game, but none wanted war with Israel.

Initial tensions on the Israel–Syria border arose in the demilitarized zone (DMZ) established between the two countries after 1948.

---

* As the resistance in Algeria was fighting French colonialism, psychiatrist and theorist Frantz Fanon published *The Wretched of the Earth*, his classic and readable treatise on revolutionary theory and decolonization. The text was influential among leaders of the time striving for national liberation. See Frantz Fanon, *The Wretched of the Earth*, trans. Richard Philcox (1963; reprint, New York: Grove Press, 2004).

Throughout the mid-1960s shooting and skirmishes along the DMZ eventually escalated to artillery and aerial combat. The tensions were chiefly the product of Israeli aggression and expansion, as noted by Israeli political scientist Zeev Maoz:

> While in the mid-1960s there was no evidence of a deliberate Israeli effort to encroach into the DMZs, the IDF did regard these areas as a Syrian soft spot and capitalized on this sensitivity to provoke Syrian response.... [T]he fact remains that Israel initi-ated most of the incidents along the border over that period, so the extent to which compellance [of Syria to desist] was working was questionable at best.[53]

Credible evidence of this mindset was revealed by Moshe Dayan, Israeli defense minister and a principal architect of the 1967 war, in interviews a decade later. Commenting on how, in his estimation, "80 percent of all those incidents there [on the border] got started":

> It worked like this: we would send a tractor to plow some place in the demilitarized zone where nothing could be grown, and we knew ahead of time that the Syrians would shoot. If they didn't shoot, we would tell the tractor to move deeper, until the Syrians got mad eventually and fired on it. And then we would activate artillery, and later on the air force.[54]

The American consulate in Jerusalem echoed these descriptions.[55]

In February 1966, yet another coup in Damascus brought to power a leadership actively supportive of Fatah and its raids. Despite that, Syria was still mindful of its own needs together with what such support could summon. As noted by political scientist Norman Finkelstein,

> Incendiary rhetoric emanating from Syria—fueled by inter-Arab rivalries—urged that a "people's war" be mounted to liberate Palestine. Yet, the basic motive behind Syrian support of the Palestinian guerillas seems to have been more prosaic—the Israeli incursions in the DMZs.

Remarks made by the then-head of Israeli military intelligence corroborate Finkelstein's observation, stating that Syria "uses this weapon of guerilla activity" because "we are bent upon establishing ... certain facts along the border."[56] Between January 1965 and the war, Palestinian guerillas carried out 122 raids, "most of them abortive." And while Syria sponsored Fatah, it preferred the organization to execute its operations from other Arab borders.[57] Again, no Arab state truly desired warfare with their Jewish neighbor, with the better part of the bombastic behavior and rhetoric being for the sake of interstate rivalries.

Among Israel's retaliatory activities, the largest was against the village of Samu, located in the Jordanian West Bank. The attack (a reprisal for three Israeli paratroopers killed in a guerilla incursion issuing from the Jordanian border) was the largest Israeli military operation since the Suez crisis, destroying over 120 houses and a school, and killing 15 Jordanian troops and three civilians.[58] In spite of King Hussein's known (and strenuous) efforts to prevent border infiltration from his country, punishment was meted out to the Hashemite kingdom, to the dismay of the UN Security Council including the United States. That Israel chose Jordan instead of Syria was curious to some, with policymakers in Tel Aviv coming under harsh criticism, domestically and internationally.[59] But the particulars notwithstanding, attacking Jordan did have the predictable consequences of further destabilizing already unhinged inter-Arab relations.[60]

The subsequent two factors contributing to Israel's justifications of its attacks on Egypt on June 5, and thus initiating the Six-Day War, were Nasser's substitution of his own forces for the UNEF presence, and his closing of the Strait of Tiran; although there were additional factors, these were among the cardinal grounds for Tel Aviv's decision. On the face of it, neither occasion warranted hostile reaction. Upon examination, Nasser's actions were mostly a show of support for Syria, coupled with a display of backbone for the sake of credibility. There were no signs that Cairo wanted war, as the Arab states along with everyone else knew who would carry the day in such an event.[61]

I highlight the initial chain of events that precipitated the June war not solely to showcase Israel's belligerence, but to illustrate the broader consideration of what set things in motion, leading to the central question of why. An array of circumstances led to rationalizations for war, and a portion of guilt can be placed at the door of all involved—Israel, the Arab states, the Palestinian guerillas, Moscow, and Washington. But a full two years before the Six-Day War Israel was looking to ratchet up regional tensions, knowing, as Moshe Dayan's remarks reveal, what response would be generated when a given button was pushed. As to why, the answer lies in the Zionist project and Israel's dissatisfaction with its borders since inception.

Israel's dismay in 1947 led to 1948's gains. The lingering indignation from independence onward was rendered evident in the June war's acquisitions: Sinai, Gaza, the West Bank, East Jerusalem, and the Syrian Golan Heights. As Ezer Weizmann, a military commander and chief of operations, asserted in a General Staff meeting on the eve of the war, "We are on the brink of a second War of Independence, with all its accomplishments." Regarding Weizmann's comments, Israeli historian Tom Segev takes notice that,

> The last few words ["with all its accomplishments"] are underlined in the minutes of the General Staff meeting, apparently to stress that this war would be unlike the first, with all its flaws, including the failure to occupy the West Bank and the Old City.

As for Egypt's alleged threat, Israeli prime minister Levi Eshkol ruminated, "It never occurred to me that large Egyptian forces near the border meant we should get up one night and destroy them. Must we live by the sword forever?" After the Old City had been conquered, David Ben-Gurion stated the following about the Palestinian residents therein: "They must be expelled. There's no need for any law. Occupation is the most effective law."

As for the new Palestinian refugee problem created by the June war, Moshe Dayan saw no problem:

> I hope they all go. If we could achieve the departure of three hundred thousand without pressure, that would be a great blessing. If we could achieve hundreds of thousands from Gaza crossing with UNRWA [UN Relief and Works Agency for Palestine Refugees] approval, we would be blessed.

The defense minister did, however, regret that the refugee situation was "awkward from a public relations standpoint."[62]

The sequence of events leading up to the war featured much back-and-forth correspondence and discussion between Israeli planners and the White House, with the former looking for a clear and official statement from the latter regarding a promise of commitment in the event of engagement, or a "green light" blessing to proceed if and when Tel Aviv chose to strike first. But much to Israeli frustration, the administration was hesitant all around, and no decree or consent was ever pledged. While standing on neither morals nor principles, Johnson and company dithered out of practical concerns, making a point of remaining vague on the subject and leaving the decision up to the Israelis. The notion of the Jewish state punishing Nasser was an attractive one in Washington, but war is always unpredictable. At the same time, it was clear to the American intelligence community that Israel had the regional upper hand, and could fight Egypt along with the rest of the Arab states. They went so far as to predict accurately how long armed conflict with Cairo would last: five to seven days.

The Jewish state predictably routed its adversaries and tripled its size in the process. In distinction to Eisenhower's response over the Suez in forcing a return, Johnson demurred over Tel Aviv's acquisitions, which to the present day not only remain contentious, but make up the core issue of the Palestine–Israel and Arab–Israeli conflicts. The UN Security Council passed Resolution 242 (November), which included American and Soviet endorsements "emphasizing the inadmissibility of the acquisition of territory by war," "[w]ithdrawal of Israeli armed forces from territories occupied in the recent conflict," and the relegation of the Palestinians to the status of a "refugee problem."[63] UN 242 has endured as the keystone of all subsequent major diplomatic initiatives, but has remained unimplemented in the intermittent "peace process."

CONSOLIDATION: NIXON–KISSINGER, 1969–74

Richard Nixon entered office inheriting a new status quo in the Middle East. The president and his national security adviser, Henry Kissinger, an academic from Harvard University, personified the concept of *realpolitik*, or practical politics. Both men were globalist in orientation and viewed foreign policy through the Cold War lens. The declared objectives of the Nixon–Kissinger team were, especially at this point in American foreign relations, fairly standard: Keep Moscow's influence to a minimum while attempting to maximize Arab cooperation with US interests. For the president and his adviser this meant maintaining Israel's regional strength, an opinion not everyone in Washington shared. This conviction was at odds with "regionalist" bureaucrats such as those in the State Department, in particular its secretary, William Rogers. State was usually regionalist in its viewpoint and was generally more inclined to regard Israel as a burden and not an asset. The thinking was that

supporting and supplying Israel heightened Middle Eastern instability, causing the radical Arab states to become agitated, thus moving
them toward the Kremlin and not away from it. But Nixon and
Kissinger dominated foreign policy, allowing Rogers scant room in
which to operate.

The State Department's perspective was the more realistic of the
two. Israeli state militancy and the American support it enjoyed
were to blame for much of the region's volatile post-World War II
history. Yet in the short term, as we learned in Chapter 1 and as
Charles Tilly encapsulated it: "coercion *works*; those who apply
substantial force to their fellows get compliance" (p. 20). Whether
the White House was actually aware of the realities or not (that
is, of the Arabs being partial to living under the thumb of neither
Washington nor Moscow), the fastest remedy from the perspective of the administration was regional stasis, erring on the side of
power and strength. In other words, it aimed at keeping the Middle
East politically frozen, using Israel as the strong-arm. As observed
by international relations scholar Camille Mansour:

> The decisionmaker may think that Israeli activism is the real
> cause of the growing strength of the Soviet Union in the Middle
> East; he may issue numerous declarations about the necessity
> of a settlement, be thoroughly convinced of this in his heart,
> and even take some steps in this direction. But since policy is
> often made up of expedient measures rather than of decisions
> deduced logically from a rational strategy, he may have no other
> alternative than to grant unconditional aid to Israel.[64]

This tenet was expressed in the Nixon Doctrine (1969). Though
announced with Vietnam in mind, the principle was applied to
the general Nixon–Kissinger formulation, including the Middle
East. The doctrine stated that the United States would "furnish
military and economic assistance" to its allies, "[b]ut we shall look
to the nation directly threatened to assume the primary responsibility of providing the manpower for its defense."[65] This hands-off
approach, keeping clients heavily armed so as to obviate physical
American involvement, was also called "Vietnamization," where the
South Vietnamese leadership was to be transitioned into taking over
for the US military. The same method would be used for Israel.

Owing to the lack of a diplomatic resolution to the 1967 war's
outcome, the years following that conflict were marked by extreme
tension on the Suez Canal, with Egyptian forces massed on the

west side and Israeli forces on the east. Nasser, in an effort to shake loose a diplomatic initiative from Washington and Moscow, initiated regular artillery bombardment along the canal. This conflict intensified and continued until summer 1970, creating a period that became known as the War of Attrition. Evidence of the breach between the White House and the State Department was never clearer than it was over this issue.

Secretary Rogers, in hopes of curbing the post-1967 violence and resuming previous diplomatic measures, proposed the Rogers Plan in December 1969, based chiefly on UN 242.[66] Meeting swift rejection from Israel—including Kissinger—Rogers continued his efforts. Despite the feasibility of the plan and its general accordance with the international consensus, diplomacy of this order was divergent from what Kissinger, and as a result Nixon, had in mind. The White House made assurances to Israeli prime minister Golda Meir that the United States would see to it that her country was not pushed into the 242 framework. The president also established with the prime minister a direct channel of communication—with Kissinger and the Israeli ambassador, Yitzhak Rabin, following suit—in order to circumvent the State Department.[67]

Nixon's assurances inspired Meir and her staff to escalate matters in the canal zone, carrying out deep penetration raids into mainland Egypt (January 1970), and thus encouraging Cairo to secure large consignments of hardware from the Soviets. Attempting in June to at least achieve a suspension of hostilities, Rogers was eventually able to secure a 90-day ceasefire at the Suez Canal, bringing the War of Attrition to an end that August. Egypt along with Jordan agreed to the second initiative by Rogers. Gaining Israel's agreement was the product of, once more, White House private commitments to Tel Aviv's protection from UN 242 as well as promises of further arms sales. Still, the Israelis were not thrilled with the ceasefire settlement.

For that matter, neither were the Palestinian guerilla groups representing the now occupied territories of the West Bank and Gaza. As Nasser was participating in an agreement with Israel and Jordan, the PLO groups such as Fatah and the Popular Front for the Liberation of Palestine (PFLP) grew concerned that they too would be confined to 242, where they existed as a "refugee problem" and nothing more. This apprehension intensified, evolving into an attempt to overthrow or at least humiliate King Hussein and sabotage the ceasefire. With a significant presence in Jordan, forming what is referred to as a "state within a state," the Palestinian groups initiated a civil war in September. Lasting over a week, the violent conflict that came to be known as "Black September" resulted in the PLO ultimately being defeated and sent out of Jordan, thereafter settling in Lebanon. Hussein's throne was rescued once more. However, this time partial credit for its preservation was owed curiously to Israel, which in the service of Washington (though it was no less anxious about the outcome than Washington) assured Amman that the IDF and the air force were mobilized and ready to assist the Jordanians in their confrontation with Syrian tank units, which had moved on the scene to aid the PLO. Hussein never had to take up Tel Aviv's offer, but the psychological edge was probably valuable. The crisis was settled by the diplomatic efforts of Nasser, who was able to forge an agreement between the PLO and the Hashemite kingdom. A day after the ceasefire, Nasser died of a heart attack.

The crisis in Jordan happened to produce an outcome that satisfied Nixon and Kissinger, despite the contributions their policies made to the upheaval in the first place. Jordan was still intact, Syria had successfully been resisted, the PLO had been scooted aside, and as an unanticipated bonus Nasser was permanently out of the picture. Egypt's vice president, Anwar Sadat, assumed the presidency and seemed to be a much more manageable figure. In addition, US–Israeli relations were at an all-time high. The cooperation provided by Tel Aviv, and especially by Rabin as ambassador to the United States, earned Israel much esteem in the eyes of the White House. Upon Rabin's departure from his position two years later, Nixon, in a blithe but irregular comment, told Meir that if Rabin was ever out of a job in Israel the United States would gladly take him on.[68]

From 1970 to 1973 a relative calm descended on the Middle East. Still, the post-1967 status quo hung like a black cloud over the region. The lingering situation had created the conditions for the recent violent episodes of the War of Attrition and the Jordan crisis, but now that a lull prevailed Kissinger somehow saw it best to tread lightly. As political scientist and former National Security Council staffer William Quandt comments, "The period of 'standstill diplomacy' from 1970 to 1973 will not go down in the annals of American foreign policy as one of the more enlightened."[69] Nixon and Kissinger were of the mind that if Israel negotiated from a position of strength, the radical Arab states, and most notably Egypt, would deem armed solutions futile and therefore simultaneously move away from the Kremlin and possibly be more amenable to Israel's conditions at the negotiating table. War seemed highly unlikely.

The UN-sponsored initiative by Swedish diplomat Gunnar Jarring that began after the Six-Day War (a component of UN 242) resumed in 1971, but to little effect owing to Tel Aviv's fixed position: "Israel will not withdraw to the pre-June 5, 1967, lines."[70] Noting the Jewish state's intransigence, Joseph Sisco (assistant secretary of state for Near East affairs) remarked, "Israel will be considered responsible for the rejection of the best opportunity to achieve peace since the establishment of the state."[71] In addition to Jarring's mission, Sadat issued a proposal of his own in February offering Israel an interim agreement to de-escalate tensions with partial withdrawals from the Suez Canal, and creating a diplomatic path leading to the implementation of UN 242.[72] The plan was to bolster the UN initiative by taking concrete measures. However, Israel's response to Sadat was no different than it was to Jarring.

Upon entering office, Sadat wanted to put 1967 behind Egypt, tend to the country's domestic concerns, and improve Cairo's relations with the United States. The Arab countries possessing territory occupied by Israel—Egypt, Syria, and Jordan—had been hoping for a resolution for six years. Sadat, though looking to avoid war, felt that if all failed, limited conflict might be enough to dissuade the United States and the USSR from fixing in place this new state of affairs. Much to the Egyptian's aggravation, the superpowers were at this time making attempts at détente, or an easing of tensions, producing in spring 1972 a joint communiqué signed by Washington and Moscow. Sadat's take on this was that it reflected superpower desire to peg the Middle East situation right where it was. In the wake of the communiqué, armament deals between Egypt and the Kremlin became hindered. Cairo was losing patience.

That summer, the Egyptian president actualized what Washington had longed to see by expelling the over 10,000 Russian advisers working in Egypt. But if he thought this would get the attention of Nixon and Kissinger, Sadat was mistaken; aside from initial meetings in DC, the gesture was ignored. This was one more instance in a list of failed attempts to break the deadlock. As had been indicated and publicly remarked upon, Sadat's frustrations if pushed far enough could result in a military dimension to his otherwise political motivations. Shortly after the expulsion, the Soviet Union resumed shipments of an array of offensive weaponry. (US shipments and military credits for Israel remained robust, increasing as much as tenfold over the course of the post-1967 period.) Egypt was planning for war and had pulled a willing Syria into the preparation.

Egypt was already resolved to wage what would be called Operation Badr, named after the Prophet Muhammad's first military victory, the presumed last straw was an Israeli settlement construction plan about to be voted on later that autumn. The Galili Document, as it was called, was an expansionist program that envisioned development, further settlement construction, and the sale of land in the territories occupied in 1967. Pointing out the salient features of the plan, historian Avi Shlaim observes: "The Galili Document was incompatible with peace with Israel's neighbors.... [It] had far-reaching psychological consequences because of its implied contempt for the Arabs."[73] This unilateral expropriation of the occupied territories displayed Tel Aviv's diplomatic inflexibility in sharp relief.

On October 6, 1973, Egypt and Syria invaded the Israeli-occupied territory the two countries were eager to reclaim. Lasting just over two weeks, the Yom Kippur War, as it became labeled, ended in an Israeli victory, but it was nothing resembling the quick and decisive one of 1967. The beginning of the Yom Kippur War did not go well for Israel, and many observers agree that it chalked up a close call for the Jewish state. In the end, though Israel was technically triumphant, Egypt emerged from the conflict satisfied and self-assured. Despite heavy losses, Cairo had given Tel Aviv a run for its money and at the same time had brought the issue of the post-1967 order front and center—Sadat's goal all along.

During the fighting, Israel had urgently requested material assistance from the United States, something on which Kissinger was hesitant. He did not want Israel to overwhelm the Egyptians, thus possibly affecting a potential postwar agreement, and preferred to avoid provoking the Russians. "The best result," said Kissinger, now secretary of state, "would be if Israel comes out a little ahead but got bloodied in the process, and if the U.S. stayed clean."[74] Nevertheless, with arms flowing into Egypt and Syria, Nixon urged an enormous airlift of weaponry into Israel, part of a $2.2 billion aid package. Such massive support for Tel Aviv did not go over well in the Arab world. After all, the war was taking place on occupied land and could have been prevented with the implementation of UN 242.

In an unprecedented event, Saudi Arabia announced the following day (in response to the highly visible and public airlift) an oil embargo against the United States, along with production cuts precipitating skyrocketing prices on the crude-oil market. With the Gulf Arab states quickly following suit, the "oil weapon" had been brandished, sending a shockwave across the globe.[75] Though discussion of such a move had taken place in the past, as well as prior to the war, the decision to carry it out came as a surprise to

Washington (Kissinger in particular); they never thought it would actually happen. For the first time, the normally isolated issues of oil and the Arab–Israeli conflict had been linked.

The 1973 war forced Kissinger to reevaluate his basic assumptions about Middle Eastern dynamics, bringing them somewhat closer to the State Department's. Israeli superiority failed to possess the deterrent capabilities required to inhibit an Arab strike. The Arab states proved capable of sophisticated communication, coordination, and combat—a performance at variance with the general racist assumptions. Furthermore, the "conservative" oil-rich nations of the region were apparently tuned in to the Arab–Israeli conflict, or more accurately stated, the conflict the United States had with the "radical" Arab governments. A peripheral Third World zone of immense strategic importance had shown solidarity by pushing back. As a result, these Arab states had gained a measure of regard in the eyes of the core (that is, the United States) by speaking the core's language.

Even so, the central principles of US policy would remain hard and fast. Israel had to be kept strong for purposes of credibility and reliability. Regardless of its rough start in October, Israel had won yet another war, overpowering two Soviet-supplied belligerents. Policy regarding Israel had to remain intact, but the Arab Middle East was in need of greater attention. Kissinger was in favor of preventing another war given the oil embargo, the likelihood of increased Soviet involvement, and the unpredictability of what a future armed conflict could produce. The secretary also sought to finally capitalize on Sadat's willingness to look to the United States for diplomatic support, which, if sustained, would help diminish Moscow's influence. From Kissinger's perspective, the situation was favorable and needed to be preserved. In other words, an *active* standstill diplomacy was in order.

Reconciling a pro-Israeli position with a posture more attentive to Arab concerns would require deft diplomatic stage-management. By this time Nixon was basically out of the picture as a result of the Watergate scandal, which in the end cost him his office in August 1974, ushering in his vice president, Gerald Ford. Consequently, Kissinger was single-handedly steering America's foreign relations, and over the remaining years of Nixon's tenure and most of Ford's, the secretary engaged in his acclaimed shuttle, or "step-by-step," diplomacy. Excluding Soviet or UN involvement, Kissinger hammered out limited settlements by traveling over the Middle East and personally negotiating with the various heads of state in, primarily, Jerusalem, Cairo, and Damascus. Two agreements between Israel and Egypt (Sinai I and II) and one agreement between Israel and Syria were achieved. The accords only featured partial withdrawals and left much to be settled, leaving the region in yet another precarious set of circumstances, where it sat until more substantial efforts were made.

DIPLOMACY, CRISIS, AND CONTINUITY: JIMMY CARTER, 1977–81

Though all administrations in general inherit from their predecessor and bequeath to their successor, the years spanning Jimmy Carter's presidency form a pivotal point in our narrative. Still, brief treatment should be sufficient to capture the sum and substance of this period. His time in office, regarding matters pertaining to the Middle East, can be viewed as bound up with two fundamental considerations: the administration's diplomatic efforts in attaining the Camp David Accords, and the critical events on the international scene that heralded a change of era.

The newly elected president decided early on that he wanted to attempt a comprehensive settlement of the Arab–Israeli conflict, which as noted above had seen little movement since (and one could argue, during) Kissinger's post-1973 shuttle diplomacy. Carter at first envisioned a multilateral initiative toward such a settlement, involving the corresponding Arab states, Israel, and the Soviet Union, all to take place in Geneva, Switzerland. But a preliminary effort to gather the various parties met with Israeli rejection of the basic parameters. The president's initial talk of a "Palestinian homeland" (a White House first) and inclusion of the PLO in the pertinent negotiations, the use of UN 242 as a touchstone, and the involvement of Moscow, were beyond anything Israel would tolerate. Moreover, elections in Israel at this time led to Menachem Begin (Likud party) becoming prime minister, empowering a more resolute commitment to building colonial settlements, especially in the West Bank, and refusal to adhere to the contents of 242—withdrawal from the Palestinian territories. Talking to the PLO was therefore not on Tel Aviv's agenda. According to the Likud party platform: "Judaea and Samaria [biblical terms for the West Bank] will not be handed to any foreign administration."[76] Acting no differently than at any time following the Yom Kippur War, Israel favored a separate peace with Egypt.[77]

Eager to engage in peace talks, Anwar Sadat decided to approach

Israel on his own, where in Jerusalem he spoke directly to the Knesset (the Israeli parliament), in November 1977.[78] The Egyptian president basically resubmitted his 1971 proposal, but incorporated the sentiment that "the Palestine question ... is the essence of the entire problem," while affirming "this people's right to self-determination, including their right to setting up their own state."[79] This of course was at variance with Israel's plans for the territories. Prime Minister Begin offered instead a plan of "administrative autonomy" for the "Arab residents ... in Judea, Samaria, and the Gaza Strip," applying to the people and not the land.[80] Amidst this divergence between Sadat and Begin, Carter invited the two leaders to Camp David, the presidential retreat in Maryland, forgoing the international conference in Geneva.

The core achievement at the two-week summit (September 5–17, 1978) was a bilateral Sinai-for-peace agreement. Issues regarding the Palestinians, while the subject of much debate, were ultimately shelved. The "frameworks" signed at the summit, and the subsequent treaty ratified at the White House in March 1979, effaced the Palestinian component of Sadat's 1977 proposal, while in effect endorsing Israel's interpretation of 242 and what was to become of the West Bank and Gaza. The accords reflected the general drift of US policy toward Israel, as well as Carter's unwillingness to stand up to domestic and Israeli pressures, along with his concern with upcoming elections and the international state of affairs (discussed below). But in spite of its deficiencies, the treaty between Egypt and Israel fostered a measure of stability in the Middle East, and has remained intact for 30 years.[81] In the global arena, however, the situation could be described as anything but stable.

There were five international upheavals that should briefly be examined, ones that took root in the period of the Carter presidency (1977–81) and would have a profound impact on the Middle East and Washington's involvement there.

Lebanon

Chaos in the small coastal state actually got underway during Ford's presidency, with a civil war breaking out in 1975, but the instability would run through the Carter era. Aside from its domestic tensions, a number of regional factors also intersected in Lebanon. As discussed earlier, the PLO had relocated there in 1970 from Jordan, and brought with them Israeli attention. Syrian scrutiny was also garnered, with Damascus looking to superintend Lebanese politics as well as minimize PLO provocation of Israel. Nevertheless, PLO cross-border raids created a pretext for a long-prepared attack by Israel in southern Lebanon. In March 1978, the IDF unleashed a week-long bombing and shelling campaign (with American arms) that killed hundreds and displaced over 100,000 Lebanese civilians and Palestinian refugees. This attack, however, was merely an overture for what was to come four years later.

Nicaragua

The repressive Somoza regime was never popular with the people of Nicaragua, but had certainly ingratiated itself with those in Washington as a dutiful client; Nicaragua under the Somozas also created (along with El Salvador, Guatemala, Honduras, and others) a weapons market for Israel. In the early 1970s, organized dissent began to take hold. A revolutionary movement called the Sandinistas eventually met with success and by 1979 had displaced the country's dictator, Anastasio Somoza. Quite similar to other such Third World developments, the Sandinistas were looking to steer an independent course, one "non-aligned" with the East–West paradigm of the Cold War. Nicaragua's problems were largely North–South in orientation, and the new leaders were seeking to renounce US sponsorship of internal oppression. Predictable American intolerance for such deviation conjures up once again the Roosevelt Corollary in the face of a falling domino. How a Central American country factors into US–Middle East relations becomes clear after Carter leaves office.

Iran

At the same time that Nicaragua was coming under new governance, a similar situation was taking place in Iran. As was touched on earlier, the shah was reinstalled by the CIA in 1953, and remained a reliable client and purchaser of American weaponry for 25 years. But growing unrest and protest evolved into revolution, one that took on an Islamic thrust and brought to power Ayatollah Ruhollah Khomeini in February 1979. Fleeing Iran, the shah, now battling cancer, was eventually admitted by the Carter administration to New York for medical treatment. Bringing validation to the internal warnings of what kind of response such a gesture could provoke, shortly after the exiled ruler's admittance the American embassy in Tehran was seized and 52 people were taken hostage for 444 days and released only minutes after Ronald Reagan took the oath of office.

Afghanistan

Adding to the volatile year of 1979, in December the Soviet Union sent roughly 100,000 troops into Afghanistan, creating a protracted war that lasted almost a decade. Among Russia's motivations were concerns over the stability of the Hafizullah Amin regime in the face of growing Islamic resistance to it, influenced in no small part by the revolution in Iran. The Kremlin's client in Kabul—possessing, at best, communist pretensions—began to teeter, creating Soviet fear of Afghanistan becoming "lost" and inviting a wave of Islamic fundamentalism moving into Central Asia toward Russia's borders. Washington, however, saw an opportunity to pull the USSR into its own "Vietnam" by supporting the Afghani Islamic guerillas, or *mujahideen*. With US aid, including large donations from Saudi Arabia and arms shipments by Israel, totaling billions of dollars, this objective was met and the Red Army was driven out of the country in 1989. It is generally agreed that the conflict claimed 15,000 Soviet and about 1 million Afghan lives.[82]

Iran–Iraq

Another after-effect of the Iranian Revolution, similar to what happened in Afghanistan, was Ayatollah Khomeini's call to Iraq's majority Shiite population to rise up and overthrow the secular Baathist regime led by Saddam Hussein. The ayatollah also provided support for the Kurdish rebellion going on in Iraq's northern extremity, an ethnic enclave desiring autonomy. At the same time, Hussein was keen on becoming the new guardian of the oil-rich Persian Gulf (replacing the shah), expanding Iraq's regional prestige, and possibly achieving for himself a Nasser-like status in the Arab Middle East. Given the rhetoric emanating from his Persian neighbor, and especially given Iran's relative political vulnerability as a result of its major transition, Hussein was eager to establish ascendancy. In September 1980, Iraq confidently invaded Iran, getting far more than it bargained for. The Iran–Iraq War would be the longest conventional war of the twentieth century, lasting until 1988 and claiming the lives of about 1 million people.

The "period" of 1979, including the adjacent years, was at once a culmination and the provenance of much that followed. The turn of the decade bore witness to the product of the European years of colonial control, American intervention (especially the

1953 coup in Iran), and the ensuing postcolonial resistance. To a degree, it could be maintained that current developments in the Middle East are transpiring in the post-1979 era.[83]

Jimmy Carter entered office on a platform based on human rights, a departure from the Nixon–Kissinger approach to foreign policy, a reduction of Cold War hysteria, and a de-escalation of nuclear proliferation and overall militarism. Over the course of his term he would move in the opposite direction to his stated objectives. As Cold War scholar John Lewis Gaddis describes the Carter administration, it was a "fusion of surface innovation with subsurface continuity."[84] In light of the turmoil of 1979, especially Russia's invasion of Afghanistan, the president announced the Carter Doctrine, stating that:

> An attempt by any outside force to gain control of the Persian Gulf region will be regarded as an assault on the vital interests of the United States of America, and such an assault will be repelled by any means necessary, including military force.[85]

(That Soviet operations in Afghanistan were cast in a Cold War light for public consumption—"a desirable and justified simplification," as the national security adviser, Zbigniew Brzezinski, put it—and that former policy architect George F. Kennan felt the invasion did not indicate further aggression, is noteworthy.[86]) In other words, Carter's reflex was reliance on state power—subsurface continuity. Shortly after, Carter signed a presidential directive (PD-59) asserting that "[t]he most fundamental objective of our strategic policy remains nuclear deterrence."[87] The defense budget and weapons sales sharply increased. Historian Walter LaFeber notes the accounting:

> After cutting $36 billion in domestic spending, Carter added $47 billion in new weapons systems. The Pentagon budget jumped from $170 billion in 1976 to $197 billion in 1981 (in 1986 dollars). To buck up both the allies and the stumbling U.S. economy, Carter also nearly doubled arms sales between 1977 and 1980 to $15.3 billion.

LaFeber then makes mention of a fundamental but mostly unacknowledged point: "Carter's defense budgets formed the roots of Ronald Reagan's policies in the 1980s."[88]

FORMALIZATION: RONALD REAGAN, 1981–89

As distinct as Jimmy Carter was from Nixon and Kissinger in his rhetoric, style, and stated intentions (despite later relapses), Ronald Reagan contrasted with Carter every bit as sharply. The former actor and Californian governor campaigned and entered office on a platform diametrically opposite to his predecessor's, pushing a program of anticommunism steeped in Cold War doctrine and with an emphasis on defense. As for style, Reagan managed his administration with a unique scarcity of energy, understanding, and attention. As described by *The Cambridge History of American Foreign Relations*, "Reagan knew little about the world in which the United States had long been the dominant power. He was uninformed—and not terribly interested."[89] Regardless, the president was effective in the realm of public relations, and was able to put a benevolent face on what were usually malevolent policies. If we divide US leaders into those who truly believed 35 years of Cold War ideology and those who were more realistic and businesslike in their views of international affairs, Reagan fitted squarely into the former camp. For the president, the world was divided along good and evil, superpower fault lines; the Americans wore the white hats, with the Soviets donning the black. Matters of foreign policy were therefore invariably cast in this light, irrespective of the realities. And while Reagan was viewing and describing foreign affairs in such terms, the advisers and planners around him had a ready-at-hand rationale for the administration's various operations, and an able PR agent to deliver it.

Within Reagan's Manichaean worldview, Israel was clearly going to be regarded as an asset. Probably more than any of the American administrations over the course of Israel's existence, Reagan not only viewed the Jewish state as a valued player on the Cold War stage, but held stronger personal devotion to Israel than had been seen in executives like Truman or Johnson. Regardless, however, of the president's—or any president's—personal orientations, US–Israeli relations followed a calculated course and had more to do with global strategy than the moral or religious fidelities of state planners.

An early aspiration of the administration was to create a regional defense alliance, something previous administrations had attempted with predictably limited results. Middle Eastern alliances sought by the United States to preempt Soviet intrusion had little to do with the Middle East per se. Cold War concerns were a Washington preoccupation and something that, as we have seen throughout the chapter, did not particularly resonate among the Arab Middle East. All the same, Reagan's secretary of state, Alexander Haig, pushed for a "strategic consensus" among Israel and pro-Western Arab states to monitor the "overriding danger of Soviet inroads" into the region.[90] In addition to aid and arms for Israel, the sale of five AWACS (Airborne Warning and Control System) airplanes to Saudi Arabia was also included in the plan. Tel Aviv cried foul. Menachem Begin maintained that the deal with the Saudis constituted a security threat to Israel. This resentment caused a period of debate (April to October 1981) within Washington, but the sale was eventually approved, with Reagan imposing a list of constraints on Riyadh regarding the use of the AWACS, for the purposes of cooling the controversy. Reagan's response to Israel's protestations was clear enough though, stating that "it is not the business of other countries to make American foreign policy."[91]

During the AWACS debate, Israel continued to cause mild consternation in Washington. In June, the Israeli Air Force (IAF) bombed Iraq's Osirak nuclear reactor. The White House ultimately censured the action, although as William Quandt notes, "many in official Washington were no doubt impressed by Israel's technical prowess, and were quietly cheering."[92] The United States supported a Security Council resolution condemning the operation, and withheld a shipment of F-16 fighter jets to Israel. All things considered, it was a light reprimand delivered mostly for appearances.

The following month the IAF was deployed, this time in southern Lebanon. Over the course of the 1970s, the PLO had moved toward a more diplomatic approach to their national struggle, gaining significant ground among the international community. In spring 1980, the European Community issued the Venice Declaration, stating that:

> The Palestinian people, which is conscious of existing as such, must be placed in a position, by an appropriate process defined within the framework of the comprehensive peace settlement, to exercise fully its right to self-determination.[93]

The declaration also mentions the PLO, and affirms that the leadership and the Palestinian people must be included in the peace process, not merely as refugees, as UN 242 indicates. Seeing that diplomacy was bearing fruit, Yasser Arafat sought to continue on that path. Accordingly, cross-border raids and tensions with Israel were in decline in this period. In spite of this, or perhaps because of it, Israel launched an attack on PLO strongholds in Lebanon, eliciting PLO response and precipitating a campaign involving bombing, rockets, and artillery. The worst of the Israeli attacks took place as far away as Beirut, killing 200–300 and wounding 600–800, the vast majority of both groups being civilians. PLO counterattacks claimed six Israeli civilians.[94] A ceasefire was negotiated that July (1981) by an American envoy—directly with Tel Aviv and indirectly with the PLO—and once again Israel had shipments of fighter aircraft withheld by the United States.

Mild dismay aside, the White House moved forward in its Cold War security measures by formalizing US–Israeli relations in a statement of "strategic cooperation," called the Memorandum of Understanding. The document established a strategic alliance which "is designed against the threat to peace and security of the region caused by the Soviet Union or Soviet-controlled forces from outside the region introduced into the region."[95] The memorandum was then suspended less than a month later after Tel Aviv unilaterally annexed and declared Israeli law in Syria's Golan Heights, occupied by Israel since 1967. The suspension of the memorandum stirred Begin's temper, expressing himself to those in Washington thus: "Are we a vassal state of yours? Are we a banana republic? Are we fourteen-year-olds who, if we misbehave, we get our wrists slapped?"[96] Reagan's secretary of defense, Caspar Weinberger, summarized the suspension of the memorandum, saying that "If there is no real cost to the Israelis, we'll never be able to stop any of their actions."[97] The view from Washington was that, for the most part, the answer to all three of the prime minister's rhetorical questions was in the affirmative. Israel's occasional intractability was perceived at the least as a necessary nuisance, at most as an asset. According to Henry Kissinger in his second volume of memoirs, which was published shortly after these events,

> Israel is dependent on the United States as no other country is on a friendly power.... Israel sees in intransigence the sole hope for preserving its dignity in a one-sided relationship. It feels instinctively that one admission of weakness, one concession granted without a struggle, will lead to an endless catalogue of demands.... And yet Israel's obstinacy, maddening as it can be, serves the purposes of both our countries best. A subservient client would soon face an accumulation of ever-growing pressures. It would tempt Israel's neighbors to escalate their

demands. It would saddle us with the opprobrium for every deadlock.[98]

Nevertheless, the repeated admonishments from Washington over Israel's persistently provocative operations caused Tel Aviv to become more prudent. Just as in 1956, when it was punished for its involvement in the Suez Canal crisis, Israel looked to Washington for permission before commencing the Six-Day War. A similar change is perceptible from 1981 to 1982.

Throughout the 1970s, Israel had its eye on the civil conflict in Lebanon. The minority group ruling the country, the Christian Maronites, was trying to maintain power in the face of growing opposition, and was viewed by Israel as a potential client with which Tel Aviv could establish a treaty. In addition, during the civil war, Syria had entered Lebanon with troops and eventually established surface-to-air missile sites just over the border; Damascus, initially supportive of the PLO, now hoped to keep its thumb on the organization and its guerillas, together with working toward hegemonic opportunities in Lebanon itself. The most pressing of Israel's concerns in Lebanon, however, was the presence of the PLO. That the Palestinian organization had been acknowledged, if indirectly, in the US-brokered 1981 ceasefire was cause for alarm. That Arafat was adhering to the ceasefire caused further apprehension. The PLO as a guerilla/terrorist outfit posed one kind of threat; as a legitimate organization pursuing its goals through diplomacy while cooperating with negotiated agreements, it posed a different kind of threat altogether to Israel. If the Israelis wanted the West Bank,[99]* they had to quash Palestinian nationalism, and for this the solution—from the perspective of Tel Aviv—was to

---

* According to two prominent Israeli journalists in a standard account of this period, Israel's grand strategy anticipated that,

> following the wholesale expulsion of the PLO ... Israel would be able to manage its conflict with the Palestinians to its own liking. The PLO leadership ... would ... lose any vestige of independence, whereupon its influence over the West Bank would promptly wither, allowing moderate local Palestinians to step forward and conduct negotiations with Israel on a constitution of autonomy for the inhabitants of the occupied territories—by Israel's rule, of course. Under these circumstances, the Palestinians would find themselves with no alternative but to seek an outlet for their political aspirations in Jordan.... [A] successful operation in Lebanon would ensure unchallenged Israeli superiority for thirty years to come, during which time Israel would be free to establish faits accomplis in its best interests.

get rid of the PLO. An official in the State Department indicated the specious logic: "The Israeli government believes it has a Palestinian problem because of the PLO; not that it has a PLO problem because of the Palestinians."[100]

Yet, as pointed out by Mark Tessler, "the PLO had shown considerable restraint during the eleven months between June 1982 and the ceasefire agreement signed the preceding July."[101] This restraint was not, it should be emphasized, for a lack of trying on the part of the IDF to provoke the PLO. Within the same period, Israel had perpetrated 2,125 airspace and 652 territorial-water violations in Lebanon.[102] Israel's motives were transparent, but communication with Washington was sustained. Israeli officials made multiple trips to DC, discussing plans and looking for a green light from the administration to commence hostilities. In essence, Tel Aviv was told that the pretext of a "significant violation" on the part of the PLO would be necessary, but that the United States would not oppose Israel's plans—with which by early 1982 Washington was well familiar—as long as there was ample justification. Otherwise stated, it had to look like the PLO started it.[103]

A Palestinian splinter faction not connected with Arafat attempted the assassination of Israel's ambassador in London. Though Israeli intelligence knew the facts, the action sufficed as a justification for Israeli planners. "Reprisal" IAF strikes in Lebanon, killing hundreds, finally triggered the desired PLO reaction. Israel invaded Lebanon on June 6, 1982. On August 11, after two months of Israel shelling southern Lebanon as well as Beirut, devastating the city and much of the country, a ceasefire agreement was forged by the Americans, despite egregious violations of the agreement by the IDF. By September 1 the Palestinian forces had left the country. Israel withdrew in summer 1985, with the exception of a strip along the southern boundary which it occupied until the year 2000. Over the course of the conflict, the IDF incurred roughly 650 casualties. Among the local and Palestinian refugee population in Lebanon, no precise numbers exist, but general, if conservative, estimates place the number in the order of 20,000 civilians killed. The wounded and displaced also numbered in the tens of thousands.[104]

Among the political results of the conflict were:

- increased, not decreased, Syrian involvement in Lebanese affairs (which remains something of a factor today)
- displacement and relocation of the PLO to its third base of operations, in Tunisia

- increased, not decreased, Palestinian nationalism in the occupied territories
- further distance between Lebanon and Israel, instead of the former becoming a client state for the latter.

The United States had become directly involved, first as part of a joint peacekeeping force. Yet the mere presence of the US military, America's sponsorship of Israel, and the administration's mounting overt support of the Maronite minority leadership (over and above the obvious backing of Tel Aviv's operations) made American personnel targets of deep resentment. Bomb attacks on the US embassy and a Marine barracks claimed some 300 lives. The United States, in turn, responded with naval bombardments, removing what little misconception was left about Washington's role.

The attacks on American sites included a rash of kidnappings throughout the mid-1980s, many of the targets of which were American—the CIA's Beirut station chief, State Department employees, as well as a number of journalists and academics. To Reagan's anticommunist agenda was added an avowed war on terrorism. However, the equivocal nature of how the word "terrorism" was used (and has been used ever since) allowed for broad application, especially in Central America.

What began as an isolated implementation of the Roosevelt Corollary, relating to resistance movements in El Salvador and Nicaragua, brought about a convergence of much of what we covered of 1979 and the after-effects of that critical period: political instability in and Israeli attacks on Lebanon, Sandinista resistance in Nicaragua, the Iranian Revolution, Iran's support of Lebanese groups like Hizballah, and the Iran–Iraq War. Throughout the early 1980s, Israel played a role in the follow-up to these developments, including its operations in Lebanon, supplying the Somoza regime in Nicaragua with weapons, and selling arms to Iran under Khomeini as a gesture against Iraq.

In October 1983, around the time of the truck-bombing of the Marine barracks in Beirut, the Reagan administration issued a policy directive (NSDD 111), in which the White House affirmed the strategic cooperation between Israel and the United States. A State Department official told the Israeli leadership after its signing that NSDD 111 applied "in Lebanon, in the Middle East generally, and everywhere."[105] Israeli prime minister Yitzhak Shamir described the matter as partly "a dialogue on coordinating activity in the third world."[106]

We now address the "everywhere" portion of this coordination. Although the following summary focuses more on Washington's handling of the Central American and Middle Eastern issues that cropped up in the first half of the decade, Tel Aviv was at Washington's side throughout.

For decades the people of El Salvador had suffered under US-sponsored oligarchic and right-wing military oppression. Attempts at resistance occurred throughout much of the twentieth century, but as we have seen in much of the Third World, revolutionary activity became more fervent and organized from the late 1950s onwards. Salvadoran guerilla organizations started to form, a group of which created the Farabundo Martí National Liberation Front (FMLN) in 1980. Washington's Cold War template viewed the FMLN and the resistance there as something exported by Cuba—which had undergone successful revolution in 1959—and thus formulated and underwritten by the Kremlin. A standard reflex in these circumstances, the United States threw its support (starting mainly under Jimmy Carter) behind the Salvadoran leadership, with Israel's contribution of helping train its secret police, established by the CIA.[107] Despite the obvious regional nature of the Salvadoran people's struggle, the Reagan administration painted the matter red and employed the conventional logic. According to the president, the "terrorists" and "outside interference" in El Salvador posed the threat of "infiltration into the [whole of the] Americas ... and, I'm sure, eventually North America."[108]

Washington could not take on Moscow. And it was hesitant to move on Cuba. But in order to stave off "the proliferation of Cuba-modeled states which would provide platforms for subversion," as it was worded in a secret administration document, any Central American movement resembling that of a "Cuba-modeled" rotten apple would have to be dealt with.[109] Among the candidates was, as described by an American ambassador working in the region, the "infected piece of meat" of Nicaragua and the Sandinistas.[110] According to Tim Weiner of the *New York Times*, in his acclaimed history of the CIA, *Legacy of Ashes*,

The White House and the agency told Congress that the goal was to defend El Salvador, run by right-wing politicians and their death squads, by cutting off Nicaraguan arms shipments to [the Salvadoran] leftists. This was a calculated ruse. The real plan was to train and arm Nicaraguans in Honduras—the

contras—and to use them to recapture their country from the
Sandinistas.[111]

As summarized by political scientist and national security specialist
John Prados:

> The matter of the Cubans must be central to any explanation
> for the Nicaragua covert action.... President Reagan believed
> the Salvadoran civil war was due to Cuban intervention, and
> that Nicaragua was the conduit for that support. The President
> was encouraged in these views by the State Department, then
> under Alexander Haig. Not able to strike directly at Cuba,
> the White House wanted to "interdict" [prohibit] aid through
> Nicaragua. In a way, then, the Nicaragua campaign is a renewed
> manifestation of the long-standing hostility toward Castro's
> Cuba.[112]

And calculated ruse it was. Meager support was being supplied, but
not enough to build a case or justify taking action. Even internal
doubters among the intelligence community acknowledged the lack
of evidence, viewed the matter as "misrepresented," and believed
"that arms interdiction had never been a serious objective."[113]

The Contras (*la contrarevolucionarios*) were mostly a proxy
army for the CIA in an effort to return Nicaragua to a form of rule
that coincided with US policy preferences in the region. Israel played
a part in supporting the Contras by selling them arms, laundering
money for the United States, and sending advisers, bolstering White
House and CIA efforts to steer around Congress. When it became
clear that the CIA was waging a secret war using the Contras to
overthrow the Sandinistas—not merely stemming an overstated
tide of gunrunning to El Salvador—Congress placed restrictions on
the agency (1982) and then cut aid to the Contras (1984). Among
the majority of Americans and members of Congress there was
scant support for Reagan's activities in Central America. Those
in charge of the operation nevertheless stood fast. As Lieutenant-
Colonel Oliver North, a chief architect of the Iran–Contra scandal
(discussed below) remarked during Congress' deliberations on the
matter, "Fuck the Congress."[114] That most of the population shared
the legislative branch's lack of enthusiasm by extension subsumes
most of the country in the colonel's utterance.

If the war was to continue, funding would have to come from
somewhere. At the same time, policymakers in Washington kept an

eye on the Iran–Iraq War, as well as contemplating what the future of Iran would be once it entered its post-Khomeini era (he died in 1989, but the event brought no change in the overall political order). The United States thought it best to woo Iranian "moderates" in the event Tehran suffered a power vacuum, though who the moderates were remained elusive. Moreover, concern in the White House increased over American hostages held in Lebanon. The abductions were being perpetrated by Shiite guerilla organizations like the newly emergent Hizballah, which had formed as a resistance movement against Israeli occupation and received support from Ayatollah Khomeini. The ideological and religious affinities were clear: an anti-Western and anti-Israeli agenda driven by Islamic sentiment.

All these developments commingled in the following way. While the United States was entertaining notions of making inroads into Tehran, Israel formed Iranian connections, not only with its arms sales during the Shah's rule, but continuing to do so ever since Khomeini rose to power. Iran, of course, was a loudly declared enemy by Washington, which made Israel's arms deals politically delicate. Nevertheless, the head of the Israeli Foreign Ministry approached White House advisers with the idea of the United States using Tel Aviv's contacts in Tehran for the purposes of warming relations there. Hence, the arms-for-hostages conspiracy was born. The United States would (secretly) provide Iran with arms, and Iran would in turn use its influence over the Lebanese terrorist organizations for the release of hostages. Though some captives were released, none of this went smoothly, and in some cases the number of hostages increased. Meanwhile, subsidizing the Contras remained a problem. The director of the CIA, William Cascy, along with Oliver North and others, saw an opportunity: the profits from the arms sales to Iran could be laundered and sent to the Contras in Nicaragua, with Congress and the American people being none the wiser. These covert operations, illegal under US law, spanned 1985–86 and were exposed in autumn 1986.

In a late 1984 memorandum to Casey, Robert M. Gates, deputy director for intelligence (now secretary of defense under Barack Obama), stated, "The fact is that the Western Hemisphere is the sphere of influence of the United States." The actions carried out in Nicaragua were to stem the Contras, as their "avowed aim is to spread further revolution in the Americas," and "to muddle along" in this endeavor is "to abandon the Monroe Doctrine" (presumably meaning Roosevelt's Corollary to it).[115] This had been the central concern from the start. Since the beginning of the twentieth century, the cardinal doctrines of American policy had remained in place. In the second half of the century, the United States had "extended the sphere" to include the Middle East, where it cultivated a client in Israel that would dutifully tend to the superpower's global programs.

CONCLUSION

Tracing US–Israeli relations over the entirety of the Cold War period, from Truman to Reagan, reveals the genesis, evolution, and nature of their association. In the interest of preventing overlap, the administrations after Reagan, from George H. W. Bush to George W. Bush, and their relationship with Israel will be covered in Chapters 5 and 6 in the context of the peace process and the Israel lobby dispute.

Though the Cold War is over, Israel remains the largest recipient of US foreign aid, further testament to the spuriousness of claims regarding the Soviet threat. According to the Congressional Research Service, "Since 1976, Israel has been the largest annual recipient of U.S. foreign assistance and is the largest cumulative recipient since World War II."[116] Israel receives roughly $3 billion annually, and "is allowed to spend 26.3% of the aid in Israel; the remainder is to be spent on U.S. arms."[117] In a 2004 CRS brief, the report states, "Israel is not economically self-sufficient, and relies on foreign assistance and borrowing to maintain its economy."[118] However, in recent years, Israel has become "more economically self-sufficient."[119] "The engine of the economy is an advanced high-tech sector," doing research and development as a junior partner with the United States in areas "including aviation, communications, computer-aided design and manufactures, medical electronics, and fiber optics."[120]

In addition to being for the most part propped up by the United States with aid and becoming an extension of American corporate power, Israel is also diplomatically protected by Washington at the United Nations. According to a report by journalist Donald Neff, between 1972 and 2005,

> the United States has cast its veto a total of 39 times to shield Israel from Security Council draft resolutions that condemned, deplored, denounced, demanded, affirmed, endorsed, called on and urged Israel to obey the world body.[121]

The aid and protection are an investment in Israel's stability, and therefore dependability as an offshore military base and R&D facility. Israel's primary value, aside from its stability and cooperation, is its military strength and aptitude. As summed up by Steven Spiegel:

> [T]he United States has interests in Israeli military performance and capability beyond exclusive concern for the Arab–Israeli balance of power. The intelligence-gathering capabilities of the Israelis are superior. The Israelis are important to the refinement and development of the American conventional deterrent. They improve American arms and advertise their superiority. Their combat experience yields important lessons.[122]

In accordance with this highly valued arrangement, it stands to reason that Washington (and the corporate sector) would be more partial to a degree of low-grade tension in the Middle East and a degree of militancy in Israel's regional conduct. This apparent preference dovetails with the diplomatic protection provided Tel Aviv by Washington, which we will examine in Chapter 5.

PART 3

DIPLOMACY AND INFLUENCE

5

THE PEACE PROCESS:
ANATOMY OF AN INJUSTICE

As we approach the subject of the peace process, we now do so with some background on the US–Israeli relationship, which should inform how diplomacy operates between the parties. In essence, the peace process is part and parcel of the special relationship.

First let us consider the phrase "peace process" itself. On the face of it, we are dealing with a process, or "a systematic series of actions directed to some end" (dictionary.com), in this case resolution of the Palestine–Israel conflict, or peace. This procedure has been unfolding since 1967,* and aside from treaties between Israel and Egypt (1979), and Israel and Jordan (1994), the occupation of the Palestinian territories maintained by Israel and tacitly supported, as well as largely financed, by the United States continues now into the twenty-first century. The process toward peace has in over 40 years produced, with respect to Israel and Palestine, no peace. Questions arise.

A review of the basic history of the conflict reveals that the main issues are clear and easy to understand, because of the salient fact that they are in themselves uncomplicated. In addition to being uncomplicated, they are well documented and accepted by scholars hailing from points far and wide on the political spectrum; there is scant legitimate contention in this allegedly highly contentious subject. With these givens in mind—the conflict's core facts being clear, substantially chronicled, and largely uncontested—a great deal of burden is placed on the word *process*. That the last four decades have yielded virtually no positive results (and a multitude of negative ones) would seem to suggest that our givens are the opposite of what they actually are: convoluted, undisclosed, and disputed. Since this is not the case, the phrase is immediately suspect. Tracing

---

* The diplomatic record of the Arab–Israeli and Palestine–Israel conflicts starts with Israeli statehood. From the 1948 war onwards, there have been hostilities and attempts at resolution of them. However, the peace process that frequently appears in the headlines pertains to Israel's occupation of the West Bank and Gaza—the Palestine–Israel conflict. For this reason, our review will begin with 1967.

the process and its outcomes down through the years renders this apparent.

My inclusion of the word "injustice" in this chapter's subtitle might imply that I am operating from a decided perspective on the matter. This is in some measure true. I will concede that the subtitle contains a minimum of opinion, that is, it reflects the past and current conditions of the occupied Palestinian territories, which spell major suffering for their inhabitants and are routinely described as a "humanitarian crisis," especially in the sealed-off and isolated Gaza Strip.[1] That this situation has been sustained since the Six-Day War and has only degenerated over time can be described conservatively, in my view, as an injustice.

As former Israeli prime minister Ariel Sharon stated candidly in a 2003 Knesset meeting, "You might not like the word occupation, but that is what it is. To hold 3.5 million Palestinians under occupation is a terrible thing for Israel, [and] the Palestinians."[2] Sharon correctly observed a facet that is seldom considered: the injustice also extends to Israel and its people. While the Palestinians have certainly borne the brunt of Zionist policies, said policies have done Israel's population little service. From 2000 to 2008, a total of 490 Israeli civilians were killed by Palestinians, mostly as a result of the Second Intifada (2000–03), which was a violent yet unsurprising expression of the grievances produced by subjugation. (By contrast, 4,805 Palestinians were killed in the same period.[3]) The injustices are by no means limited to and calculable only by body counts; these particular data are presented here merely to provide a sample index of what has been at stake. Injustices account for a range of effects, from emotional to economic, and regardless of whether there is a disparity between how much harm each side has incurred, the Palestinian territories and Israel are the worse for the conflict and its protraction. The subtitle attempts to encompass these prefatory thoughts.

PROLOGUE

Western Europe became the seat of world power in roughly 1500, and has dominated global affairs for the last 500 years. Its projection of power across the continents was direct, driven by expansionism and acquisition, and ruthless in its methods. As an outcome of European, and in particular British, establishment in the New World, a seed was planted in the early seventeenth century that by the twentieth germinated and transformed into a separate state, one more powerful than anything Europe had hoped to become. After two savage internal conflicts that resulted in near self-immolation, Europe devolved into a second-rate power in the mid-twentieth century, facing ever-declining authority in international affairs while situated between two non-European "superpowers": the United States and the Soviet Union. After the second European conflict these two superpowers formed a tacit agreement—with the United States possessing the upper hand—whereupon the USSR would exercise leverage over its Eastern European periphery and the United States would manage and oversee Western Europe, Japan, and all associated Third World peripheral zones. According to Cold War historian Melvyn Leffler, "The terms laid out by the Truman administration for a cooperative relationship [with Moscow] were clearly skewed to sustain America's preponderant position in the international system."[4] Far from novel, these exploits were a continuation of Manifest Destiny and the Open Door Policy.

In a tense discussion in 1821, John Quincy Adams, as secretary of state, told a British diplomat that America did not contest London's holdings in Canada, but the Oregon territory was going to be hands off. Adams told his counterpart, "Keep what is yours [Canada] and leave the rest of the continent to us." The improved position the United States held after the War of 1812 was not dissimilar to the position it found itself in after World War II. As historian George C. Herring observes,

> Americans after the War of 1812 became even more assertive in foreign policy. They challenged the European commercial system and sought to break down trade barriers. Above all, they poised themselves to take control of North America and seized every opportunity to remove every obstacle. Indeed, only to the powerful British would they concede the right to "keep what is yours." They gave the Spaniards, Indians, and Mexicans no such consideration.[5]

This historical analog proves apt once the appropriate substitutions are made: World War II for the War of 1812, the world (less the Soviet sphere) for North America, the Soviets for the British, and the three groups receiving "no such consideration" for any and all outside the White House–Kremlin framework. Though the British in the 1820s were the predominant world power, the comparison obtains. The established patterns of US policy elucidate and demystify modern developments. Almost 350 years of American expansion and hegemony (from Jamestown on) were not going to be discontinued when the world was finally, in 1945, at its disposal.

The Washington–Wall Street objective of global preponderance was for the most part met, and enjoyed considerable success well into the postwar period, though a trend of decreasing supremacy set in during the 1970s and continues into the present.[6] In its post-1945 aims, the United States attempted to secure the open door by positioning Western Europe as a junior partner in the Cold War arrangements, as well as the Third World regions peripheral to Europe. American economic schemes required that the Third World, on which the United States (and the core in general) depended for natural resources, remained cooperative with First World ambitions. Yet, the threat to this "stability" became a mounting issue over time. This was a function of these previously colonial entities gaining independence from their former European overlords, a phenomenon that began to take place on a larger scale after World War I, becoming more acute after World War II. Owing to its petroleum resources and being a hotbed of national liberation movements, the Middle East became, after American oil firms first blazed the trail in the early 1930s, a central priority in Washington.

By this chapter, the story is now a familiar one. Despite coverage of the peace process continuously implying otherwise, American diplomacy in the Middle East is not separate or detached from the original motives that brought it into the region at the outset. With now decades of US involvement in the Middle East to refer to, and over two centuries of its general approach to foreign relations at hand, it stands to reason that the diplomatic style will fit within these currents. At least four basic observations can be extrapolated to our present study.

- Policymakers in Washington have in general aimed to preserve the status quo in the Middle East. Henry Kissinger's management of regional affairs in the 1970s serves as an ideal illustration. Things were kept as they were unless a fire needed extinguishing (for instance, the 1973 Yom Kippur War), in which case "standstill diplomacy" and shuttle diplomacy were used to effect minimal alteration.
- In a related aspect of this tendency—present throughout much of its history, but starkly visible in the postwar era—the United States has endeavored to control and/or thwart independent self-determination in the Third World. This has also applied

to the Palestinians. The emergence of a legitimate state in the territories also factors into the first point above: Keeping the territories politically inert preserves the balance, whereas a Palestinian state would add an unpredictable element.

- A level of tension in the region, especially where it concerns Israel, has brought the benefit of creating a source of leverage used to regulate Tel Aviv's behavior. The tensions have increased Israeli wants from the United States, which in turn could be granted, delayed, or denied depending on the circumstances. This also provides pretext and justification for the United States remaining involved in the region, historically a matter of Cold War preoccupation, now a concern over terrorism and Islamic extremism—both persistently stated thorns in Washington's side, yet both to a large extent the by-products of American interference. That these tensions also financially accrue to the domestic weapons industry is also a factor that should not be overlooked.

- The Palestinians have been a low (if mostly non-) priority, and have generally only received US attention when the situations in the West Bank and Gaza were agitated to an extent beyond what planners in Washington felt was benign. Rhetoric and diplomacy supporting the Palestinians have also served immediate purposes, for example, allaying Arab indignation owing to popular sympathy in the region for the plight of the Palestinians. In other words, the occupied territories are a useful source for PR and propaganda.

These four points of reference—regional stasis, restraint of national liberation, keeping Israel militant, and periodic Palestinian utility— while certainly expandable, form a minimal set of considerations that we should well expect to persist in the diplomatic domain, where we now turn.

Before getting into the specific elements that make up the record, it will be advantageous to start with a bird's-eye view of the whole process. The peace process as it exists today is the product of the following proposals and agreements, listed chronologically and clustered into three phases:

1. The 1967 phase

- UN 242 (1967)
- Anwar Sadat proposal (1971)

- Gunnar Jarring (UN) mission (1971)
- Arab–PLO proposal (1976)
- Anwar Sadat proposal, reissued (1977)
- Camp David I (1978)

2. The Madrid–Oslo phase

- Shamir Plan (1989)
- Madrid conference (1991)
- Oslo Accords I and II (1993, 1995)
- Camp David II (2000)
- Clinton Plan (2000)
- Taba statement (2001)

3. The Post-Taba Phase

- Saudi proposal (2002)
- People's Voice/Ayalon–Nusseibeh plan (2003)
- Geneva Accord/Beilin–Rabbo plan (2003)
- Road Map (2003)
- Saudi proposal, reissued (2007)
- Annapolis (2007).

While this list is not exhaustive, and does not include some of the smaller events (such as the follow-up agreements to Oslo II, responses to the Shamir Plan, and the string of plans during and after Israel's 1982 invasion of Lebanon), it does map out the main nodes; the smaller instances will nevertheless be touched upon in the chapter. The clustering into phases will be a useful way to order and simplify the history. As will be demonstrated, this does not imply that the items in a given grouping are directly linked in a chain, but simply designates a rough periodization. While the diplomatic record can appear elaborate, if impenetrable at times, the gist of what is being negotiated, once distilled to the essentials, is fairly straightforward.[7]

THE 1967 PHASE, 1967–78

After the June war, Israel had acquired the Sinai Peninsula and Gaza from Egypt, the Golan Heights from Syria, and the West

Bank (including East Jerusalem) from Jordan. Roughly a week after the war ended, Israeli heads of state convened secret discussions over what should be done about the postwar situation, in particular its territorial gains. On June 19, a cabinet decision was made consisting of a peace initiative to be proposed to Egypt and Syria, based on the international border between Israel and the two Arab states—Sinai and the Golan Heights—with Gaza retained under Israeli sovereignty. The West Bank was not mentioned in the decision. Two days later the proposal was communicated to the US secretary of state, Dean Rusk. The secretary later notified Israel that Cairo and Damascus demanded unconditional Israeli withdrawal and therefore rejected the proposal. However, this forwarding and response are not confirmed.[8] Nevertheless, as historian Avi Shlaim observes,

> One is left with the impression that [Israeli ambassador Abba] Eban was more interested in using the cabinet decision of 19 June to impress the Americans than to engage the governments of Egypt and Syria in substantive negotiations.

Shortly afterwards, the decision's momentum died among its authors, with plans for keeping portions or all of the acquired territory taking precedence instead. Tel Aviv also undertook plans for developing settlements in the Golan, and by doing so, according to Shlaim, "reversed their own policy and embarked on the road toward creeping annexation. The decision of 19 June became a dead letter even before its formal cancellation in October."[9]

That July, among other offered strategies for how to manage the West Bank, the Israeli minister of labor, Yigal Allon, produced the Allon Plan. Neither accepted nor rejected internally, Allon's formulation envisioned the West Bank as being divided into east and west sectors. The eastern areas along the Jordan River would belong to Israel, while the territory's western interior would be separated again into north and south cantons (by a corridor stretching from Jerusalem to Jericho) and designated as Jordanian. The current situation in the West Bank, with respect to borders, subdivision of Palestinian areas, and wall construction, closely resembles what was outlined by Allon over four decades ago.

Unlike 1956, Israel was not ordered by the United States to relinquish the territories it now occupied as a result of its decisive victory. What was established instead was UN Security Council Resolution 242. (Decisions by the Council are legally binding, unlike General

Assembly resolutions.) The essence of UN 242 is "[w]ithdrawal of Israel armed forces from territories occupied in the recent conflict," in accordance with "the inadmissibility of the acquisition of territory by war." All parties are to adhere to the resolution's call for the "[t]ermination of all claims or states of belligerency." The Palestinians are mentioned indirectly, in the context of the resolution calling for "a just settlement of the refugee problem."[10] Israel's interpretation was withdrawal from some of the land it now occupied. Egypt and Jordan (Syria rejected 242) shared the UN interpretation, namely, that Israel should withdraw from all of the occupied land. The Americans were located somewhere in the middle of the two, though closer to the UN–Arab understanding. Following passage of the resolution, Swedish diplomat Gunnar Jarring was placed in charge of overseeing 242's implementation. His mission lasted until April 1969, meeting diplomatic deadlock owing to a great extent to Israel's interpretation of how much territory was to be returned.[11]

By this time Egyptian frustrations with the lack of diplomatic movement had given way to escalation along the Bar-Lev line, where Israeli troops were stationed on the eastern side of the Suez Canal. Hostilities had taken place along the canal since the end of the Six-Day War, but in spring 1969 were intensified by Egypt, creating the War of Attrition (see page 97). In response to the conflict, the newly inaugurated Richard Nixon administration put forward two proposals through its secretary of state, William Rogers. The first, called the Rogers Plan (December 1969), was based on UN 242, calling for cessation of hostilities, return to international borders, commitments to peace, and negotiations. The initiative met with immediate and categorical rejection by Tel Aviv. Egypt never accepted the plan but remained open to its possibilities, being ultimately wary that the American proposition might spell a bilateral peace and not a comprehensive one. Rogers then communicated a second plan (known as Rogers B) in June 1970, in the form of a ceasefire, along with a call for a resumption of Jarring's efforts. The United States gained reluctant Israeli agreement after assurances of protection from UN 242 were made, as well as promises of aid.[12] With the inclusion of Arab agreement, a 90-day ceasefire was implemented, bringing the War of Attrition to a close and reintroducing Jarring to the diplomatic scene.

Jarring's mission resumed in early 1971 with him sending a memorandum to both Israel and Egypt in an attempt to take a temperature reading of where each party stood. In the diplomatic message, or aide-memoire, "parallel and simultaneous commitments" of both sides were sought: for Israel to withdraw to the "former international boundary," and for Egypt to "enter into a peace agreement with Israel."[13] Cairo accepted the memo, which marked the first public agreement to work toward a treaty with its Jewish neighbor. Tel Aviv rejected the memo, stating that "Israel will not withdraw to the pre-June 5, 1967, lines."[14] This rejection brought the Jarring initiative to a halt. It is instructive to note that during this period—before and after—the United States had markedly increased military and financial assistance to Israel.[15] According to historian Nadav Safran, "the State Department did not even attempt to apply pressure on Israel by manipulating the supply of arms to it, as it had done for much less reason in the past." Yet, disappointment registered from William Rogers and the State Department. Safran locates the source of State's irritation:

> The sharpness of the secretary of state's verbal reaction to Israel's response to Jarring was in a sense a measure of his frustration in the face of a developing tendency in the administration as a whole to view military assistance to Israel mainly as a function of meeting the Soviet challenge in the area and deterring war, thus largely taking it out of the play of immediate Arab–Israeli diplomacy.[16]

Whether Rogers (or Safran) truly believed the underlying rationale of Nixon and Kissinger ("the Soviet challenge"), the administration's priorities, and what was worth sacrificing for them, are beyond question. These three factors—Israeli refusal to withdraw, US supply and support of Israel, and ultimate American non-support of the peace process—will remain fixed points for the duration of the chapter.

Though Jarring's mission was over, the possibility of resolve lingered a little longer because of the diplomatic trial balloon floated by President Anwar Sadat, Nasser's former vice president. Days before Jarring sent off his memos, Sadat in a speech to the Egyptian National Assembly offered his own interim initiative, whereby both sides would agree to a 30-day ceasefire extension and Egypt would set to opening the Suez Canal on the following condition, perhaps the paramount sentence in the speech:

> We demand that during this period of with-holding fire a partial withdrawal of the Israeli troops on the eastern bank of the Suez Canal will be realised as a first step in a timetable to be laid

down with a view to implementing the rest of the provisions of the Security Council Resolution.[17]

In other words the condition meant partial withdrawal for partial peace, all with a view toward implementing 242, or full withdrawal. After months of discussion among the Americans, among the Israelis, between the two, and between the State Department and Cairo, Israel's prime minister, Golda Meir, remained inflexible and dedicated to the notion that a partial withdrawal was not going to lead to full withdrawal to the pre-June 5 borders. Looking to sustain the territorial status quo—and reassured by Nixon that Israel would receive the Phantom jets recently delayed to increase Tel Aviv's diplomatic cooperation[18]—Meir ran out the clock on Sadat's initiative, thus rejecting it and moving the Egyptian leader in the direction of increasingly militant pronouncements. One way or another, Sadat wanted Israel out of Egypt.

The deadlock led perhaps unsurprisingly, though not so for the Israelis, to the 1973 Yom Kippur War. The three-week conflict ended with the passage of Security Council Resolution 338, calling for an end to hostilities, implementation of 242, and immediate negotiations.[19] The negotiations portion took place in Geneva with US–Soviet oversight, but the peace conference ended up being more ceremonial and pro forma than anything substantive, mainly a consequence of Kissinger's mismanagement and overall US interest in ending the oil embargo (see page 100).[20] The willingness of Egypt (and Syria) to resort to armed conflict, especially in light of the US–Israeli assumption that the Arab states were deterred by Israel's military might, moved Kissinger to pursue his shuttle diplomacy, eventually achieving limited postwar improvements in the so-called Sinai I and II agreements.

During this time, the Palestine Liberation Organization (PLO) was gaining diplomatic ground, with its leader, Yasser Arafat, speaking before the UN General Assembly in autumn 1974. The assembly in turn responded with two resolutions in support of the Palestinians. The first confirmed their "right to self-determination without external interference" and "[t]he right to national independence and sovereignty." The second conferred upon the PLO UN observer status.* Though the resolutions were legally non-binding, they reflected the global consensus.[21]

---

* Observer status is granted by the General Assembly, welcoming certain nonmember states, international organizations, and liberation

Up until this point in the peace process, the Palestinians had not been a factor, except in UN 242 as a "refugee problem." But as the PLO achieved increased recognition, the subject of the occupied territories began to enter the discourse on how to create peace in the Middle East. In January 1976, during a Security Council "debate on the Middle East problem including the Palestinian question," Egypt, Syria, Jordan, and the PLO presented an initiative which became a draft proposal to be voted on by the council.[22] The proposal (S/11940) affirmed three overriding items:

- the Palestinian people's "inalienable national right of self-determination, including the right to establish an independent state"
- "The right of Palestinian refugees wishing to return to their homes" or to receive compensation
- "That Israel should withdraw from all the Arab territories occupied since June 1967."[23]

The draft was singly vetoed by the United States.[24]

In 1977, the United States and Israel both underwent a change in leadership, ushering in the Jimmy Carter administration (January) and the premiership of Likud member Menachem Begin (June). The two leaders immediately diverged in their stated intentions. Carter entered office quickly showing interest in reconvening the Geneva conference and comprehensively addressing the Arab–Israeli issue, which as far as US involvement was concerned had been sitting in limbo since Kissinger's limited efforts. Included in the White House's rhetoric was talk of a Palestinian "homeland." Begin and the Likud party, on the other hand, stated in their policy platform that "Judaea and Samaria [the West Bank] will not be handed to any foreign administration; between the Sea and the Jordan there will only be Israeli sovereignty." The platform also emphasized that settlement construction "in all parts of the Land of Israel is the focal point of the Zionist effort," while dismissing the PLO as "no national liberation organization but an organization of assassins ... [whose] aim is to liquidate the State of Israel."[25] It should be mentioned that prior to Likud's electoral victory the PLO had indicated that it envisioned a Palestinian state in the occupied territories. The head of the PLO's Political Department, which managed foreign affairs, spoke in the

---

movements to participate in the assembly, but without the right to vote on resolutions.

Egyptian press (*Al-Ahram*) of "the establishment of an independent Palestinian state in the territories from which Israel withdraws," a tacit recognition of Israel and something on which diplomacy could have been built, but it was instead ignored.[26]

Nevertheless, Carter and his staff worked to reconvene the 1973 Geneva peace conference, trying to establish among the involved parties a consensus about the conference's principles and procedures. Much of the difficulty that ensued revolved around how the Palestinians were going to be included, and what language was to be used to describe their involvement. Another sticking point regarding language was the issue of withdrawal; these were items that were central to Middle Eastern peace and on which Israel was most unyielding. Preparations also involved the Soviets. Eventually Washington and Moscow produced a joint communiqué containing the intended principles for the summit, and making mention of "resolution of the Palestinian question, including insuring the legitimate rights of the Palestinian people."[27] Tel Aviv's response was immediate, forceful rejection.

During this phase, Sadat was seeking a detour around what was looking more and more like a dead end. Israel and Egypt were working the back channel, both of them out of frustration with how preparations for Geneva were shaping up. Israel wanted to achieve separate agreements, especially with Cairo, while Egypt viewed Geneva as something that was, given the emphasis on procedure, going to offer nothing more than it did the first time. With preparations bogging down, Sadat decided to strike off on his own. On November 9, 1977, in another address to the Egyptian National Assembly, the president stated, "I am ready to go to Geneva.... I am even ready to go to the Knesset and discuss [the matter] with them."[28] Begin took notice and issued an invitation to the Egyptian leader, who addressed Israel's parliament ten days later. In his speech, Sadat laid out a five-point peace agreement, amounting in the end to a reiteration of UN 242 as well as an invocation of "the fundamental rights of the Palestinian people and their right to self-determination, including their right to establish their own state."[29] Back and forth discussion between the Egyptians, Israelis, and the White House proceeded, continuing to hang on the usual issues, with Israel offering counterproposals that steered wide of the subject of the West Bank and Gaza. The ever-dimming prospects further clouded over at an Israeli-held dinner in Jerusalem honoring Egypt's foreign minister. At the event, which was to open further dialogue between Cairo and Tel Aviv, Begin made the following remarks:

The Arabs have enjoyed self-determination in twenty-one Arab countries for a very long time. Is it too much for Israel to have one country among twenty-one? NO, I declare in my loudest voice, NO to withdrawal to the 1967 lines, NO to self-determination for the terrorists.[30]

Carter decided to move to direct negotiations between Sadat and Begin. Invitations were issued to both leaders, and the three met at Camp David, where from September 5–17, 1978, two accords were established. The first placed "the resolution of the Palestinian problem in all its aspects" in a five-year framework to be settled by Egypt, Israel, and Jordan. The second accord set in motion a peace treaty between Egypt and Israel, which was signed at the White House on March 26, 1979.[31] Though an improvement, Camp David provided Israel with what it had desired all along: a bilateral agreement with Egypt. The Arab–Israeli conflict had been neglected. The Golan Heights remained occupied. The Palestinians had been consigned to a murky and ambiguous five-year plan based on "full autonomy" and containing no mention of the PLO. In other words, Tel Aviv's inflexibility had paid off. Not only did Israel continue to enjoy the material benefits of its relationship with the United States, but from June 1967 forward Washington had made certain that diplomatic hurdles were kept to a minimum. Throughout the literature, there are frequent descriptions of US presidential and staff frustrations with the various episodes of Israel's recalcitrance, yet, as the record shows, the Jewish state was routinely and consistently rewarded. Similarly, Arab initiative and creativity in undertaking a path toward conflict resolution was not only dismissed, but has since been effaced and superseded with rhetoric suggesting that Israel is besieged and lacks a "partner in peace."

Arafat continued his diplomatic efforts at the United Nations. Similar to the comments made to the Egyptian press, the PLO chairman made a diplomatic gesture toward Carter through Illinois congressman Paul Findley in October 1978, making the following statement:

The PLO will accept an independent Palestinian state consisting of the West Bank and Gaza, with connecting corridor, and in that circumstance will renounce any and all violent means to enlarge the territory of that state. I would reserve the right, of course, to use non-violent means, that is to say, diplomatic and democratic means, to bring about the eventual unification of all of Palestine.[32]

Arafat also asserted, "We will give de facto recognition to the State of Israel," and that "we would live at peace with all our neighbors." International relations scholar Seth Tillman notes that "Neither the statement made to Findley nor the substance of the writer's interview with Arafat ... elicited a response from the Carter administration." Indeed, Carter himself had stated that spring in a press conference, "We do not and never have favored an independent Palestinian nation." Tillman summarizes: "Carter during this period ... was showing mounting irritation with Begin's insistence on his plan for the West Bank and Gaza, and the resulting confusion may have obscured the fact that the president was hardly less firm than Begin himself in his rejection of an independent Palestinian state."[33]

It is critical for readers to bear in mind that at any time in the period covered in this section, from 1967–78, the United States could have reversed the entire situation with the mere behest of the executive branch for Israel to withdraw to the pre-June 1967 borders.

INTERLUDE: THE REAGAN YEARS

After Camp David, Israel was more or less through with the peace process. Abba Eban, in a 1982 article citing "Government policy guidelines" passed by the Knesset, stated that "after the transition period laid down in the Camp David accords, Israel will raise its claim and *will act to fulfill its rights* to sovereignty over Judea, Samaria and the Gaza" (original emphasis).[34] Tel Aviv had not withdrawn from the West Bank and Gaza, nor would it. A requisite within this programmatic retention of the Palestinian territories was to address the symbol of Palestinian desire for self-determination, independence, and statehood. The PLO would have to be checked. Israeli negotiator, historian, and former foreign minister Shlomo Ben-Ami observes in his account of the peace process, *Scars of War, Wounds of Peace*:

> When Begin brought the peace process to a halt he knew that he could rely on the strategic gains he had made through his peace with Egypt. He had taken Egypt out of the war cycle and he could rest assured that the collapse of the [Palestinian] autonomy talks would not lead to war.... He would now be free to destroy the Iraqi nuclear reactor and to invade Lebanon in order to do away with the military and political challenge

posed by the PLO.... Begin was free to realise his real political
Weltanschauung [world view].[35]

Camp David and the treaty with Cairo had taken Egypt, the
Arab state with the most heft, out of the picture. Egypt had been
neutralized.

In our tripartite division of the peace process, the end of the first
phase (1978) and the beginning of the second phase (1989) leapfrog
over the entirety of the Reagan years. Much of this has to do with
Israel's military involvements in Lebanon, which stretched from the
late-1970s to the mid-1980s. Tensions along the Israel–Lebanon
border were animated mostly by the PLO having relocated there
after their flight from Jordan in 1970. These tensions were a product of provocative and reprisal cross-border attacks by Israel and
the PLO, along with both sides' involvement in the volatile internal
situation in Lebanon.

Israel's enormously disproportionate actions included air strikes
and bombing throughout southern Lebanon in the late 1970s—
during the preparation and convention of Camp David—claiming
thousands of lives and displacing hundreds of thousands of people
(mostly civilians in both instances) while occupying southern Lebanon for months at a time. This policy of clearing out the south by
punishing the refugee populations, all in an effort to displace the
PLO, culminated in Israel's 1982 invasion. In short, the Reagan
administration spent its tenure granting the opportunity for, and
therefore assisting, Israel to carry out its designs on the occupied
territories and subsequent aim of flushing the PLO out of Lebanon
into a third place of exile—a continuation of Carter's handling of
the situation.

Diplomatic movement by the White House in the 1981–85
period was meager, and as was now standard for 20 years, rejection-
ist. During the violence in Lebanon, the president issued the Reagan
Plan, calling for Israeli withdrawal from the West Bank and Gaza
according to UN 242, but envisioned the Palestinian territories
becoming linked with Jordan instead of achieving statehood. The
Israelis rejected the plan on account of its call for withdrawal, while
King Hussein of Jordan and Arafat were receptive. At an Arab summit
in Fez, Morocco, a proposal called the Fez Plan was produced,
based on a 1981 Saudi proposal called the Fahd Plan (named after
the Saudi crown prince). The eight-point Fahd and Fez plans both
called for full Israeli withdrawal, a Palestinian state based on the
Green Line, or 1967 borders, and normalization of region-wide

relations.[36] Soon thereafter, the Soviet Union issued the Brezhnev Plan, basically a reiteration of the Fez proposal. All three plans—the 1981 Fahd Plan, along with the Fez and Brezhnev plans—were rejected by Israel. Some time later, in early 1985, a joint Jordanian–PLO initiative was made, modeled on the Reagan Plan, but met with American rejection instead.

The remaining years of the Reagan administration and much of those of George H. W. Bush (1989–93), in terms of the Palestine–Israel conflict, were focused on the Intifada, an Arabic term meaning a "shaking off." Palestinian desire for an end to the occupation and a new life in a state called Palestine gave rise to this period of grassroots resistance, rebellion, and protest in the territories, spanning 1987 to 1991. This was not a PLO stimulus; the Palestinian people in their political isolation had decided to speak for themselves.

In spring 1988, Reagan's secretary of state, George Shultz, issued a somewhat abstract peace plan: "The agreed objective is a comprehensive peace providing for the security of all the States in the region and for the legitimate rights of the Palestinian people."[37] Negotiations would be based on 242, transitional periods, final status talks, and conducted between Israel and a joint Jordanian–Palestinian delegation. There was no mention of the PLO, and for this reason the plan was unpopular with the Palestinians. However, Shultz was most irritated with the spurning of the initiative by Israeli prime minister Yitzhak Shamir, who went so far as to reject the essence of 242, and was quoted in the *New York Times* as saying "this expression of territory for peace is not accepted by me."[38] Yet, for all the secretary's disappointment, the administration promptly reinforced its strategic agreements with the Jewish state and carried through with shipments of fighter aircraft.[39]

As the Intifada persisted, the local leadership in the territories and the external PLO leadership, now in Tunis after fleeing Lebanon, sought to further pursue the diplomatic path and create an alternative agenda running parallel with the people's uprising in the territories. Throughout 1988 both Palestinian governments issued a host of multi-pointed plans, statements in the media, and documents calling for Israeli withdrawal, creation of a Palestinian state, willingness to adhere to the pertinent UN resolutions, and peaceful recognition of Israel. On November 15, at a Palestinian National Council (PNC; the PLO's legislative body) meeting held in Algiers, Arafat and the council declared independence for the state of Palestine, embracing a two-state solution—Israel and Palestine—including acceptance of all UN resolutions dating back to 1947, and recognition of Israel. The declaration was then reissued in a "political communiqué" elucidating the particular points agreed to by the PNC.[40]

Regardless of the PLO's campaign and its increased moderation and acceptance of 242 (which dismisses Palestinian concerns), along with State Department confirmation that Fatah had not recently been involved in terrorism[41]—which Arafat continued to repudiate verbally—Reagan's people were dissatisfied and further insisted the PLO do more in this area. As Arafat and the Palestinian organization complied with past and present dictates on their behavior, additional hoops were continuously presented, through which they were to jump, and repeatedly did.

At the end of the year, after sustained cooperation with White House demands, the administration eventually opened an indirect dialog with the PLO through the American ambassador in Tunis. It was during this contact that George H. W. Bush took office.

THE MADRID–OSLO PHASE, 1989–2001

The US–PLO dialogue was less than substantive, and discontinued on the American side within the first year of the new administration. The Bush White House carried over many staff members who had run Reagan's administration, and there was little that was going to be different. However, the president and his secretary of state, James Baker, were pragmatic, business-like politicians and neither harbored much in the way of personal devotions toward Israel. Nevertheless, and as we have seen continuously, US policy adhered to certain doctrinal conventions; Israel was a client and would be supported, and a Palestinian state added something new and uncertain to the status quo, which was best avoided. In his discussions and signals toward trying to get the Israelis to engage diplomatically, Baker was described in the *New York Times* as going "out of his way to reiterate his opposition to a Palestinian state."[42]

During the short-lived US–PLO dialogue, Prime Minister Shamir sought to reroute any possible movement and issued a peace plan of his own. The Shamir Plan, officially dated May 14, 1989, predictably rejected upfront a Palestinian state, negotiations with the PLO, and any "change in the status of Judea, Samaria and Gaza."[43] The plan called for democratic elections in the territories, "a transitional period of self-rule" under the elected leadership, and negotiations toward a "permanent solution." What the plan spelled was continued Israeli occupation of the territories, with the Palestinian leadership handling day-to-day management. But even the scope of their authority would be monitored and restricted. As summarized by Shamir:

> If the elected representatives try to stray from the course which will be allowed for them, and will try to deal with other subjects like trying to establish a Palestinian state, Israel will prevent them, even though they have been elected.[44]

The Palestinians opposed the plan, as did President Hosni Mubarak of Egypt (who replaced Sadat after he was assassinated in 1981) and King Hussein of Jordan.

In spite of his opposition, Mubarak that autumn tried to prevent a diplomatic impasse by offering his own ten-point plan (September 4), which used Shamir's election concept as a point of departure, but included mention of "territory for peace" and called for a halt to Israeli settlement in the territories.[45] Palestinian response was mostly negative because the ten points neglected to mention the PLO or statehood, although Arafat and company remained open to further discussion and development in connection with Mubarak's initiative, and began working with the Egyptian president on the matter. The Israelis dismissed the plan entirely.

The following month Secretary Baker floated his own initiative (October 10), this one a five-point plan aiming to create an Israeli–Palestinian dialogue in Cairo based on Shamir's formula of elections and negotiations, where the "Palestinians would be free to raise issues that relate to their opinions on how to make elections and the negotiating process succeed."[46] Similar to their response to Mubarak's plan, the Palestinians were receptive to the possibilities and began working in that direction. Also similar was Israel's opposition to Baker's five points, which like Mubarak's initiative was based on the Shamir Plan in the first place. No matter. In June 1990, the Shamir Plan was scuttled within the Israeli government by the prime minister's own party and cabinet, with the prime minister's help. Regardless of Baker's irritation over Israel's increasing right-wing intransigence, the United States at this time once again suspended its dialogue with the PLO. The decision was based on acts of terrorism carried out by Palestinian groups not associated with Arafat, which again was confirmed by the State Department.

At the turn of the decade, the limited diplomacy that had been achieved in the late 1980s was now idle. During this dormancy significant changes were taking place in the international scene, in particular the disintegration and demise of the Soviet Union and tensions in the Persian Gulf. As the Cold War was becoming a thing of the past, the Middle East was entering a new phase of external influence, with the United States now being the world's sole super-power. The standard roles played by Washington, Moscow, and the Middle Eastern states (especially those that looked to the USSR for support) were now being redefined, a period captured by Bush and his staff with the vague, if disconcerting, phrase "new world order."

After the long and brutal Iran–Iraq War, both countries had endured hundreds of thousands killed and heavy financial costs. Iraq's efforts in attacking and fighting the Iranians were rewarded with massive loans and support from the gulf states of Saudi Arabia, the United Arab Emirates, and Kuwait; aid was also supplied by the Soviets and the United States, with both occasionally playing both sides during the conflict. At the war's end, Iraq's leader, Saddam Hussein, was looking for debt relief as well as for Kuwait to lower oil production and thus increase market prices, much needed by Baghdad for reconstruction. Meeting with opposition, the Iraqi leader's anger was aroused along with his view that Kuwait's creation by the British in 1922 was illegitimate in the first place. In Hussein's eyes, the obvious solution to all these and more prob-lems and grievances, in addition to his overall designs on regional superiority, was to annex Kuwait.

In all likelihood not anticipating an aggressive US response, having been told by the American ambassador to Baghdad that "we have no opinion on the Arab–Arab conflicts, like your border disagreement with Kuwait," Iraqi forces poured over the border in August 1990 and annexed the gulf emirate.[47] After discussion in the United Nations, but little exploration in the way of possible diplomatic solutions to the crisis, US and coalition forces unleashed Operation Desert Storm in January 1991, driving Hussein's occupa-tion back over the border as well as subjecting Iraq to devastating destruction in a spectacle of American military power. Following the conflict, Bush and Baker shifted focus to the Arab–Israeli peace process.

During the Gulf War, a number of Arab states had joined the US-led coalition forces, in particular Egypt, Saudi Arabia, and Syria, out of political motivation, financial incentives from the United States, or both. Israel, too, supported the war effort—and favored the termination of Hussein's regime, which the United

States decided instead to preserve by not supporting a Shiite uprising that sought just that aim after the war—but Tel Aviv's role was something of a curiosity. In an extraordinary episode in the history of international relations, as 39 Iraqi Scud missiles were successfully launched against Israel's coastal cities, Washington ordered Israel not to respond, a command the Jewish state met with compliance. The PLO and those in the territories, while not in favor of Hussein's occupation of Kuwait, shortsightedly championed the Iraqi leader, more for his defiant anti-Western rhetoric and linkage of his presence in Kuwait with Israel's in the West Bank and Gaza, suggesting he would withdraw if Israel did. Jordan's King Hussein also pointed out the contradiction of the United States protecting Israel in its occupation of the Palestinian territories with its eagerness to punish Arab aggression, for which the king was reprimanded and Jordan denied aid by Washington.

To sum up, Arab states (even Syria) had cooperated with the United States; Israel had also cooperated by not responding, causing some observers to question the "strategic asset" conception (for contrary evidence, see the block quotes on page 171); the PLO and the Palestinians had rooted for the wrong side and now could be counted on to be more amenable than usual. For similar reasons Jordan could also be relied upon to be accommodating. Iraq firing on Israel opened a new chapter and set a new precedent, the repetition of which the White House was eager to prevent. Furthermore, Bush's popularity was at an all-time high, and US elections were approaching the following year into the bargain. In an effort to address the above points and reduce regional tensions—one similar to Kissinger's efforts in 1973—Baker and the White House set to invigorating the peace process.

From spring to autumn 1991, Bush and (mostly) Baker began attempts to gain the approval of all involved parties for an October conference. After the president's announcement in March, Baker embarked on his Kissingeresque shuttling around the Middle East, holding preliminary talks with the region's leaders. Of the stumbling blocks, the most difficult were predictably how the Palestinians were going to be represented in the conference, and Prime Minister Shamir's expected impediments: "I don't believe in territorial compromise."[48] Concerning the Palestinian representatives, still tarnished with having voiced support for Saddam Hussein, it was decided that the (exclusively) non-PLO delegates attending the summit would be part of a joint delegation with the Jordanians and would remain in contact with the PLO in the background. Eventual Israeli agreement was acquired, mostly after Bush announced a 120-day delay on $10 billion in loan guarantees Tel Aviv had requested after the Gulf War. The president wanted the conference in Madrid to happen, and pushing Israel, the Israel lobby in Washington, and Congress was no concern when the White House had particular interests. That Bush had majority support among the American population for the loan delay only strengthened his position. By October, after strenuous preliminary efforts, all were on board.

It was abundantly clear Bush and Baker wanted the conference to convene, but what followed brought to light that it was the *conference* the White House desired. At almost the quarter-century mark, anyone observing this episode of the peace process could not be faulted for incredulity. But when the White House wanted something, it got results. The peace process, however, yielded no results simply because there had never been an earnest and austere demand for peace on the part of the Oval Office, its principal staff, or its advisers. What was desired was process, not product. The Israeli former deputy mayor of Jerusalem and noted political scientist and analyst Meron Benvenisti offers his assessment of the Bush–Baker contribution to Arab–Israeli diplomacy:

> Had the Bush administration intended to impose a peace, it would not have frittered away its prestige with interminable shuttle trips and Byzantine negotiations with the region's most experienced hagglers. The pose of being an "impartial mediator," and U.S. efforts to drag the rivals to a peace conference even without an agenda, gave cause to suspect that what the Bush administration really wanted was to create the impression that it was making peace while avoiding the unpleasant necessity of actually doing so.[49]

Convened on October 30, 1991, in Madrid's Royal Palace, co-chairs President Bush and Mikhail Gorbachev (last leader of the Soviet Union) presided over the opening ceremony attended by Egypt, Israel, Syria, Lebanon, the joint Jordanian–Palestinian delegation, various representatives from Europe, the United Nations, and plenty of journalists. That the Israelis and their Arab neighbors were all present was indeed a first. After a day of speeches, with the Palestinian address by Dr. Haidar Abdul Shafi standing out among the rest for its eloquence and vision, and a couple days of bilateral negotiations, the conference span off into different multilateral talks extending over the next year and a half.

Ultimately, the conference and subsequent talks received inadequate support from their White House sponsors. Bush and Baker pulled back, ostensibly to allow the parties to work out solutions themselves, but lending credence to Benvenisti's insights. The various talks were also hampered by Israel's call for Palestinian "autonomy," along with an unwillingness to pursue land-for-peace solutions and a dedication to building ever-increasing numbers of settlements in the occupied territories. Despite Bush's prolonged delay of the loan guarantees in hopes of checking Israel's now deeply rooted program of confiscation by way of building on Palestinian land, the Shamir government was inexorably committed: "No force in the world will stop this construction."[50] The Bush administration, though underwhelmed by this remark, made no direct response.

As described by former *Los Angeles Times* and *Time* magazine correspondent Donald Neff, "with a wiliness born of a lifetime in politics, Bush launched a subtle campaign to demonstrate to Israel's supporters how tough it could get if Shamir continued his obstructive ways." Reports, public and leaked, began to surface about the Jewish state's violations of its pledges on settlement construction in the territories, and its re-exporting and selling US weapons technology on the side, a contravention of established agreements and US law.[51] A quarter-century of free rein and American support had accommodated Israel's expansionist objectives, a lifestyle to which it had become accustomed. As was revealed by the prime minister after his June 1992 electoral defeat: "I would have conducted the autonomy negotiations for 10 years, and in the meantime we would have reached half a million souls in Judea and Samaria."[52] Development of settlements since the late Israeli leader's tenure has brought his ambitions close to the desired mark, with 462,000 settlers living in the West Bank and East Jerusalem as of the end of 2007.[53] While the unavailing post-Madrid talks continued, a highly secretive situation developed in Tel Aviv, moving to London and finally to Oslo, Norway.

The Norwegian sociologist Terje Rød-Larsen, in discussion with an Israeli government official, offered the possibility of taking the existing talks in a different direction. As described later in the *New York Times*,

> Norway could be a bridge between Israel and the P.L.O., not as a mediator but as an expediter, one graced with diplomatic

sophistication, familiarity with the key figures and distance from the region and prying cameras.[54]

After preliminary back-channel talks were conducted to secure the go-ahead from the primary leaders, namely, the newly elected Prime Minister Yitzhak Rabin (replacing Shamir) and Yasser Arafat, the Oslo channel commenced in January 1993.

The 14 meetings took place in and near the city of Oslo, spanning eight months and carried out in absolute secrecy. Informal fireside-type discussions which sometimes spread over days at a time, these gatherings were conducted by a small number of people so as to insure against leaks. From the host country there was Rød-Larsen and the Norwegian foreign minister and his wife; from Israel, two university professors; and from the PLO, its treasurer, Ahmed Qurei. With a few others joining later, including a member of the Israeli Foreign Ministry, and contacts back home, this was the extent of those involved, all with the silent blessing of the "grandfathers"—Rabin and Arafat.

By summer an agreement had been reached and then shown to Warren Christopher, secretary of state for President Bill Clinton (1993–2001), who had entered the White House roughly when the Oslo meetings began. The administration had been informed of the proceedings in Norway and loosely kept abreast of their progress, but never had detailed knowledge or direct involvement. Nevertheless, Clinton assumed the role of impresario at the White House on September 13, 1993, where Rabin and Arafat signed the Declaration of Principles (DOP) and shook hands, with the American president standing behind them as master of ceremonies.

While the signing of the DOP, or Oslo Accord, did fit the repeated descriptions of the event being "historic" and "momentous," the substance of the actual document was less sensational than the image of what transpired on the White House lawn that morning. The accord was composed of two parts: an exchange of letters of recognition between Rabin and Arafat, and the DOP. One could have then probably have guessed— what is now nothing more than a truism—that the letters alone served as an omen presaging more of the same. Arafat's letter expressed recognition of the state of Israel, whereas Rabin's letter to Arafat expressed recognition of the PLO, not Palestine. The second component was the DOP itself. About twelve pages in length, the declaration was an agreement on "interim self-government arrangements." What it lays out is the establishment of a Palestinian self-government authority, Israeli withdrawal from Gaza and the West Bank town of Jericho, a five-year transitional period, and "permanent status negotiations" to "cover remaining issues," such as Jerusalem, refugees, settlements, and borders. Not a treaty, and not the creation of a Palestinian state, Oslo granted the PLO civil authority over Gaza and Jericho. Israel retained everything it did before, including military access through these areas, but no longer had to administer them. To reach agreement in Norway, the central and core issues of the Palestine–Israel conflict were simply deferred.[55]

From Israel's right wing, the government was condemned for giving up portions of biblical Israel, while from the Palestinian extremist end of the spectrum, such as Hamas and Islamic Jihad, the PLO was reviled for cooperating with the Israelis and the Americans and selling out the dream of a Palestinian state; for that matter, this was also the criticism of the Palestinian mainstream. The respected and late Palestinian poet Mahmoud Darwish resigned from his position in the PLO Executive Committee in protest, stating he was "under no obligation to take part in this gamble," and that the PLO's "institutions, departments and bureaus ... are up for auction."[56] Edward W. Said, the noted and late Palestinian-American scholar and former member of the Palestinian National Council (from which he resigned out of protest), expressed his critical analyses of the accord in essays and articles published during the Oslo period, later collected in a book entitled *Peace and Its Discontents*, which he referred to as "a record of dissent."[57]

It was clear enough that Arafat read into the accord what he wanted to see, despite protestations and warnings from a number of his advisers. In addition to his optimistic interpretation of the agreement, the simple fact was that Oslo brought Arafat in from the cold. With Israeli recognition, he and the PLO would no longer be a leadership in exile, and with the pittance of territory the Palestinians were allowed to administer, and the vague implication that there was more territory coming, Arafat could justify signing the DOP. This came at a cost. Oslo was not an agreement negotiated by equal powers; it was a back-channel deal transacted between a major client of the United States and the leadership-in-exile of the territories occupied by that client. Arafat and his Tunis-based staff could relocate to the West Bank and Gaza, if they were to do so as superintendents in the employ of Israel. As Shlomo Ben-Ami observes:

Conspicuously, as one of the chief Israeli negotiators in Oslo,

Uri Savir, acknowledged, Arafat was chosen as a partner by the Israelis with the hope that he would use his new power base in the territories to "dismantle Hamas and other violent opposition groups." The Israelis conceived of Arafat as a collaborator of sorts, a sub-contractor in the task of enhancing Israel's security. For Israel this would be the main test of Arafat's performance.[58]

Meron Benvenisti draws the same inference:

Rabin did not act out of compassion or empathy [in agreeing to the DOP]: in fact, he despised and mistrusted Arafat. He needed him as a partner in managing the raging intercommunal strife [e.g. the Intifada].... Rabin calculated that Arafat's demise would usher in Hamas and that by saving Arafat he was taking only a small risk.... He knew that by moving to the territories, Arafat would become even more dependent on the Israelis than he had ever been on the countries of his exile—Jordan, Lebanon, and even Tunisia.[59]

Arafat envisioned an eventual Palestinian state, but in reality had been outsourced to mitigate against the very pressures yearning for one. He was now an occupation governor. (This situation continues into the present, with Mahmoud Abbas, the leader succeeding Arafat after his death in November 2004 and current Palestinian Authority president, playing an identical role.) Almost 30 years of unwavering US–Israeli rejection of any kind of peaceful and just settlement of the conflict had finally inveigled the chairman into taking what he could get, all at the expense of peace.

Over the next two years Israel withdrew from Gaza and Jericho, and Article VII of the DOP, called the "Interim Agreement," was negotiated and signed on September 28, 1995, again at the White House though with less fanfare.[60] In all its lengthy detail, this agreement, known as Oslo II, addresses two main issues. The first is the structure, powers, and responsibilities of the Palestinian "Council," which eventually became the Palestinian Authority (PA). The second is the "redeployment" of Israeli forces from, and subsequent PA jurisdiction in, various areas in the West Bank. In brief, the areas are designated A, B, and C:

• Area A (3 percent of the West Bank) comprised larger population centers, where the PA would have full jurisdiction.

- Area B (24 percent) comprised about 450 towns and hamlets, where there would be dual jurisdiction in matters of security, with the PA handling internal matters and the IDF handling external.
- Area C (73 percent) encompassed the remainder of the West Bank—"except for the issues that will be negotiated in the permanent status negotiations, [Area C] will be gradually transferred to Palestinian jurisdiction in accordance with this Agreement."[61]

In other words, 73 percent was left to be handled at a later date.

Edward Said described Oslo as a "modified Allon Plan," though what it ended up being was something far worse than what the labor minister envisioned in 1967.[62] As the Oslo Accords were being implemented, the Palestinians in the West Bank and Gaza watched their situation decline. Areas A and B were now islands of PA territory, surrounded by Israeli-held and IDF-controlled territory—Area C. Movement for the residents became restricted, with checkpoints creating atomized isolation and the attendant economic strangulation. The Allon Plan, after all, allowed for contiguity in roughly half of the West Bank; the Oslo situation featured fragmented islands on 27 percent. What seemed outrageous in 1967 looked idyllic in 1995, and still does in 2009.

On November 4, 1995, Yitzhak Rabin was assassinated by a Jewish extremist. The subsequent two premierships of Shimon Peres (1995–96) and Benjamin Netanyahu (1996–99) brought the pace of implementation of Oslo II to a crawl. Peres provoked terrorist reprisals by assassinating a Hamas bomb maker during a period of calm in the territories. This also stirred Hizballah in southern Lebanon to act, creating a justification for Israel to unleash in April 1996 its fourth (after 1978, 1982, 1993) attack on Lebanon, killing almost 200 civilians. Netanyahu, a strident opponent of the Oslo process, continued along the path of provocation, along with blatant delay of the interim agreement protocols and outspoken dedication to settlement expansion. He signed limited agreements connected with Oslo II—the Hebron Agreement and the Wye River Accord—but only under American pressure to reduce the bloodshed and instability that had done nothing but intensify over the Peres and Netanyahu years, a mere prelude for what lay ahead.

The Camp David II summit in July 2000 was presented, and perceived by many, as something separate from the Oslo track. Fair arguments can be made to support this view, as it was a deviation from the Oslo program, much like Oslo was from Madrid. Though not a terribly critical issue, it is included here as a continuation of the Madrid–Oslo process insofar as it was convened in the derailed context of Oslo II over the course of the Peres and Netanyahu years, and against the background of growing Palestinian anger and discouragement. The day-to-day realities of Oslo spelled a harsher version of occupation—closures, searches, confinement, economic hardship, territorial encroachment of settlements and their corresponding road network (which expropriated even more land), harassment, humiliation, and beatings at checkpoints by Israeli security officials—instead of alleviation of it.

Camp David was summitry conducted by a coalition of the weak. The tenure of Israeli prime minister Ehud Barak, who entered office in July 1999, was on shaky ground, with fractures forming beneath Labor's control of the Knesset, opening a possibility for Likud's emergence in the event of elections. President Clinton was in the last moments of his eight-year term and was looking to secure a legacy, and perhaps burnish his image after the Monica Lewinsky scandal and subsequent impeachment in the House of Representatives (he was acquitted in the Senate). He also remained vigilant of Israeli politics and Barak's teetering government, hoping to use a peace settlement as a way of preserving the prime minister's office; Clinton had played a role in Barak's election and was keen on his survival. Both were looking for an end-run around the incremental, interim-based Oslo process, and the answer lay in an attempt to achieve a final-status agreement. With Arafat growing less popular among Palestinians as a result of Oslo's effects on the territories, and therefore possibly growing more willing to accept any proposal that gave hope of improvement, Barak and Clinton saw an opportunity.

In May 2000, unofficial talks between the Israelis and the Palestinians led to exploring the possibilities of a summit. In Sweden, a map was produced by the Israeli negotiators indicating Palestinian control in 76.6 percent of the West Bank, with this percentage being divided into three separate pieces, and all three set apart from East Jerusalem and Gaza.[63] The Palestinians rejected the map outright. A "state" on three-quarters of the West Bank with no territorial contiguity was unacceptable at the minimum. The nature of this impasse would be imported into Camp David and contribute to the demise of negotiations there.

On July 5 Clinton phoned in invitations to Arafat and Barak for a summit at Camp David (July 11–25) to reach a permanent-status agreement. For two weeks in the Catoctin Mountains, the three delegations made considerable progress in as far as they discussed topics such as Jerusalem and refugees, though little actual movement was achieved on these subjects. The issues of borders and settlements tended to fold into one discussion of what the West Bank would look like as part of the state of Palestine. What was "offered" at Camp David was fundamentally what had been presented to the Palestinian negotiators in May. The percentage had increased from 76.6 to roughly 91 percent of the West Bank, but as in May the territory would be broken into three cantons, with an Israeli salient, or jutting slice of land, cutting from Jerusalem to the Jordan River, and another in the north. The 91 percent offer was in actuality about 77 percent, or approximately the May map.[64]

The summit ground to a standstill, and Clinton called it to a close. Immediately after, the president and Barak began placing blame for Camp David's failure at Arafat's doorstep, something the Palestinian delegation had feared and which Clinton repeatedly said he would not do.[65] The essence of this blame, now an extant myth, was that Barak had made a generous offer while Arafat issued no counterproposals and was unwilling to negotiate or show flexibility. As has been documented in the realistic literature, these charges are inaccurate. The so-called generosity on the subject of territory, though greater than had ever been discussed, was less than charitable. Moreover, the word "offer" itself is also suspect. Robert Malley, an American negotiator and Clinton adviser, and Hussein Agha, a Palestinian scholar based at Oxford, in a *New York Review of Books* article entitled "Camp David: The Tragedy of Errors," elucidated Barak's negotiating style, heavily influencing the summit's procedures:

> [S]trictly speaking, there never was an Israeli offer. Determined to preserve Israel's position in the event of failure, and resolved not to let the Palestinians take advantage of one-sided compromises, the Israelis always stopped one, if not several, steps short of a proposal. The ideas put forward at Camp David were never stated in writing, but orally conveyed. They generally were presented as US concepts, not Israeli ones; indeed, despite having demanded the opportunity to negotiate face to face with Arafat, Barak refused to hold any substantive meeting with him at Camp David out of fear that the Palestinian leader would seek to put Israeli concessions on the record. Nor were the proposals detailed. If written down, the American ideas at Camp

David would have covered no more than a few pages. Barak and the Americans insisted that Arafat accept them as general "bases for negotiations" before launching into more rigorous negotiations.[66]

Curiously, and in spite of the PR effort to cast Arafat as stonewalling peace and opportunity, Clinton later said in 2003 while dining with a prominent Israeli, "If Yitzhak Rabin were alive, I would have gotten an agreement out of Camp David."[67]

On all other major permanent-status matters—East Jerusalem and religious sites (that is, the Temple Mount/Haram al-Sharif), Israeli retention of settlements in blocs in the West Bank, land swaps, refugee right of return—the Palestinian delegation showed a willingness to take into account Israel's demographic and security needs. They had produced their own map, which was rejected, largely because it hewed closer to international law, which in turn failed to allow enough accommodation for Israeli settlers in the West Bank.[68] For the Palestinian team, UN 242 was supposed to be the basis for negotiations—a correct assumption—but at Camp David the American and Israeli delegations moved away from 242. The PA's chief negotiator was even reprimanded by Clinton for bringing it up.[69] Resolution 242 was, for the Palestinians, a major concession. Recognizing Israel, accepting a state in 22 percent of Palestine—the West Bank and Gaza—showing willingness to compromise on all major points, and still meeting with accusations of creating diplomatic deadlock at the summit made them realize that Camp David was a continuation of the "peace process" as it had existed since 1967.[70] As political scientist Jeremy Pressman summarizes in an article published in the *International Security* journal, entitled "Visions in Collision":

> The evidence suggests that the Palestinian narrative of the 2000–01 peace talks is significantly more accurate than the Israeli narrative. At Camp David, Israel's position—whether intended or not—was arguably an extension of the occupation under a different guise.[71]

Though members of the delegations would continue to meet in the back channel, they were now doing so as the Second Intifada's explosive violence raged in the background. Ehud Barak's political opponent, Likud's Ariel Sharon, had paid a provocative visit to the Temple Mount/Haram al-Sharif (September 28, 2000) with roughly 1,000 police and military members, igniting the Palestinian resistance. Discussion of the visit had taken place, with the American leadership, Palestinian leadership, and even Israeli intelligence predicting what such a gesture would precipitate. All knew that the situation in the occupied territories was deteriorating and this had lowered the flashpoint of possible unrest.

The negotiators maintained contact, meetings took place between Clinton and each leader separately in November, and on December 23, with all present at the White House except Barak and Arafat, the president read what became known as the Clinton Plan. The essence of the president's set of parameters was:

- a Palestinian state in Gaza and a contiguous 94–96 percent of the West Bank, with land swaps to compensate Palestine for annexed territory
- 80 percent of Israeli settlers in the West Bank in blocs
- a solution for Jerusalem based on the principle that "Arab areas are Palestinian and Jewish ones are Israeli"
- Palestinian sovereignty over the Haram al-Sharif and Israeli sovereignty over the Western Wall
- the Palestinian state as the focal point for refugees choosing to return.[72]

Barak and Arafat, both with reservations, accepted Clinton's parameters.

Israeli–Palestinian talks continued, but with no American involvement. From January 21–27, 2001, at the Egyptian town of Taba on the Gulf of Aqaba, the two sides closed further the gaps in their respective positions. Primarily based on the Clinton Plan, what is known as the Taba statement represents where the two sides would pick up in the event of another round of negotiations in the future.[73] With Barak's suspension of the talks, they were not allowed to seek their potential, which might well have spelled the end of the Palestine–Israel conflict.

CONCLUSION: THE POST-TABA PHASE, 2002–07

Taba was the closest the peace process has come in its decades-long odyssey to producing something that could have brought peace. Independent initiatives have since been the bulk of diplomatic movement. Among the most important was the 2002 Saudi peace proposal. The plan was initially summarized in a February article by *New York Times* columnist Thomas Friedman, who had dinner with then-Crown Prince (now King) Abdullah of Saudi Arabia and discussed a proposal on which the crown prince had been working.[74] The plan was made official when it was presented to and adopted by all 22 members of the Arab League at the organization's summit in Beirut the following March. The initiative was a quid pro quo. From Israel: "Full Israeli withdrawal from all the territories occupied since 1967, including the Syrian Golan Heights to the lines of June 4, 1967 as well as the remaining occupied Lebanese territories in the south of Lebanon," "a just solution to the Palestinian Refugee problem," and "acceptance of the establishment of a Sovereign Independent Palestinian State." The Arab League, in turn, "[will] [c]onsider the Arab–Israeli conflict ended, and enter into a peace agreement with Israel, and provide security for all the states of the region," as well as "[e]stablish normal relations with Israel in the context of this comprehensive peace."[75] The response from Tel Aviv was further suppression of the Second Intifada under the premiership of Ariel Sharon. The Arab League would reissue the proposal in 2007, to a similar reaction.

Taba also served as a model for various track-II initiatives. Two noteworthy instances of this—both of which mention the Saudi/Arab League proposal—were the People's Voice (or Ayalon–Nusseibeh plan) and the Geneva Accord. The People's Voice was authored by a retired Israeli naval and intelligence officer and a Palestinian academic in 2002, but presented in June 2003. It laid out a basic framework calling for two states, Israel and a demilitarized Palestine, whose borders would be based on the Green Line, an open Jerusalem that would serve as capital to both states, no sovereignty over holy sites, and refugee return to Palestine only. The plan has gathered hundreds of thousands of signatures from both populations, but exists only as a possibility and point of reference.[76]

The Geneva Accord (or Beilin–Rabbo plan) was brokered by an Israeli negotiator and chief architect of the Oslo Accords and a former PA minister before People's Voice, but publicly released shortly after. This "Eighth Day of Taba," as it was conceived, spelled out in greater detail a comparable proposal based on similar treatment of the core issues.[77] The accord attracted broad international attention, with a number of world leaders voicing support, and attained majority approval among both Israeli and Palestinian populations. Like the Arab League initiative and People's Voice, the

Geneva Accord is now an item in the post-Taba gallery of unrealized independent diplomacy.

US-sanctioned initiatives since Taba have been few and far between, with the few occasions lacking substance. The George W. Bush administration (2001–09), on the eve of invading Iraq in spring 2003, followed a suggestion by British prime minister Tony Blair and proposed the so-called Road Map. Co-sponsored by the United Nations, the European Union, Russia, and the United States—together known as the Quartet—the Road Map established a three-phase set of abstract benchmarks and a corresponding time-line that would result in a two-state solution.[78] Though possibly a workable document, which could return the diplomatic situation to a Taba-like atmosphere, the Road Map received no follow-up, no support, and no implementation.

Near the end of its second term, the Bush II administration, and in particular its secretary of state, Condoleezza Rice, initiated an international conference to settle the conflict. In her own contribution to shuttle diplomacy, Rice met with leaders from both sides as well as regional heads of state. The conference was convened on November 27, 2007, in Annapolis, Maryland, at the United States Naval Academy, and was attended by over 40 countries and national organizations.[79] As stated by President Bush at the summit:

> In furtherance of the goal of two states, Israel and Palestine, living side by side in peace and security, we agree to immediately launch good-faith, bilateral negotiations in order to conclude a peace treaty resolving all outstanding issues, including all core issues, without exception, as specified in previous agreements.[80]

The Annapolis conference's encouragement to "launch negotiations" produced short-lived talks after the conference that became hampered by Israeli settlement expansion.[81] With no American support, Annapolis bore considerable resemblance to its predecessor in Madrid. As Rice commented prior to the event, "Frankly, we have better things to do than invite people to Annapolis for a photo op."[82] As to the secretary's meaning, conjecture is the only available recourse.

As we have seen over the course of this summary, there has been a gross disparity between opportunities for peace and bringing these opportunities to fruition on the part of those holding the cards—

Washington and Tel Aviv. Arab proposals were generally ignored; suspicions as to their legitimacy remained a possible bluff never called. Israeli proposals, few in number and disingenuously seeking to exclude the Palestinian territories from discussion, were undermined from within. American initiatives tended to gain the most publicity and pageantry, but upon even superficial examination have preserved Israel's agendas in the West Bank and Gaza, with even Carter's Camp David success serving as an example of such rejectionism. And in the background of the US-led (or endorsed) diplomatic efforts, Washington's financial and military support of Israel—alongside Tel Aviv engaging in settlement expansion in the West Bank—only further drives home the point that the "peace process" has been political theater.

Yet the Clinton Plan, the Taba statement, the Saudi proposal, and the Geneva Accord signal cause for some optimism. The framework for a two-state settlement is well known and within the realm of possibility. In addition, the modalities of such an agreement have worldwide support: majorities of Americans, Israelis, and Middle Easterners all support such a framework. Beyond polling data, this is also visible in the United Nations. The UN General Assembly regularly votes on what is called the "Peaceful settlement of the question of Palestine," which it deems "the core of the Arab-Israeli conflict." At the time of writing this, the most recent resolution (63/29) was passed on January 22, 2009. It called for Israel to halt construction of settlements and the separation wall in the West Bank, and states that the United Nations "[r]eaffirms its commitment, in accordance with international law, to the two-State solution of Israel and Palestine, living side by side in peace and security within recognized borders, based on the pre-1967 borders." The voting record for 63/29 was more or less what it has usually been. Of the 192 member states of the General Assembly, 164 of them voted in favor of the resolution (with a small number abstaining or not voting), while seven countries voted against it. The list of these seven is, if anything, thought provoking. The dissenting votes came from the United States, Israel, the Marshall Islands, Micronesia, Nauru, Palau, and, this time, Australia.[83]

As this book goes to print, the Barack Obama administration has sent officials to the region, with Secretary of State Hillary Clinton voicing Washington's commitment to "a comprehensive peace between Israel and its Arab neighbors and we will pursue it on many fronts."[84] It is too early to tell. We have noted Carter's "fusion of surface innovation with subsurface continuity" (see page 106). George C. Herring, noting earlier but similar patterns, states, "In spite of his radical preelection image, [Thomas] Jefferson retained the instruments and followed the basic thrust of his predecessor's foreign policy."[85] It remains to be seen whether Obama's approach to the peace process and Arab–Israeli diplomacy will hew toward innovation, or whether his administration will retain the instruments.

6

THE ISRAEL LOBBY: ANATOMY OF A CONTROVERSY

Our final chapter addresses a subject that is roughly as old as the peace process discussed in Chapter 5, but in recent years has become increasingly contentious. The contention is predominantly academic and simply revolves around how much influence the Israel lobby wields, and to what degree it affects American foreign policy in the Middle East.

The goals in this chapter are to arrive at a basic understanding of what the lobby is and what it does, and then look at the various positions taken by scholars and writers in the continuing debate over the lobby effect. These positions are then considered in the context of the history covered throughout the book.

THE LOBBY

The word "lobby" can be used as both a noun and a verb, and means "to solicit or try to influence the votes of members of a legislative body" (dictionary.com), or an individual (lobbyist) or organization that performs such undertakings. According to the United States Senate's website,

> Lobbying is the practice of trying to persuade legislators to propose, pass, or defeat legislation or to change existing laws. A lobbyist may work for a group, organization, or industry, and presents information on legislative proposals to support his or her clients' interests.[1]

Lobbying is nothing new in American politics, and dates back to the late eighteenth century.

Lobbies are legally authorized groups carrying out legally sanctioned activities; what they do is well within the law. In the United States, lobbying is protected under the First Amendment, enshrining the right "to petition the Government for a redress of grievances." While our focus is the lobby dedicated to US–Israeli relations—the "Israel lobby" or "pro-Israel lobby"—it bears mention that this lobby is only one in a very long list of entities operating in Washington, DC, with hopes of advancing a given cause.

At the top of the lobbying flowchart, there are what are called sectors, which are general categories pertaining to lobbying: for example, health, transportation, communications/electronics. Under each sector, there is a list of industries. In the case of communications/electronics, one of the (many) industries within that sector is telecommunications. This particular industry is composed of dozens upon dozens of corporations and organizations, many of which are familiar to anyone owning a cellular phone: Motorola, Sprint-Nextel, T-Mobile, Verizon, and others. In an effort to carry out lobbying, these corporations hire lobbying firms specializing in telecommunications. Motorola, for example, in the past has hired a firm called Ogilvy Government Relations. Ogilvy employs lobbyists who then work with clients (in this case Motorola) to advance that company's legislative agenda on Capitol Hill. However, Motorola hires multiple firms, not just Ogilvy; likewise, Ogilvy has a long list of clients coming from an array of industries (and sectors), not just telecommunications. For instance, it also handles the "single-issue" sector, under which fall industries such as gun rights, and therefore attracts clients like the National Rifle Association (NRA), for which Ogilvy performs lobbying services. When one begins to add up the list of clients and firms, it is well into the thousands. The flowchart therefore becomes overwhelmingly labyrinthine, and databases are needed to keep track of the details.[2]

Motorola and the NRA differ in the world of lobbying insofar as the former, as mentioned, hires firms to do its lobbying. While the NRA hires firms as well, it also acts as its own client and registers "in-house" lobbyists with the government to do its own advocacy work in Washington. Concerning our present study, the Israel lobby bears more resemblance to the NRA than a telecom corporation. The Israel lobby resides under the single-issue sector (like the NRA) but belongs to the pro-Israel industry. Within the pro-Israel industry there are a handful of firms, all acting as their own clients, doing lobbying in the interest of advancing their cause of expanding US support for Israel—or decreasing support for Israel's adversaries. The most prominent of these firms by far is the American Israel

Public Affairs Committee, or AIPAC (pronounced *ay-pak*), whose tag line is "America's Pro-Israel Lobby."

On its website AIPAC describes itself thus:

> For more than half a century, the American Israel Public Affairs Committee has worked to help make Israel more secure by ensuring that American support remains strong. From a small pro-Israel public affairs boutique in the 1950s, AIPAC has grown into a 100,000-member national grassroots movement described by *The New York Times* as "the most important organization affecting America's relationship with Israel."[3]
>
> AIPAC is registered as a domestic lobby and supported financially by private donations. The organization receives no financial assistance from Israel, from any national organization or any foreign group. AIPAC is not a political action committee. It does not rate, endorse or contribute to candidates. Because it is a lobby, contributions to AIPAC are not tax deductible.

As noted in the second paragraph of the quote above, AIPAC is not a political action committee, or a PAC, an occasional source of misunderstanding on account of the acronyms. A PAC is "a political committee organized for the purpose of raising and spending money to elect and defeat candidates."[4] AIPAC works in conjunction with these committees—alerting congressional candidates to pro-Israel PACs who will be forthcoming with campaign contributions, or notifying PACs as to which candidates are most in line with the pro-Israeli agenda—but does not function as one.

AIPAC's activities are varied, and given the size of its staff (200 lobbyists, researchers, and organizers), it can perform a wide range of tasks. In addition to hosting lavish events, at which American and Israeli heads of state routinely appear and give speeches and talks, AIPAC also functions as an information clearing house, conducting analyses on a variety of issues concerning Israel and the Middle East, and publishing reports and periodicals such as the *Near East Report*, all available on its website. In short, AIPAC is big, well funded (with an annual budget of roughly $47 million), well staffed, well connected, and very busy.[5] Not only is AIPAC a dominant force within its own industry, it has been ranked by *Fortune* magazine as one of the top five most powerful lobbies in Washington, surpassed only by behemoths such as AARP (the American Association of Retired Persons) and the NRA.[6] But it is important to point out that, irrespective of how one may view its objectives, what AIPAC does is legal, visible, registered, and documented.

As mentioned, AIPAC is not the only pro-Israeli lobbying force working on the Hill. It is joined by other smaller lobbying organizations such as the American Jewish Committee, the American Jewish Congress, and the Zionist Organization of America (ZOA), all of which are involved in other advocacy, educational, and charitable activities, not just direct lobbying in Washington. In addition, the Israel lobby's efforts are supplemented by numerous Jewish organizations working to further America's backing of Israel, such as the Anti-Defamation League (ADL). Serving as a hub to many of these organizations, numbering in the order of 50, is the Conference of Presidents of Major American Jewish Organizations. As stated on the Conference of Presidents' website, it is:

> American Jewry's recognized address for consensus policy, collective action, and maximizing the resources of the American Jewish community. When events in the U.S., Israel and elsewhere affect the American Jewish community, the Conference of Presidents take the lead to explain and analyze issues, provide a link between American Jewry and the U.S. government, and marshal a coordinated community response.[7]

There are also what are referred to as Christian Zionist organizations, such as Christians United for Israel (CUFI), that are involved in promotion of pro-Israel interests and work in concert with their Jewish counterparts.

Taken in aggregate, and despite the lack of a precise definition, one starts to get a picture of what is meant by the Israel lobby. Yet, it must be noted that such an aggregate does not suggest or reflect any kind of monolithic uniformity among the lobby's constituent parts; diversity and disagreement exist throughout the various lobbies and the committees, associations, and institutes making up the Conference of Presidents. On balance, however, these are the people and groups who are doing organized advocacy for the US–Israeli alliance. In that, there is uniformity. It should also be pointed out that, strictly speaking, the "lobby" means specifically those groups such as AIPAC and ZOA that are registered and carrying out actual lobbying of the government. The network of supportive Jewish and Christian groups does engage in advocacy, and therefore performs a kind of lobbying, but does not technically constitute a lobby.

Though it got its start in the 1950s, AIPAC only attained the clout it now possesses over the course of the Carter and Reagan years. As its influence increased, so too did the attention paid to its activities and ever-expanding prominence. In the mid-1980s among some academics and political activists, this attention turned critical, and over the following years this criticism intensified. During George W. Bush's second term in the White House, the debate rose to a crescendo in response to the publishing of an essay by two prominent political scientists, catapulting the dispute to a whole new level and creating a fulcrum on which the matter has pivoted ever since.

THE EARLY DEBATE

Upon the birth of Israel, American Jews identified with the nascent Zionist enterprise, but not necessarily enough to relocate there as citizens of it. While supportive, Jewish Americans in general considered themselves American Jews, and had found a place to live and raise their families where anti-Semitism was far less severe—though by no means absent—and where they were, as a minority group (2–3 percent), professionally and financially successful. To this day, Jews are one of the most affluent American minority groups.[8] And, as is typically the case, prosperity and political influence tend to go hand in hand.*

With the emergence of the Jewish state, Jews in America found something around which to gather politically. As described by historian Howard M. Sachar,

> For the Jews of the United States, the success of their Israeli kinsman in winning and defending their homeland generated an upsurge of self-esteem too profound to be described as vicarious.... With each passing year, commitment to Israel's growth and welfare would become the emotional and ideological focus of Jewish communal life.[9]

---

* Pointing out these realities concerning the Jewish population is sometimes a sensitive matter, as similar observations throughout history have been employed by anti-Semitic ideologues to create arguments justifying the persecution of Jews; the Third Reich, the most salient example, viewed Jews as a threat to Germany, owing to their financial prominence. Yet a clear distinction exists between dispassionate consideration and using those considerations for nefarious, hate-inspired doctrine.

Moreover, Israel was greatly in need of support. The United States was a clear candidate for supplying it, principally on account of American Jewish largesse and political influence. According to Sachar, "For American Jews ... fund-raising for Israel became a decisive expression of Jewish peoplehood itself."[10] Jewish prosperity, organization, and concern for Israel all focused this community's political energies, which were and are relatively considerable.

Journalist Edward Tivnan notes in his 1987 book, *The Lobby*, that Jewish political power in America has basically three sources. The first is what he terms "a political weapon of last resort," namely, "Jews can brand—and thus ignore—their or Israel's critics by labeling them 'anti-Israel,' 'pro-Arab,' or worse, 'anti-Semitic.'" This tactic, says Tivnan, "may be the most powerful, and most abused by the hardliners." The second source is that Jews vote. Though a small minority, they exhibit a very high turnout in a country that has a rather low level of voter participation. This has the potential of occasionally swinging election outcomes. Third, in light of their financial success and political awareness and activity, American Jews are inclined to donate money to campaigns. Tivnan observes that, while corporations tend to wait somewhat detachedly to assess the overall situation before donating to campaigns, hovering to determine likely candidates, Jewish donations are made earlier and are commonly based on "who they believe will support their interests." This is done even if the candidate is unlikely to succeed; early "seed" money is critically important to a campaign.[11]

Though American Jewry's devotion to Israel was significant throughout the first two decades of the state's existence, the picture changed after the June 1967 war, and not just for Jews. Israel's lightning victory in the Six-Day War got the attention of official Washington and the intellectual classes (particularly the media, universities, and think tanks). The Jewish state's performance sealed its role in the region, expanded official and popular American respect for it, and increased Jewish American support. For Jews in the United States, Israel had very much become a team for which it was worth rooting. For some, it was based on the simple reason that Israel was not going anywhere and knew how to handle itself. However, according to J. J. Goldberg, the editorial director of the Jewish newspaper the *Forward*, the Six-Day War did not inspire the same confidence among Jews that it did for others. It had the opposite effect, and showed "that Israel might be destroyed at any moment ... that the world was a hostile and dangerous place, that nobody cared about the Jews, and the Jews should care about nobody."[12] Yet, regardless of the response or interpretations, aid and support for Israel in the United States dramatically increased across the board, governmental and private.

Over the next 20 years, AIPAC expanded its staff, budget, and level of operations. The Ford, Carter, and Reagan administrations all experienced a degree of occasional pressure by way of AIPAC's highly dedicated lobbying efforts among members of Congress. In addition to encouraging the legislative branch to augment aid to and intensify relations with Tel Aviv, battles were waged over, for example, the issue of the United States selling arms to Arab states, with AIPAC creating enough agitation to get even the attention of the White House. As AIPAC's size and reputation increased, so too did its visibility. Some writers and academics began to wonder whether maybe the Israel lobby was gaining too much sway in Congress; if it was tarnishing America's image in the Middle East; if it was pushing the Palestine–Israel conflict farther away from resolution; and if it was working counter to US national interests. By the mid-1980s, critical examination of the lobby was getting under way.

In 1985, Paul Findley, a former representative from Illinois, published an exposé entitled *They Dare to Speak Out*. In it, Findley recounts the lobby pressure brought to bear on his campaign for re-election in 1982 as punishment for his contact with the PLO (see page 133), pressure which contributed to his defeat. The book goes on to catalog the methods and instances of the pro-Israel lobby carrying out its agenda, its sometimes questionable techniques, and highlights people who resisted lobby pressure and the occasional costs of such defiance. According to Findley, "It is no overstatement to say that AIPAC has effectively gained control of virtually all of Capitol Hill's action on Middle East policy."[13]

The following year, independent scholar Cheryl Rubenberg, then at Florida International University, included an analysis of the lobby issue in her book *Israel and the American National Interest*. In it she dedicates a chapter to the subject, putting forth a thesis in line with Findley's. For Rubenberg, the Israel lobby has a "virtual stranglehold" on the formation of US policy in the Middle East:

That organized pro-Israeli groups have been able to translate their premise into American policy, to have kept the perception of Israel as a strategic asset dominant in American political culture, and to have obtained American support ... for every one of

Israel's policy objectives is, to a great extent, a reflection of their ability to influence the domestic political process.

Rubenberg maintains that Israel has not acted in the national interest and is therefore a strategic liability, not an asset. Owing to US support for Israel and the lobby's strong-arm encouragement of that support, when Israel carries out acts of aggression in the region—settlement expansion in the West Bank, attacks against Lebanon, and so on—this has "resulted in American credibility in the Arab world plummeting to unprecedented depths."[14]

We have already mentioned Edward Tivnan's 1987 book on the subject, which is more of a journalistic, historical look at the lobby and US–Israeli relations. Tivnan's account examines the three-way dynamic between the United States, Israel, and the lobby, suggesting that this triad behaves in the interests of neither the United States nor Israel, and that the strategic asset thesis is questionable by virtue of Israel's expansionist, aggressive behavior, citing the example of Tel Aviv annexing the Syrian Golan Heights in 1981. Of this, Tivnan asks rhetorically, "What kind of strategic asset was this that ignored totally U.S. interests [for instance, UN 242] in the region?"[15] Though broader in consideration than the previously mentioned analyses, and perhaps less denunciatory, Tivnan's book still resides at the critical end of the spectrum, functioning more as a warning that the Washington–Tel Aviv–lobby interconnection is toxic in nature and does not serve the interests of the United States, Israel, or Jews.

Discussion and analysis continued, with authors seeking to assign the appropriate level of influence to the lobby's role in Washington. Into the 1990s there were works such as *The Passionate Attachment* (1992) by George W. Ball, undersecretary of state under Johnson and Kennedy, and his son, Douglas, which continued the critical approach to the lobby and the US–Israeli relationship. They conclude that AIPAC "operates a virtual reign of terror among congressional members."[16] There also emerged books that attempted to take a more moderate tack. J. J. Goldberg's *Jewish Power: Inside the American Jewish Establishment* (1996), despite its provocative title, attempts to demonstrate otherwise by deconstructing Jewish power in the United States, concluding that AIPAC and others wield something less than the dominance Findley, Tivnan, and the Balls contend, all of whom he mentions.[17]

Though the dispute was predominantly taking place in the literature more intended for specialists, by the middle of the decade, the poles of the debate had basically been established. Everyone agreed the lobby was making *an* impact on policy; the discrepancy was between whether it was a little or a lot, and if the national interest was being served or not.

MEARSHEIMER AND WALT

A year after the September 11 terrorist attacks, the *Atlantic Monthly* invited two political scientists, John Mearsheimer (University of Chicago) and Stephen Walt (Harvard University), to author an article on the Israel lobby and its influence on American foreign policy. Submitting a draft about two years later, the professors met rejection, with the magazine refusing publication. Mearsheimer and Walt then approached the *London Review of Books*, which ran the over-12,000-word essay—"The Israel Lobby and U.S. Foreign Policy"—in March 2006. The piece was also posted for download on the website of Harvard's John F. Kennedy School of Government, this version featuring over 200 endnotes. A year later, the two scholars published a book under the same title, significantly expanding the essay and its notations.[*18]

Mearsheimer and Walt assert that "Israel has become a strategic liability for the United States. Yet no aspiring politician is going to say so in public, or even raise the possibility."[19]

Many policies pursued on Israel's behalf now jeopardize U.S. national security. The combination of unstinting U.S. support for Israel and Israel's prolonged occupation of Palestinian territory has fueled anti-Americanism throughout the Arab and Islamic world, thereby increasing the threat from international terrorism and making it harder for Washington to deal with other problems, such as shutting down Iran's nuclear program. Because the United States is now so unpopular within the broader region, Arab leaders who might otherwise share U.S. goals are reluctant to help us openly, a predicament that cripples U.S. efforts to deal with a host of regional challenges.

This situation, which has no equal in American history, is due primarily to the activities of the Israel lobby.[20]

---

* All quotes from Mearsheimer and Walt throughout are taken from their book, *The Israel Lobby and U.S. Foreign Policy* (New York: Farrar, Straus and Giroux, 2007).

Mearsheimer and Walt also maintain that "the lobby's impact has been unintentionally harmful to Israel as well," insofar as support from Washington, with the lobby's persuasion, has prolonged the conflict with the Palestinians.[21] They also note the divergence between American popular opinion and US policy toward Israel:

> The American people are certainly not demanding that their politicians support Israel down the line. In essence, there is a gulf between how the broader public thinks about Israel and its relationship with the United States, and how governing elites in Washington conduct American policy. The main reason for this gap is the lobby's formidable reputation inside the Beltway [Washington]."[22]

The authors point out that, "We do not believe the lobby is all-powerful, or that it controls important institutions in the United States." What they do draw from the "abundance of evidence [is] that the lobby wields impressive influence." The core of their thesis is summarized as follows:

> the United States provides Israel with extraordinary material aid and diplomatic support, the lobby is the principal reason for that support, and this uncritical and unconditional relationship is not in the American national interest.[23]

Mearsheimer and Walt then embark on a cost–benefit analysis, suggesting that the United States is not getting enough in return for what it is paying. Support for Israel has not been "a cost-effective way for the United States to deal with countries that Washington had previously identified as hostile." The United States has not "received substantial benefits," nor has "the value of these benefits exceeded the economic and political costs of U.S. support." Americans have not been made "more secure or more prosperous," nor has "backing [Israel] won America additional friends around the world."[24] For the strategic value Israel possessed during the Cold War, and therefore justifying for Mearsheimer and Walt the American support it received over that period, "that justification ended when the Soviet Union collapsed." "The case for Israel's strategic value from 1967 to 1989 is straightforward."[25] (They do concede that "the case is not ... open and shut," and that, for example, Israel, while checking Soviet client states like Egypt, Syria, and Iraq, also "played a significant role in pushing those states into Moscow's arms in the first place.")[26] Mearsheimer and Walt endeavor to make the case that, in the post-Cold War era, "[v]iewed objectively, Israel is a liability in both the 'war on terror' and in the broader effort to deal with so-called rogue states," as well as "the related effort to democratize the Middle East."[27]

After preliminary consideration of US–Israeli relations, the authors set to defining what they mean by the "Israel lobby." Acknowledging "that the lobby's boundaries are somewhat fuzzy," they include in the lobby's "core" those groups mentioned in the previous section, namely, the lobby firms like AIPAC, Jewish groups such as the ADL, the Christian Zionist organizations like CUFI, and think tanks like the Washington Institute for Near East Policy (WINEP). The authors also include individuals, such as "a journalist or scholar who predictably takes Israel's side and devotes a significant amount of his or her writing to defending steadfast U.S. support for Israel," who tend to be well known in their field. In general, Mearsheimer and Walt recognize that the label "Israel lobby" is a "convenient shorthand term" and choose to use it because it "is used in common parlance" and has become a convention, like "gun lobby."[28]

The book then offers a review of how the lobby functions, how it affects legislation, and how it helps ensure that the public discourse—utilizing the press, think tanks, and advocacy on college campuses—maintains a pro-Israeli point of view: "The [lobby's] goal is to convince the public that America's and Israel's interests are the same."[29] Mearsheimer and Walt argue that absent this influence, pro-Israel coverage in the media would be less consistently so. After these discussions, Mearsheimer and Walt approach the focal point of their study.

As outlined above, the central argument of the Mearsheimer and Walt analysis is that the Israel lobby's objectives and line of action are at variance with US national interests, similar to the critical literature of the 1980s and 1990s. More specifically, they identify three main American interests in the Middle East: "keeping Persian Gulf oil flowing to world markets, discouraging the spread of weapons of mass destruction, and reducing anti-American terrorism originating in the region."[30] The authors maintain that, even though the lobby has supported these interests in the past,

> many policies that organizations in the lobby have promoted over time have ultimately left the United States worse off. That was not their intention, of course, and the groups and

individuals who pushed for these policies undoubtedly believed
that the actions they favored would be good for the United
States. They were wrong. Indeed, although these policies were
intended to benefit Israel, many of them have damaged Israel's
interests as well.[31]

Mearsheimer and Walt conclude that in the post-9/11 era, Israel and
the lobby have needed to "convince" the White House of Israel's
strategic value; "policy makers had to be shown that it made good
strategic sense for the United States to try to rid the Middle East
of Israel's foes, which were said to be America's foes." "The Bush
administration eventually embraced the lobby's views about the new
threat environment." For Mearsheimer and Walt, this is not a matter
of two groups—the US government and the lobby—heading in the
same direction, working on similar goals, for reasons of comparable
interests, beliefs, and world views. This assumption they term the
"conventional wisdom," that the lobby, according to the wisdom,
is merely "overdetermining" events and policies that would have
more or less been the same without its influence. In other words,
for Mearsheimer and Walt, the United States "adopt[ing] Israel's
policy preferences" is not a case of Israeli and American heads of
state seeing "the world in essentially the same way."[32]

The remainder of the book is spent examining the particular
instances where the lobby, according to the authors, moved the
United States away from its own post-9/11 interests. The case
studies they review are the Palestine–Israel conflict, the 2003 US
invasion of Iraq, policy and approaches concerning Syria and Iran,
and the 2006 Israel–Hizballah conflict (called the 34-Day War, or
commonly, if inaccurately, the Second Lebanon War). Brief summaries of the Mearsheimer and Walt positions on these points should
suffice.

- Concerning Palestine–Israel, lobby forces have, Mearsheimer
  and Walt allege, discouraged the United States from pursuing
  a more even-handed policy toward a diplomatic settlement to
  the conflict, thus allowing Israel to instead run roughshod and
  increase anti-Americanism and resentment against Israel.
- Regarding Iraq, the authors de-emphasize the issue of oil,
  and hold that without lobby pressure "the war would almost
  certainly not have occurred."[33] Though the "driving force"
  behind the war was the influence of the neoconservatives[34] in
  the Bush administration (many of whom are Jewish), without

the lobby's supportive efforts, "America would probably not be in Iraq today."[35]

- Similar to the Palestine–Israel conflict, the aggressive posture Washington has adopted toward Syria and the lack of progress with regard to the peace process and Israel's occupation of the Golan Heights—all of which "has damaged America's position in the Arab and Islamic world"—are functions of neoconservative and lobby machinations.[36]

- On the topic of Iran, Mearsheimer and Walt contend that "the United States, Israel, and Iran's Arab neighbors ... have an independent interest in keeping Iran non-nuclear and preventing it from becoming a regional hegemon." However, the authors infer that "Israel and the lobby have pushed the United States to pursue a strategically unwise policy toward Iran," which to date has mainly been belligerent rhetoric "about using military force to destroy Iran's nuclear facilities. Unfortunately, such rhetoric makes it harder, not easier, to stop Iran from going nuclear.... Were it not for the lobby, the United States would almost certainly have a different and more effective Iran policy."[37]

- Finally, US support for Israel's summer 2006 war with the Lebanese guerilla organization Hizballah is evaluated along the same lines as the previous cases, with the authors asserting that "the lobby played the critical role" in this backing "despite the strategic costs." The notion of the United States benefiting from the war is dismissed: "the claim that American policy makers [viewed] Lebanon as a dry run for Iran makes little sense, as the assigned tasks in these two scenarios have little in common."[38] The war in Lebanon, like the other cases, has, it is argued, exacerbated terrorism, reduced US credibility, and ended up hampering the war on terror.

Providing such a brief synopsis of a 350-page book (not including back matter) can pose certain risks, but I hope it offers a serviceable overview of reasonable fidelity. As mentioned, the work by John Mearsheimer and Stephen Walt on this subject ended up creating an axis around which subsequent debate revolves.

THE CURRENT DEBATE: REACTION TO MEARSHEIMER AND WALT

When the *London Review of Books* essay was published, the response was fervent, with the book only inviting additional clamor.

A torrent of articles, essays, and op-ed pieces hit mainstream and independent outlets alike. In a number of cases spin-off debates occurred, where writers engaged one another in back-and-forth dialogues. Commentary came from all points on the spectrum, and in some instances journalists, scholars, and pundits who ordinarily would be miles apart on similar issues ended up making parallel arguments. While the debate was most heated in 2006–07, the matter remains contested.

In a very general sense, the responses can be grouped into three categories. This grouping is a device of my own choosing in an effort to clarify the literature for the newcomer. The three categories have been established in relation to the Mearsheimer and Walt interpretation: those writers who were *strongly critical*, those who were *moderately critical*, and those whose assessments were *compatible* with the interpretation (see the box on page 177). Items in a given category should be viewed as bearing only broad and loose resemblance; there is substantial variation within each group. A further generality that becomes visible as a result of classifying the commentary is where the authors tend to originate politically. This I mention only as a further clarification. Those writers who were strongly critical tend to sit somewhere right of center. Those who were moderately critical more often reside left of center. The responses that were more or less compatible with Mearsheimer and Walt, barring exceptions, could in general be described as centrist, or liberal (a now nebulous term I use here with caution). In the interest of brevity, we will look only at the two camps that deviate from Mearsheimer and Walt.

Strongly critical

These critiques, in the main, adopted a protective or defensive posture. The general view here was to cast Mearsheimer and Walt as condemning Israel and/or approximating anti-Semitic arguments made in the past about Jewish power and manipulation. Jeffrey Goldberg, a correspondent for the *Atlantic* magazine, argues in the *New Republic* that Mearsheimer and Walt adopt a "Judeocentric" position suggesting "Jews exercise disproportionate control over world affairs." He continues: "Judeocentrism is a single-cause theory of history, and as such it is, almost by definition, a conspiracy." This tradition "has now found a couple of unexpected new tribunes" in Mearsheimer and Walt.[39] Eliot Cohen, a professor from Johns Hopkins University and neoconservative counselor to former secretary of state Condoleezza Rice, makes a parallel, if less varnished, estimation of Mearsheimer and Walt's "wretched piece of scholarship" in a *Washington Post* op-ed entitled "Yes, it's Anti-Semitic."[40] Abraham Foxman, the national director for the Anti-Defamation League, in his book *The Deadliest Lies: The Israeli Lobby and the Myth of Jewish Control*, states: "In 2006, two mild-mannered university professors inaugurated a new era of anti-Jewish scapegoating—whether they did it intentionally or not." For Foxman, the Mearsheimer and Walt essay is "a classic conspiratorial analysis invoking the canards of 'Jewish power,' 'Jewish self-interest,' and 'Jewish control.'"[41]

Concern for what is viewed as an unrealistic, aggressive condemnation of Israel made by Mearsheimer and Walt also appears throughout this literature. The response is typically to cast the Palestine–Israel conflict as more symmetrical in character. Foxman:

> The fact that Israel exercises a degree of control over the lives and movements of Palestinian people in the territories under its jurisdiction is an uncomfortable reality for the Israeli people. The Jews created Israel not in order to have dominion over any other people but simply in order to have a homeland they could call their own and in which they could live in peace, ruling themselves as they saw fit. In self-defense, the Israelis were forced to take control of some Palestinian lands, which to this day are a source of attacks against Israel. Against its will, Israel was put in the position of being a conqueror.[42]

Prominent Israeli historian Benny Morris, writing in the *New Republic*, undertakes a corrective to Mearsheimer and Walt's historical review in their essay. He maintains that "Israel is the weaker party in the Arab–Israeli conflict"; that Israel's military victories were "decided by the failure of the significantly stronger and more populous Arab world"; in the Second Intifada, "the Palestinians ... enjoyed the propaganda benefit of underdog status"; that Israel fought the Second Intifada "with both hands tied behind its back," and so on throughout the article.[43]

Perhaps unsurprisingly, this group suggests a much lower level of lobby influence than Mearsheimer and Walt describe. As Jeffrey Goldberg quotes from a discussion with former secretary of defense Donald Rumsfeld, when asked about the lobby's role in pushing the United States into Iraq: "I suppose the implication of that is the president [George W. Bush] and the vice president [Dick Cheney] and myself and [Secretary of State] Colin Powell just fell off a turnip truck to take these jobs."[44] This particular assessment is a point of contact between the strongly and moderately critical writers.

Moderately critical

The writers here tend in general to feel that the discussion opened wide by Mearsheimer and Walt is a worthwhile one. As Walter Russell Mead, a senior fellow at the Council on Foreign Relations, remarks, "Mearsheimer and Walt have admirably and courageously helped to start a much needed conversation on a controversial and combustible topic." However, Mead also comments in his evaluation: "This is not serious scholarship."[45] Stephen Zunes, a political scientist at the University of San Francisco, contends that the essay "has been met by unreasonable criticism from a wide range of rightist apologists for U.S. support of the Israeli occupation [of the Palestinian territories].... The article has [also] garnered unreasonable praise from many in progressive circles."[46] Noted MIT linguist and political analyst Noam Chomsky asserts that Mearsheimer and Walt "deserve credit" for taking "a courageous stand, which merits praise, [but] we still have to ask how convincing their thesis is. Not very, in my opinion."[47]

Many authors in the moderate camp, like those who were strongly critical, acknowledge that Mearsheimer and Walt approach the classical anti-Semitic arguments. Mead states that "charges [of anti-Semitism] go too far.... [However,] [t]he authors do what anti-Semites have always done: they overstate the power of Jews."[48] Zunes issues a similar verdict, stating that it is not the case "that Mearsheimer, Walt, or anyone else who expresses concern about the power of the Israel lobby is an anti-Semite, but the way in which this exaggerated view of Jewish power parallels historic anti-Semitism should give us all pause."[49] Michelle Goldberg, writing for *Salon*, says she recognizes that Mearsheimer and Walt "are not anti-Semites, or aligned with anti-Semitic forces. They seem, however, somewhat oblivious as to why the issue they've taken on is so horribly sensitive, and they make little effort to address the causes of the taboo they're trying to dislodge."[50]

One of the key criticisms for this group is the impression that the lobby has to convince Washington that Israel is still a strategic asset in the post-Cold War 9/11 era. Joseph Massad, a professor of modern Arab politics at Columbia University, observes that "the United States spends much more on its military bases in the Arab world, not to mention on those in Europe or Asia, than it does on Israel." He then notes:

> Critics argue that when the US had to intervene in the Gulf, it could not rely on Israel to do the job because of the sensitivity of including it in such a coalition which would embarrass Arab allies, hence the need for direct US intervention and the uselessness of Israel as a strategic ally. While this may be true, the US also could not rely on any of its military bases to launch the invasions on their own and had to ship in its army. American bases in the Gulf did provide important and needed support but so did Israel.[51]

Zunes addresses this point in more detail:

> Rather than being a liability, as Mearsheimer and Walt claim, the 1991 Gulf War once again proved Israel to be a strategic asset: Israeli developments in air-to-ground warfare were integrated into allied bombing raids against Iraqi missile sites and other targets; Israeli-designed conformal fuel tanks for F-15 fighter-bombers greatly enhanced their range; Israeli-provided mine plows were utilized during the final assaults on Iraqi positions; Israeli mobile bridges were used by U.S. Marines; Israeli targeting systems and low-altitude warning devices were employed by U.S. helicopters; and Israel developed key components for the widely-used Tomahawk missiles.[52]

Zunes also cites similar evidence that Israel has been of service to the United States in the war on terror and in Iraq, calling into further question Mearsheimer and Walt's reasoning that the Jewish state is more a liability than an asset (as planners see it). Independent scholar and political scientist Norman Finkelstein holds that the strategic liability thesis "misses the big picture":

> Sometimes what's most obvious escapes the eye. Israel is the only stable and secure base for projecting U.S. power in this region. Every other country the U.S. relies on might, for all anyone knows, fall out of U.S. control tomorrow.[53]

(Regarding this question, Mead points toward a "potential shift"—that is, Israel's "option of diversifying its great-power base of support"—being a "major concern to the United States."[54])

According to Chomsky, Israel is performing the same services it has always performed, mitigating against "radical nationalism." He argues that although the Cold War rationale has become obsolete—and was questionable to begin with—the United States is "pursuing about the same policies as before," its alliance with Israel being a "logical corollary" of opposition to "radical nationalism."[55] That the US regional interest is oil is something emphasized throughout this category.

Since many of these writers note the continuity of American foreign policy over the decades and eras, especially as it pertains to the Middle East, the common conclusion is that Mearsheimer and Walt have done policymakers in Washington a favor by choosing to underline the lobby's role in what, according to many in this group, the government would have been doing in large part anyway. The analysis here is that the lobby's prestige was instead derived from Israel's standing as a US client. As Massad states, the "attraction" to the Mearsheimer and Walt interpretation "is that it exonerates the United States' government from all the responsibility and guilt that it deserves for its policies in the Arab world." "One could argue ... that it is in fact the very centrality of Israel to US strategy in the Middle East that accounts, in part, for the strength of the pro-Israel lobby and not the other way around." Chomsky: "The thesis M–W propose does ... have plenty of appeal. The reason, I think, is that it leaves the US government untouched on its high pinnacle of nobility." Zunes: "What progressive supporters of Mearsheimer and Walt's analysis seem to ignore is that both men have a vested interest in absolving from responsibility the foreign policy establishment that they have served so loyally all these years."[56]

EVALUATION AND CONCLUDING REMARKS

This overview mostly stated the positions of the various writers, infrequently including or citing the evidence they provided in support of their positions. To include the evidentiary particulars would have made this chapter overwhelmingly long, and more than likely would not have made the issue any clearer for those readers new to the subject.

The Israel lobby issue, like many issues in the field of history and political science, and in the humanities in general, does not offer the opportunities found in the physical sciences like chemistry and physics, counting on measurability and predictability. The lobby dispute is a matter of interpretation of the data; it is a judgment call. Many of the scholars and journalists offering responses to Mearsheimer and Walt, irrespective of their general category, pointed toward proof supporting their arguments. Mearsheimer and Walt, as mentioned, provided over 200 endnotes in their essay (and more in the book) to substantiate their claims; probably as many more were thrown back at them in a bid to discredit their thesis. Of course, not everyone can be right at the same time. But on the surface, most every writer furnished evidence suggesting that they were on the right track. This provides for a mountain of information and point-counterpoint. Pulling back from the nearly endless quotes, facts, figures, and anecdotes can help us see the forest for the trees.

We might first look at some of Mearsheimer and Walt's basic premises as well as some of the terms and concepts that come up in the lobby debate. Two commonly invoked concepts are "national interest" and "strategic asset." Focusing on Mearsheimer and Walt, as we covered, they argue that Israel is not serving the former and is no longer the latter. For the authors, because of this and the fact that disproportionate and uninterrupted support for Israel continues, something must be amiss. In other words, the government is working at cross-purposes with itself, and therefore there must be another force at work. This would stand to reason were they using the terms "national interest" and "strategic asset" consistently, which they are not.

Mearsheimer and Walt are using these terms as we the people might apply them, not as they are used by state planners. As we have observed, there is a visible continuity in American foreign policy that spans the life of the country. In the case of the Middle East, this has involved power projection there for the sake of natural resources, prevention of independent/progressive nationalism, and preemption of other external powers usurping American regional primacy (not just the USSR). None of these objectives, of course, wins a country friends. Yet these objectives are the national interest—from the perspective of Washington and the White House. That the United States' quasi-imperial conduct inspires terrorism is unsurprising to power, as revenge throughout history has always been the standard response; what the CIA calls "blowback." But based on the consistency of US policy in the Middle East, the policymakers that have been responsible for this consistency—all administrations since 1945—obviously feel blowback is an acceptable downside.

As a result, Mearsheimer and Walt's discussion of whether Israel is a liability or an asset in the "war on terror" and the "effort to democratize the Middle East" is wide of the history.[57] As was covered at the end of Chapter 2 and the beginning of Chapter 4, American Cold War fears of Soviet tentacles were overstated. The real concerns of the foreign policy agenda in the region received much less public attention. And for these policy goals, Washington came to appreciate (and further develop) a well-armed, politically stable client state in Israel. Mearsheimer and Walt themselves quote Henry Kissinger, stating that:

> Israeli strength does not prevent the spread of communism in the Arab world.... So it is difficult to claim that a strong Israel serves American interests because it prevents the spread of communism in the Arab world. It does not. It provides for the survival of Israel.[58]

Israel's strength and stability are part of its value.

As we observed in Chapter 4, quoting Kissinger (see page 109), causing low-level tension has been part of Israel's job all along; it is expected to be (slightly) incorrigible. Its main function, however, is to simply exist in the region as a military power, as an adjunct to US objectives in the region. But have those objectives changed since the fall of the Soviet Union? According to then-General (res.) Shlomo Gazit, Israel's first coordinator of government operations in the occupied territories (1967–74) and head of military intelligence (1974–79), in a 1992 article in the Israeli press, the Jewish state's post-Cold War agenda was to bear little contrast to its prior agenda:

> Israel's main task has not changed at all, and it remains of crucial importance. The geographical location of Israel at the centre of the Arab-Muslim Middle East predestines Israel to be a devoted guardian of stability in all the countries surrounding it. Its [role] is to protect the existing regimes: to prevent or halt the processes of radicalization and to block the expansion of fundamentalist religious zealotry.

He continues:

> Israel has its "red lines", which have a powerful deterrent effect by virtue of causing uncertainty beyond its borders, precisely because they are not clearly marked nor explicitly defined. The

purpose of these red lines is to determine which strategic developments or other changes occurring beyond Israel's borders can be
defined as threats which Israel itself will regard as intolerable to
the point of being compelled to use all its military power for the
sake of their prevention or eradication.[59]

This is further confirmation of what we have observed throughout.

Similar to the standard Cold War rhetoric, is the new rhetoric—the war on terror and spreading democracy—capturing a new
reality or merely creating camouflage for the usual policies? Based
on the regularity, it would seem the latter is the case. Iraq quickly
becoming the primary concern in the wake of 9/11 indicates a lack
of interest in fighting terror or spreading democracy. As the intelligence community predicted, invading Iraq would increase the
likelihood of terrorism, and invading and occupying a sovereign
nation is not, on any planet, a democratic gesture. What we do see
is a rotten apple (Saddam, after his adventure in Kuwait and thus
being branded unreliable) being disposed of—and Iraq's immense
oil reserves are no secret.

Furthermore, American policy in the Middle East for the last
six decades has not signaled any preoccupation among planners
with concepts like America's standing, credibility, or reputation in
the Arab world. Were it concerned with how it is viewed in the
region—and with terrorism—it would simply cease to intervene
there. As Osama bin Laden clarified in a 2004 address to the
American people, just prior to US elections:

> Security is an important pillar of human life. Free people do not
> relinquish their security. This is contrary to [President] Bush's
> claim that we hate freedom. Let him tell us why we did not
> strike Sweden, for example.... We fought you because we are
> free and do not accept injustice. We want to restore freedom to
> our nation. Just as you waste our security, we will waste your
> security.[60]

The kind of credibility that US policy architects have been mindful
of is not the kind Mearsheimer and Walt, and those who hold similar interpretations, are talking about. The credibility on the minds
of planners, as we have touched on over the course of the book, is
the kind conveyed by state power. In Frank Herbert's classic science
fiction novel *Dune*, a character belonging to a mystic order briefly
demonstrates the depth of her powers, whereupon she says to her

unnerved interlocutor, "You've glimpsed the fist within the Bene Gesserit glove." She establishes in that moment credibility; and her credibility, no different than in international relations, is based on the fist—and the phlegmatic willingness to avail oneself of it. Heads of state tend to not agonize over things like trustworthiness and the opinions of others (save those of the domestic population, and usually not out of sincerity).

If the fundamental premises postulated by Mearsheimer and Walt do not stand up to historical scrutiny, the authors' verdict on the degree of the lobby's power is, by necessity, in some measure dubious. As mentioned above, their argument hinges on something in US policy formulation being amiss, which the historical record by and large does not support. Control of resources, punishment of deviation, and general regional hegemony are the guiding principles of policy formulation. Mearsheimer and Walt are correct that America's policies in the Middle East are not in the national interest: that is, the interest of the American population. After all, we pick up the tab: the tax payers foot the bill for foreign aid (which is then spent on US weaponry), innocent people will suffer any future terrorist attacks, and the rank-and-file members of the military bear the direct burden of these imperial adventures. The population shoulders these costs, not the architects. But this is a change in topic, important as it is. The Mearsheimer and Walt analysis suggests that the national interest of the state and of the people is one and the same, and because this interest is being harmed, it must be by dint of a third party. However, this conflation of interests is at direct variance with the historical realities. Two prominent political scientists must certainly be aware of the record, so one would be within bounds to ask why it is these scholars perform such a reordering.

That the lobby is powerful is clear. That it has, in some instances, exacerbated policy is also clear. As we covered in Chapter 5, because the Palestinians do not rank very highly on the list of US priorities, the lobby has likely had influence in helping Israel advance its expansion in the occupied territories. That the lobby issue needs to be addressed and discussed would be a fair-minded assertion. Mearsheimer and Walt have contributed to this, and in so doing also provided a realistic rendering of the history of the Palestine–Israel conflict. But proposing a high degree of lobby power and influence is to move away from the historical evidence, which is well documented and quite clear. That being the case, we can only conclude that the lobby's stature and reputation were built on something preexisting, namely, the increasing value of Israel as a Middle Eastern client state, off-shore military base, and junior partner in the realms of finance, research and development, and intelligence for the world's sole superpower—a status the United States did not achieve by being naive and easily manipulated.

Israel lobby—bibliographic note

For readers looking to study the issue further, below is a bibliographic guide to the commentary that appeared in periodicals in response to Mearsheimer and Walt. The articles (and two books) are grouped into three general categories, which, it must be emphasized, *roughly* serve as a means of giving the reader a basic framework. Articles within a category should not be viewed as being in perfect accordance with one another or interchangeable; diversity within a given heading can be significant. These lists are not comprehensive, but are reasonably representative of what was being published at the time when the lobby debate was at its greatest intensity (2006–07). The criteria used in my choices were to include those articles that were authored by noteworthy scholars and writers, or tend to crop up in the past or present discourse, or I felt would be useful to readers embarking on broader inquiry. Most are available online.

The three classifications—compatible, moderately critical, and strongly critical—are based on the commentator's proximity to the Mearsheimer and Walt thesis. The articles are presented in alphabetical order according to author.

Compatible: Kathleen and Bill Christison, "The Power of the Israel Lobby: Its Origin and Growth," *CounterPunch*, June 16/18, 2006; Richard Cohen, "No, it's not Anti-Semitic," *Washington Post*, April 25, 2006; Tony Judt, "A Lobby, Not a Conspiracy," *New York Times*, April 19, 2006; Michael Massing, "The Storm over the Israel Lobby," *New York Review of Books*, 53, no. 10 (June 8, 2006); M. J. Rosenberg, "It's Lobbying, but is it Really Pro-Israel?" *Haaretz*, September 21, 2007; and George Soros, "On Israel, America and AIPAC," *New York Review of Books*, 54, no. 6 (April 12, 2007);

book: James Petras, *The Power of Israel in the United States* (Atlanta, GA: Clarity Press, 2006).

Moderately critical: Noam Chomsky, "The Israel Lobby?" *ZNet*, March 28, 2006; Norman G. Finkelstein, "The Israel Lobby: It's Not Either/Or," *CounterPunch*, May 1, 2006; Michelle Goldberg, "Is the 'Israel Lobby' Distorting America's Mideast Policies?" *Salon*, April 18, 2006; Joseph Massad, "Blaming the Lobby," *Al-Ahram*, March 23–29, 2006; Walter Russell Mead, "Jerusalem Syndrome: Decoding the Israel Lobby," *Foreign Affairs*, November/December 2007; Sherry Wolf, "The Watchdog, Not the Master," *International Socialist Review*, March–April 2007; and Stephen Zunes, "The Israel Lobby: How Powerful is it Really?" *Foreign Policy in Focus*, May 16, 2006.

Strongly critical: Eliot A. Cohen, "Yes, it's Anti-Semitic," *Washington Post*, April 5, 2006; Alan Dershowitz, "Debunking the Newest—and Oldest—Jewish Conspiracy: A Reply to the Mearsheimer–Walt "Working Paper," Harvard University/ John F. Kennedy School of Government, April 2006; Jeffrey Goldberg, "The Usual Suspect," *New Republic*, October 8, 2007; Benny Morris, "And Now for Some Facts," *New Republic*, May 8, 2006; and Michael B. Oren, "Quiet Riot: Tinfoil Hats in Harvard Yard," *New Republic*, April 10, 2006; *book*: Abraham H. Foxman, *The Deadliest Lies: The Israel Lobby and the Myth of Jewish Control* (New York: Palgrave Macmillan, 2007).

Other: "The War over Israel's Influence" (Roundtable), *Foreign Policy*, July/August 2006; and Glenn Frankel, "A Beautiful Friendship?" *Washington Post*, July 16, 2006.

CONCLUSION

As the quote by historian Howard Zinn in the Preface indicates, the goal of this book is not to dwell on, for example, the genocidal policies targeted against Native Americans. Our moral sphere extends only as far as our actions will affect outcomes. Judging Andrew Jackson might offer a certain satisfaction, but it does no one any tangible good; only in the present do our judgments and actions offer possible results. Popular pressure from within the country's boundaries is one of the only ways Washington will adjust its foreign courses of action. However, the populace is lacking basic information on the matter—and one cannot help but note the convenience of this reality. However it must be noted that most Americans are in agreement with one another, and largely in disagreement with the leadership when it comes to foreign policy issues (as well as a host of others). Close and constant polling of the American public reveals that their preferences are politically left of even the so-called "liberal" leadership, and cut across partisan divisions (Democrat–Republican, liberal–conservative), which are mainly artificial constraints on how we discuss politics in the United States. The vast polling literature that exists, as well as books like *The Foreign Policy Disconnect* by Benjamin Page (Northwestern University) and Marshall Bouton (Chicago Council on Foreign Relations), place this matter well beyond dispute.[1] Even in the haze that exists around how American foreign affairs are presented, and especially those pertaining to the Middle East, most people in the United States still have a rational sense of justice regarding the subject. But as to the specifics of past and current involvements, we remain to a large extent in the dark.

In all six chapters we looked at subjects that are regrettably under-discussed in the context of basic history. Topics like nation-states, American foreign relations, and Israel are frequently taken as givens, with discourse and analysis starting with assumptions instead of fundamentals. In just about any discipline, intellectual or not, fundamentals are the first things people tend to become rusty on, forget, or never firmly possess in the first place. Yet,

analyses that are based on assumptions, which in turn are typically
ideological—nationalism, racism, theism, etcetera—tend to simplify
matters, and therefore are attractive. Such arguments neatly parcel
the good guys and bad guys, and set the default position for "our
side" as being righteous, or at least well-intentioned. This might be
comforting, but it is not necessarily historical. Basic questions will
always prove the best method of inquiry, as doctrinal beliefs do not
fare very well in their presence. There is no better testament to just
how tenuous arguments based on ideology are.

But beyond being tenuous, ideological assumptions pose a
danger. As also observed in the Zinn quote, the "moral proportion" provided by custom-tailoring our history to tell an acceptable
tale is "deadly." For one, such tailoring makes it easier for heads
of state to wage unnecessary wars, as well as inspire the terrorism
that goes with them. In the interim, a certain tranquility is provided
by engaging in romantic conceptions of one's country, its past and
present, and its leaders' personalities. Our sense of nationalism—
which by the time we are old enough to read and write is already
becoming integrated into our thinking—creates a connection to the
government (state) that transforms it into an extension of ourselves
(country); the state apparatus becomes attached to our homeland,
the source of our roots, the land of our fathers, and so on. This
composite forms the nation: that is, a group of people bound in
sovereignty. The nation has been described in a standard work on
the subject as "an imagined political community ... conceived as a
deep, horizontal comradeship."[2] This sense of community, however,
is something that generally occurs after the fact, though there are
exceptions (Palestinians, Kurds, Basques). First comes the state,
then comes the nationalist mindset. In 1861, after the unification of
Italy, a prominent statesman remarked: "We have made Italy, now
we have to make Italians."[3] While our fond notions of homeland
are not wrong, fusing them with the state's political machinery can
generate blind spots, together with an inability or unwillingness to
view the state's behavior as something separate from the country's
well-being. This is perhaps the primary source of our cultural reluc-
tance to consider the record in earnest.

Upon suspension of this tendency, the conversation is rebooted,
as it were, especially when we return to the beginning and retrace
our steps from a given point in history to the present. Starting from
scratch helps deprogram our study of current events by mitigating against cultural trends not unrelated to nationalist doctrine.
In American political culture, there is an encouragement to, for

example, participate in the liberal–conservative opposition (nurtured and augmented by uninterrupted commentary and opinion on television and radio), which tends to focus the attention on the individual and what "side" they are on. This polar dynamic, another example of ideological orientation, creates the false impression that there are only two available positions. Some might attempt to finesse the situation by offering a "shades of gray" proposition, but this nevertheless takes place within the established parameters. This is not to say that there are not legitimate political disagreements or differences among the population, but the blue–red fault line in American politics inhibits recognition among the population that the commonalities within itself are both greater than the divisions and quite threatening to the extant power structures.

In addition to the distorting effect of this opposition, it is also calibrated to the right. Liberalism is for the most part a centrist position on the political spectrum, but in the current fashion the center has become the left, and almost everything previously left of center removed from legitimate consideration, providing additional constraint. As mentioned, the population generally sits to the left of the liberal camp in Congress. Were the center adjusted to correspond to majority public opinion, the liberal lawmakers on Capitol Hill, now considered left, would be located right of center.

Another factor impinging on our becoming informed is that it is time-consuming to sift through books on a given subject, which is necessary if we wish to leaven our news intake with some context. The media present the news almost strictly as *new*, regardless of whether that is indeed the case. In this book I attempted to provide both a distillation and a conduit between the current events coverage and the bulkier and/or specialist historical literature. It is interesting to observe the relative quality of scholarship available in academic and scholarly works. Owing to the unparalleled access to information in the United States, the historical record is not hidden from public view in state archives or destroyed. Historians are allowed access, and the literature as a result is fairly rich. Despite nationalist proclivities—strong and deep among the academic and intellectual class—affecting at times how the history is told, honest historical information sits just beneath the surface. In many cases, the sources that appear in the endnotes in this book are titles any undergraduate or graduate student might use in their studies in political science and history—degrees commonly held by members of government, incidentally. When former secretary of state Condoleezza Rice responded to Russian president Dmitri Medvedev's 2008 visit to

Caracas, Venezuela, invoking the language of Cold War planners and the title of a standard work on that period—"I just don't think there's any question about who has the *preponderance of power* in the Western Hemisphere"—she let her education show.[4]

The aim of this book has been to show the connectivity and relative consistency over the last 500 years, and specifically the last 60 or so involving the pinnacle of American power and its replacement of British and French hegemony in the Middle East. As we saw in Chapter 3, that region's nation-state configuration is comparatively recent. Also touched on later in the book was the development of the Arab world's resentment toward the United States—another somewhat recent phenomenon. The involvement of the United States in the Middle East, including Israel's proxy role, has brought that resentment into Israel and now the United States in the form of 9/11, innocents suffering the costs of state policy as usual. However, the egregious suffering that lies at the source of that resentment warrants careful attention; if not out of human sympathy, at least out of practical self-preservation. The burden of liability is two-fold: The power unwelcomely projected into the Middle East is "ours," as it relates to the state apparatus; and the only authority that can alter our foreign policy is "ours," as it pertains to the country. Yet the solutions are simple, and begin with calling a halt to policies of such projection.

NOTES

PREFACE

1 Howard Zinn, *A People's History of the United States: 1492–Present*, rev. ed. (New York: Harper Perennial, 2003), 19.

CHAPTER 1

1 Immanuel Wallerstein, *World-Systems Analysis: An Introduction* (Durham, NC: Duke University Press, 2004), 16. Another valuable primer is Thomas Richard Shannon, *An Introduction to the World–System Perspective*, 2nd ed. (Boulder, CO: Westview Press, 1996). For in-depth study of world-systems analysis, consult Wallerstein's magnum opus on the subject, *The Modern World-System*, 3 vols. (New York: Academic Press, 1974, 1980, 1989).

2 J. M. Roberts, *The New Penguin History of the World*, 4th ed. (London: Penguin, 2002), 118.

3 Fernand Braudel, *A History of Civilizations*, trans. Richard Mayne (London: Penguin, 1993), 43.

4 Walter C. Opello, Jr. and Stephen J. Rosow, *The Nation-State and Global Order: A Historical Introduction to Contemporary Politics*, 2nd ed. (Boulder, CO: Lynne Rienner, 2004), 22. The Opello and Rosow text is an informative and accessible examination of the nation-state that those looking for further study will find valuable.

5 Thomas H. Greer and Gavin Lewis, *A Brief History of the Western World*, 9th ed. (Belmont, CA: Thomson Wadsworth, 2005), 115.

6 Plutarch, *Tiberius and Caius Gracchus*, bk. IX, ch. 5; quoted in Perry Anderson, *Passages from Antiquity to Feudalism* (1974; reprint, London: Verso, 1996), 57n4.

7 Norman Davies, *Europe: A History* (New York: HarperPerennial, 1996), 302.

8 F. L. Ganshof, *Feudalism*, trans. Philip Grierson, 3rd ed. (New York: Harper & Row, 1964), xvi. Ganshof's brief account is referred to by many historians and serves as a valuable account of a subject that is at times challenging to define and describe. The quote cited above also appears in Davies, *Europe*, 311.

9   Anderson, *Passages*, 148.
10 Opello and Rosow, *The Nation-State*, 61.
11 The issue of capitalism, and the where, when, and how of its arrival, can be a thorny and contentious one; in addition, or as a result, the literature is vast. For a short and illuminating discussion of the subject and an examination of the classic debates, see Ellen Meiksins Wood, *The Origins of Capitalism: A Longer View* (London: Verso, 2002).
12 German physicist Otto von Guericke writing during the time of Westphalia; quoted in H. G. Koenigsberger, *Early Modern Europe, 1500–1789* (London: Longman, 1987), 122.
13 Charles Tilly, *Coercion, Capital, and European States, AD 990–1992*, rev. ed. (Cambridge, MA: Blackwell, 1992), 70. For fair attribution, political analyst Noam Chomsky cites this quote frequently in lectures and interviews, which probably influenced my gravitation to the passage in Tilly's book.
14 Quoted in Anders Stephanson, *Manifest Destiny: American Expansionism and the Empire of Right* (New York: Hill & Wang, 1995), 96.

CHAPTER 2

1   Thomas H. Greer and Gavin Lewis, *A Brief History of the Western World*, 9th ed. (Belmont, CA: Thomson Wadsworth, 2005), 332.
2   Hugh Seton-Watson, *Nations and States: An Enquiry into the Origins of Nations and the Politics of Nationalism* (Boulder, CO: Westview Press, 1977), 193.
3   Tzvetan Todorov, *The Conquest of America: The Question of the Other*, trans. Richard Howard (1984; reprint, Norman, OK: Red River/University of Oklahoma Press, 1999), 42, 142–3.
4   Quoted in ibid., 21, 46.
5   Quoted in ibid., 142.
6   See Howard Zinn, *A People's History of the United States: 1492–Present*, rev. ed. (New York: Harper Perennial, 2003), 77–89.
7   See Walter LaFeber, "The Constitution and United States Foreign Policy: An Interpretation," *Journal of American History*, 74, no. 3 (Dec. 1987): 695–717; cited in Bradford Perkins, *The Cambridge History of American Foreign Relations*, vol. 1, *The Creation of a Republican Empire, 1776–1865* (Cambridge, UK: Cambridge University Press, 1993), 58.
8   *The Federalist* is accessible online at the Avalon Project at Yale Law School: http://www.yale.edu/lawweb/avalon/federal/fed.htm. I have used the commonly available Rossiter edition throughout: Alexander Hamilton, James Madison, and John Jay, *The Federalist Papers*, ed. Clinton Rossiter (1961; reprint, New York: Penguin/Signet Classic, 1999).

9 All quotes from *Federalist* No. 10.
10 Charles A. Beard, *An Economic Interpretation of the Constitution of the United States* (1913; reprint, Mineola, NY: Dover Publications, 2004), 13.
11 Quoted in ibid., 199.
12 "Letter from Gouverneur Morris, New-York, to Mr. Penn," May 20, 1774, *American Archives*, series 4, ed. Peter Force (Washington, DC), 1:324. *The American Archives: Documents of the American Revolution, 1774–1776* database is available online from Northern Illinois University Libraries, http://dig.lib.niu.edu/amarch. The quote also appears in Richard Hofstadter, *The American Political Tradition: And the Men who Made it* (1948; reprint, New York, Vintage, 1989), 7.
13 *United States Magazine and Democratic Review*, vol. 17, issue 085–086 (July–August 1845): 5–10. An archive of scans of the magazine is available online at Cornell University Library's site, http://cdl.library.cornell.edu/moa/browse.journals/usde.html.
14 Walter LaFeber, *The American Age: U.S. Foreign Policy at Home and Abroad, 1750 to the Present*, 2nd ed. (New York: W. W. Norton, 1994), 120.
15 This quote frequently appears in the general literature. See Perkins, *Cambridge History*, 160.
16 Quoted in Zinn, *People's History*, 77.
17 Theodore Roosevelt, *The Winning of the West*, 4 vols. (1889, 1894, 1896; reprint, New York: G. P. Putnam's Sons/Knickerbocker Press, 1928), 1:17, 1:331, 1:333, 3:41, 3:44.
18 Lewis Cass quoted in Thomas G. Paterson et al., *American Foreign Relations: A History*, vol. 1, *To 1920*, 6th ed. (Boston, MA: Houghton Mifflin, 2005), 91. William T. Sherman quoted in Michael H. Hunt, *Ideology and U.S. Foreign Policy* (New Haven, CT: Yale University Press, 1987), 55. Georgia governor quoted in Anders Stephanson, *Manifest Destiny: American Expansionism and the Empire of Right* (New York: Hill & Wang, 1995), 26. Andrew Jackson quoted in LaFeber, *American Age*, 99.
19 Quoted in V. G. Kiernan, *America: the New Imperialism, From White Settlement to World Hegemony* (1978; reprint, London: Verso, 2005), 40. Kiernan's book is an informative and lively analysis of American foreign relations from the settlers to the 1970s.
20 Thomas R. Hietala, *Manifest Design: American Exceptionalism and Empire*, rev. ed. (Ithaca, NY: Cornell University Press, 2003).
21 Paterson et al., *American Foreign Relations*, 1:115.
22 The text of the Monroe Doctrine is available on the Avalon Project: http://www.yale.edu/lawweb/avalon/monroe.htm.
23 Dexter Perkins, *The Monroe Doctrine, 1823–1826* (1927; reprint, Gloucester, MA: Peter Smith, 1965), 43–4.
24 Quoted in ibid., 44.
25 Quoted in Hunt, *Ideology*, 101.

26 Perkins, *Monroe Doctrine*, 98. For discussion of Adams, South America, and the two-spheres principle, see 53–4, 72–4, 78–9, 100–3, 141–2, 143.

27 Quoted in Perkins, *Cambridge History*, 157.

28 Zinn, *People's History*, 258.

29 A. T. Mahan, "The United States Looking Outward," *Atlantic Monthly*, December 1890, 816–24. Mahan is best known for his classic statement on naval strategy, *The Influence of Sea Power upon History, 1660–1783* (1890; reprint, Mineola, NY: Dover, 1987).

30 Frederick J. Turner, "The Problem of the West," *Atlantic Monthly*, September 1896, 289–97. See also Turner's *The Frontier in American History* (1920; reprint, Mineola, NY: Dover, 1996), especially the first chapter, which is his influential essay "The Significance of the Frontier in American History."

31 Richard F. Grimmett, "Instances of Use of United States Armed Forces Abroad, 1798–2007," Congressional Research Service (Report RL32170), September 12, 2007; downloadable at the Federation of American Scientists site, http://www.fas.org/sgp/crs/natsec/RL32170.pdf. See also William Blum, *Killing Hope: U.S. Military and CIA Interventions since World War II*, rev. ed. (Monroe, ME: Common Courage Press, 2004), 454–62 (appendix II).

32 Hietala, *Manifest Design*, xvii.

33 William Appleman Williams, *The Tragedy of American Diplomacy*, rev. ed. (New York: W. W. Norton, 1972), 45.

34 Ibid.

35 A readable and lively account can be found in the first four chapters of Stephen Kinzer, *Overthrow: America's Century of Regime Change from Hawaii to Iraq* (New York: Times Books/Henry Holt, 2006). For a brief, thematic analysis by a leading specialist, readers would do well to consider Thomas Schoonover, *Uncle Sam's War of 1898 and the Origins of Globalization* (Lexington, KY: University Press of Kentucky, 2003).

36 See Paterson et al., *American Foreign Relations*, 1:218; and LaFeber, *American Age*, 215–16.

37 Stephanson, *Manifest Destiny*, 98.

38 Schoonover, *Uncle Sam's War*, 99. His discussion of power's use of language bears comparison with similar insights made by George Orwell in his classic essay on writing entitled "Politics and the English Language" (1946):

> In our time, political speech and writing are largely the defence of the indefensible. Things like the continuance of British rule in India, the Russian purges and deportations, the dropping of the atom bombs on Japan, can indeed be defended, but only by arguments which are too brutal for most people to face, and which do not square with the professed aims of the political parties. Thus political language

has to consist largely of euphemism, question-begging and sheer cloudy vagueness. Defenceless villages are bombarded from the air, the inhabitants driven out into the countryside, the cattle machine-gunned, the huts set on fire with incendiary bullets: this is called *pacification*. Millions of peasants are robbed of their farms and sent trudging along the roads with no more than they can carry: this is called *transfer of population* or *rectification of frontiers*. People are imprisoned for years without trial, or shot in the back of the neck or sent to die of scurvy in Arctic lumber camps: this is called *elimination of unreliable elements*. Such phraseology is needed if one wants to name things without calling up mental pictures of them. (George Orwell, *Why I Write* (New York: Penguin Books, 2005), 114–15. Emphasis in original)

39 Three valuable accounts of some of the various interventions are: Blum, *Killing Hope*; Kinzer, *Overthrow*; and John Prados, *Presidents' Secret Wars: CIA and Pentagon Covert Operations from World War II through the Persian Gulf,* rev. ed. (Chicago: Elephant/Ivan R. Dee, 1996). See also Tim Weiner, *Legacy of Ashes: The History of the CIA* (New York: Doubleday, 2007).

40 See the Department of Defense's *Base Structure Report*, available online at the website of the Office of the Deputy Under Secretary of Defense: http://www.acq.osd.mil/ie/irm.

41 Williams, *Tragedy*, 55.

42 For the text of the Roosevelt Corollary, see the Our Documents initiative, run in part by the National Archives and Records Administration: http://www.ourdocuments.gov. This is a good source for early American documents (1776–1965), featuring downloadable scans of the originals.

43 Walter LaFeber, *Inevitable Revolutions: The United States in Central America*, 2nd ed. (New York: W. W. Norton, 1993), 38.

44 Akira Iriye, *The Cambridge History of American Foreign Relations*, vol. 3, *The Globalizing of America, 1913–1945* (Cambridge, UK: Cambridge University Press, 1993), 30.

45 The Kellogg–Briand Pact is published by the Avalon Project: http://www.yale.edu/lawweb/avalon/kbpact/kbpact.htm.

46 See Wilson's Fourteen Points, issued after World War I, at the Avalon Project: http://www.yale.edu/lawweb/avalon/wilson14.htm. His "War Message," delivered upon entering World War I, is published in Michael Waldman, ed., *My Fellow Americans: The Most Important Speeches of America's Presidents, from George Washington to George W. Bush* (Naperville, IL: Sourcebooks, 2003), 81–6.

47 Frank Ninkovich, *Modernity and Power: A History of the Domino Theory in the Twentieth Century* (Chicago: University of Chicago Press, 1994), 53, 54, 68.

48 FDR's first inaugural address is available on the Avalon Project: http://www.yale.edu/lawweb/avalon/presiden/inaug/froos1.htm.

49 Thomas G. Paterson et al., *American Foreign Relations: A History*, vol. 2, *Since 1895*, 6th ed. (Boston, MA: Houghton Mifflin, 2005), 152.
50 David F. Schmitz, *Thank God They're on our Side: The United States and Right-Wing Dictatorships, 1921–1965* (Chapel Hill, NC: University of North Carolina Press, 1999), 6.
51 Melvyn P. Leffler, *A Preponderance of Power: National Security, the Truman Administration, and the Cold War* (Stanford, CA: Stanford University Press, 1992), 5. Leffler's is a standard text, though newcomers might find it cumbersome. See also his "The American Conception of National Security and the Beginnings of the Cold War, 1945–48," *American Historical Review*, 89, no. 2 (April 1984): 346–82; and *The Specter of Communism: The United States and the Origins of the Cold War, 1917–1953* (New York: Hill & Wang, 1994).
52 Quoted in Walter LaFeber, *America, Russia, and the Cold War, 1945–2006*, 10th ed. (New York: McGraw Hill, 2008), 31.
53 Quoted in Leffler, *Preponderance*, 6.
54 For an excellent corrective analysis of the Cold War, addressing this and related themes, see "Cold War: Fact and Fancy," in Noam Chomsky, *Deterring Democracy* (New York: Hill & Wang, 1992), ch. 1. Chomsky's work on the Cold War simply says out loud what most historians either hint at or try their best to ignore, and therefore he himself is ignored on the topic. As he notes in his *Fateful Triangle* (p. 34; see Bibliography) about Gabriel and Joyce Kolko, first-rate scholars who also accurately describe history and are at times dismissed for it, their books

> remain invaluable for understanding the general wartime and postwar period, though much useful work has appeared since, including much documentation that basically supports their analyses, in my view, though the fact is rarely acknowledged; since they do not adhere to approved orthodoxies, it is considered a violation of scholarly ethics to refer to their contributions.

Regrettably, this observation also applies to its author.
55 "X" [George F. Kennan], "The Sources of Soviet Conduct," *Foreign Affairs*, 25 (July 1947): 566–82. The article was published anonymously, hence the X and bracketed name.
56 Months later, a dispatch similar to Kennan's was sent by the Soviet ambassador in Washington, Nikolai Novikov, to his superiors in Moscow. Novikov's cable, also noting threats posed by the other, cites particular and realistic evidence of American designs on the Middle East and its oil, and "plans for world dominance"—expansion of the armed forces, massive military budget increases, and establishment of worldwide bases, all within close proximity to Russia's borders. See Rashid Khalidi, *Sowing Crisis: The Cold War and American Dominance in the Middle East* (Boston, MA: Beacon Press, 2009), 65–9. Khalidi observes (p. 69):

While the Soviets saw American initiatives in the Middle East as part of a move toward world hegemony, and as directly threatening the security of their homeland, the Americans saw Soviet moves there as aggressive threats not to their national security in the narrowest sense, but rather to their increasingly powerful posture in this region and to the resources it contained, which were so vital to America's newfound dominant position in the world.

In other words, Soviet "threats" were to US interests, whereas actual expansionist behavior on the part of the US military appeared, perhaps understandably, threatening to Moscow itself, and not many miles away. The subject of US interests in Middle Eastern oil will be picked up in Chapter 4.

57 Warren I. Cohen, *The Cambridge History of American Foreign Relations*, vol. 4, *America in the Age of Soviet Power, 1945–1991* (Cambridge, UK: Cambridge University Press, 1993), 39–40.

58 Quoted in John Lewis Gaddis, *Strategies of Containment: A Critical Appraisal of American National Security Policy during the Cold War*, rev. ed. (New York: Oxford University Press, 2005), 35.

59 Blum, *Killing Hope*, 35.

60 The president's "Truman Doctrine" speech (March 12, 1947) is on the Avalon Project: http://www.yale.edu/lawweb/avalon/trudoc.htm. See also Truman's speech given at Baylor University (March 6) discussing the economic aspects of his foreign policy plans, on the corresponding website to LaFeber, *America, Russia*: http://www.mhhe.com/lafeber. See pp. 62–3 for discussion.

61 See Paterson et al., *American Foreign Relations*, 2:240; and Leffler, *Preponderance*, 143.

62 Quoted in LaFeber, *America, Russia*, 64.

63 Gabriel Kolko, *Century of War: Politics, Conflicts, and Society Since 1914* (New York: New Press, 1994), 379–80.

64 Dean Acheson, *Present at the Creation: My Years in the State Department* (1969; reprint, New York: W. W. Norton, 1987), 219.

65 Quoted in Schmitz, *Thank God*, 17

66 Quotes from National Security Council paper 68 (NSC-68), authored in April 1950 and declassified in 1975. NSC-68 is perhaps the essential and fundamental statement of the US's Cold War policy. The document's at times evangelical, cosmic language becomes more extraordinary when attempts are made to square it with the surrounding historical realities. For its text see the Federation of American Scientists website: http://www.fas.org/irp/offdocs/nsc-hst/nsc-68.htm.

CHAPTER 3

1 See William L. Cleveland, *A History of the Modern Middle East*, 3rd ed. (Boulder, CO: Westview Press, 2004), 49; and Donald Quataert, *The*

Ottoman Empire, 1700–1922, 2nd ed. (Cambridge, UK: Cambridge University Press, 2005), 24.

2   Re at Kasaba, *The Ottoman Empire and the World Economy: The Nineteenth Century* (Albany, NY: SUNY Press, 1988), 18. Kasaba's is a short but scholarly analysis that some readers new to the subject may find slightly technical. However, his first and second chapters are worth considering.

3   Arthur Goldschmidt Jr. and Lawrence Davidson, *A Concise History of the Middle East,* 8th ed. (Boulder, CO: Westview Press, 2006), 172.

4   Quataert, *Ottoman Empire*, 189–90. Cf. James L. Gelvin, *The Modern Middle East: A History* (New York: Oxford University Press, 2005), 56–8.

5   Cleveland, *History*, 89.

6   Rashid Khalidi, *Resurrecting Empire: Western Footprints and America's Perilous Path in the Middle East* (Boston, MA: Beacon Press, 2005), 16.

7   Quoted in Charles D. Smith, *Palestine and the Arab–Israeli Conflict*, 6th ed. (Boston, MA: Bedford/St. Martin's, 2007), 60.

8   Albert Hourani, *A History of the Arab Peoples* (New York: Warner, 1991), 283.

9   The correspondence is reproduced in George Antonius, *The Arab Awakening: The Story of the Arab National Movement* (1938; reprint, New York: Capricorn Books, 1965), 413–27.

10 See Smith, *Palestine*, 68.

11 The text of the Sykes–Picot Agreement is available on the Avalon Project, http://www.yale.edu/lawweb/avalon/mideast/sykes.htm. See also Walter Laqueur and Barry Rubin, eds., *The Israeli–Arab Reader: A Documentary History of the Middle East Conflict,* 6th ed. (New York: Penguin, 2001), 13–16.

12 Quoted in Smith, *Palestine,* 80.

13 The text of the Covenant of the League of Nations is available on the Avalon Project, http://www.yale.edu/lawweb/avalon/leagcov.htm.

14 Cleveland, *History*, 164.

15 Benny Morris, *Righteous Victims: A History of the Zionist–Arab Conflict, 1881–2001* (New York: Vintage, 2001), 73.

16 Justin McCarthy, *The Population of Palestine: Population Statistics of the Late Ottoman Period and the Mandate* (New York: Columbia University Press, 1990), 10.

17 Morris, *Righteous Victims*, 49. For substantive documentation of the idea of population transfer in Zionist thinking, see Chapter 2 in Morris's *The Birth of the Palestinian Refugee Problem Revisited* (Cambridge, UK: Cambridge University Press, 2004), 39–61; and Nur Masalha, *Expulsion of the Palestinians: The Concept of "Transfer" in Zionist Political Thought, 1882–1948* (Washington, DC: Institute for Palestine Studies, 1992).

18 Raphael Patai, ed., *The Complete Diaries of Theodor Herzl*, trans.

Harry Zohn (New York: Herzl Press and Thomas Yoseloff, 1960), 1:88; cited in Morris, *Birth*, 41.

19 Quoted in Masalha, *Expulsion*, 32 (see 9). See also Simha Flapan, *Zionism and the Palestinians* (London: Croom Helm, 1979), 67–70.

20 Quoted in Kathleen Christison, *Perceptions of Palestine: Their Influence on U.S. Middle East Policy* (Berkeley, CA: University of California Press, 2001), 93.

21 Quoted in John J. Mearsheimer and Stephen M. Walt, *The Israel Lobby and U.S. Foreign Policy* (New York: Farrar, Straus & Giroux, 2007), 96.

22 Flapan, *Zionism*, 141.

23 Quote from the summary "Report of the Palestine Royal Commission," available on the United Nations Information System on the Question of Palestine (UNISPAL) website, http://domino.un.org/unispal.nsf. Excerpts from the actual report are printed in Smith, *Palestine*, 161–5; and Laqueur and Rubin, *Israeli–Arab Reader*, 41–3.

24 See Henry L. Feingold, *The Politics of Rescue: The Roosevelt Administration and the Holocaust, 1938–1945* (New York: Holocaust Publications; New Brunswick, NJ: Rutgers University, 1970).

25 McCarthy, *Population*, 36.

26 Avi Shlaim, *The Iron Wall: Israel and the Arab World* (New York: W. W. Norton, 1999), 25.

27 For text and discussion of Plan Dalet (and Plan Gimmel, or Plan C), see Walid Khalidi, "Plan Dalet: Master Plan for the Conquest of Palestine," *Journal of Palestine Studies*, 18, no. 1 (Autumn 1988). There is disagreement among scholars as to whether Plan Dalet constituted a premeditated objective for expulsion. The leading scholar on the subject, Benny Morris, rejects this notion, yet states, perhaps curiously, that

> The essence of the plan was the clearing of hostile and potentially hostile forces out of the interior of the territory of the prospective Jewish State.… The Haganah regarded almost all the villages as actively or potentially hostile.… Plan D provided for the conquest and permanent occupation, or leveling, of villages and towns.… The plan gave each brigade discretion in its treatment of villages in its zone of operations.… [I]t constituted a strategic-doctrinal basis and carte blanche for expulsions … by commanders.… and it gave commanders, post facto, formal, persuasive cover for their actions.
>
> (Morris, *Birth*, 164–5. See also 60–1, 166–7)

For a well-reasoned analysis of Morris's conclusions, see Norman G. Finkelstein, *Image and Reality of the Israel–Palestine Conflict*, 2nd ed. (London: Verso, 2003), 51–87. Cf. Masalha, *Expulsion*, 175–99; and Simha Flapan, *The Birth of Israel: Myths and Realities* (New York: Pantheon, 1987), 83–118.

CHAPTER 4

1 Quoted in Joyce Kolko and Gabriel Kolko, *The Limits of Power: The World and United States Foreign Policy, 1945–1954* (New York: Harper & Row, 1972), 71.

2 See "Robert Fisk Criticizes 'Experts' Cited in Iraq Study Group Report" (keynote, Muslim Public Affairs Council, December 16, 2006), Democracy Now!, December 20, 2006, http://www.democracynow. org.

3 Quoted in Stephen Kinzer, *All the Shah's Men: An American Coup and the Roots of Middle East Terror* (Hoboken, NJ: John Wiley & Sons, 2003), 39.

4 Daniel Yergin, *The Prize: The Epic Quest for Oil, Money, and Power* (New York: Free Press, 1991), 393. Yergin's is a leading account of oil, its corresponding industry, and the role they have played around the world from the late nineteenth century to the 1991 Gulf War.

5 Quoted in ibid., 394.

6 Quoted in ibid., 393.

7 David S. Painter, *Oil and the American Century: The Political Economy of U.S. Foreign Oil Policy, 1941–1954* (Baltimore, MD: Johns Hopkins University Press, 1986), 34, passim (e.g. see 116). For the birth of US foreign oil policy, and the attendant relations between public and private power, Painter's is a standard study. In the United Kingdom, the book was published with a slightly more descriptive title, *Private Power and Public Policy: Multinational Oil Corporations and U.S. Foreign Policy, 1941–1954*.

8 Yergin, *The Prize*, 424. Cf. ibid., 425; and Melvyn P. Leffler, *A Preponderance of Power: National Security, the Truman Administration, and the Cold War* (Stanford, CA: Stanford University Press, 1992), 419.

9 Quoted in Gabriel Kolko, *Confronting the Third World: United States Foreign Policy, 1945–1980* (New York: Pantheon, 1988), 70.

10 Quoted in Painter, *Oil*, 17.

11 Warren I. Cohen, *The Cambridge History of American Foreign Relations*, vol. 4, *America in the Age of Soviet Power, 1945–1991* (Cambridge, UK: Cambridge University Press, 1993), 31.

12 Quoted from NSC-68 (sections V-C, VII-B). See Chapter 2, note 61 for reference.

13 Quoted in Kolko, *Confronting*, 70.

14 Painter, *Oil*, 209.

15 Nikki R. Keddie, *Modern Iran: Roots and Results of Revolution* (New Haven, CT: Yale University Press, 2003), 125.

16 For a readable account of the story of Operation Ajax and the overthrow of Mossadeq told in narrative style, see Kinzer, *All the Shah's Men*, cited in note 3. Brief but useful overviews can be found in Keddie, *Modern Iran*, ch. 6; Stephen Kinzer, *Overthrow: America's*

Century of Regime Change from Hawaii to Iraq (New York: Times
Books/Henry Holt, 2006), 117–28; Tim Weiner, *Legacy of Ashes: The
History of the CIA* (New York: Doubleday, 2007), ch. 9; and Yergin,
The Prize, ch. 23.
17 Kinzer, *Overthrow*, 4.
18 Kathleen Christison, *Perceptions of Palestine: Their Influence on
U.S. Middle East Policy* (Berkeley, CA: University of California Press,
2001), 87.
19 Quoted in Steven L. Spiegel, *The Other Arab–Israeli Conflict: Making
America's Middle East Policy, from Truman to Reagan* (Chicago:
University of Chicago Press, 1985), 20. See also Andrew Cockburn
and Leslie Cockburn, *Dangerous Liaison: The Inside Story of the U.S.–
Israeli Covert Relationship* (New York: HarperCollins, 1991), 26.
20 For a realistic summary of Truman's decision making, see Ian J.
Bickerton and Carla L. Klausner, *A History of the Arab–Israeli
Conflict*, 5th ed. (Upper Saddle River, NJ: Pearson Prentice Hall,
2007), 82–3. See also Charles D. Smith, *Palestine and the Arab–Israeli
Conflict*, 6th ed. (Boston, MA: Bedford/St. Martin's, 2007), 186,
201–2; and Spiegel, *The Other*, 38–9.
21 Spiegel, *The Other*, 44.
22 Quoted in Camille Mansour, B*eyond Alliance: Israel and U.S. Foreign
Policy*, trans. James A. Cohen (New York: Columbia University Press,
1994), 70.
23 Quoted in Cockburn and Cockburn, *Dangerous Liaison,* 32.
24 Uri Bialer, *Between East and West: Israel's Foreign Policy Orientation,
1948–1956* (Cambridge, UK: Cambridge University Press, 1990),
241.
25 The text of the Tripartite Declaration Regarding the Armistice Borders
is available at the Avalon Project at Yale Law School, http://www.
yale.edu/lawweb/avalon/Middle East/mid001.htm. See also the UN
Information System on the Question of Palestine (UNISPAL), http://
domino.un.org/unispal.nsf.
26 See Mansour, *Beyond Alliance*, 76–7.
27 See Bialer, *East and West*, 200–2.
28 Howard M. Sachar, *A History of Israel: From the Rise of Zionism to
our Time*, 3rd ed. (New York: Alfred A. Knopf, 2007), 460.
29 Livia Rokach, *Israel's Sacred Terrorism*, 3rd ed. (Belmont, MA: AAUG
Press, 1986), 15. Rokach's book is a slender but invaluable analysis
of Sharett's diaries, offering rich documentary insight into what Israeli
elites were planning in the 1950s.
30 Quoted in Spiegel, *The Other*, 53.
31 Quoted in Salim Yaqub, *Containing Arab Nationalism: The Eisenhower
Doctrine and the Middle East* (Chapel Hill, NC: University of North
Carolina Press, 2004), 41; Smith, *Palestine*, 247.
32 See Stephen Green, *Taking Sides: America's Secret Relations with a
Militant Israel* (New York: William Morrow, 1984), 99–105; and Mark

Tessler, *A History of the Israeli–Palestinian Conflict* (Bloomington, IN: Indiana University Press, 1994), 338–9.

33 Quoted in Avi Shlaim, *The Iron Wall: Israel and the Arab World* (New York: W. W. Norton, 1999), 78.

34 Rokach, *Sacred Terrorism*, 45.

35 Benny Morris, *Righteous Victims: A History of the Zionist–Arab Conflict, 1881–2001* (New York: Vintage, 2001), 270; see also 269–79. For his standard text on the subject, see Benny Morris, *Israel's Border Wars, 1949–1956: Arab Infiltration, Israeli Retaliation, and the Countdown to the Suez War*, rev. ed. (Oxford: Clarendon Press, 1997).

36 Quoted in Smith, *Palestine*, 242.

37 Quoted in Spiegel, *The Other*, 83.

38 Quoted in Green, *Taking Sides*, 134; ibid., 137. For further internal comments and documentation about what US planners and intelligence officials suspected regarding Israel's goals and intentions, see Abraham Ben-Zvi, *Decade of Transition: Eisenhower, Kennedy, and the Origins of the American–Israeli Alliance* (New York: Columbia University Press, 1998), 43, 161–2n64–5.

39 Ben-Zvi, *Decade*, 61, 65, 66.

40 Quoted in Noam Chomsky, *World Orders Old and New*, rev. ed. (New York: Columbia University Press, 1996), 79.

41 For text of the Eisenhower Doctrine, see "Special Message to the Congress on the Situation in the Middle East," January 5, 1957 (section VI), published by the American Presidency Project (University of California at Santa Barbara), http://www.presidency.ucsb.edu/ws/index.php?pid=11007.

42 Kolko, *Confronting*, 84–5.

43 Yaqub, *Containing*, 270.

44 Spiegel, *The Other*, 93.

45 Quoted in Ben-Zvi, *Decade*, 80.

46 Quoted in Cockburn and Cockburn, *Dangerous Liaison*, 91.

47 Green, *Taking Sides*, 151; see also 154–7 (and ch. 7 in toto for US–Israeli nuclear concerns, 1948–67). For Eisenhower, see also Cockburn and Cockburn, *Dangerous Liaison*, 89.

48 Green, *Taking Sides*, 151, 159.

49 Seymour M. Hersh, *The Samson Option: Israel's Nuclear Arsenal and American Foreign Policy* (New York, Random House, 1991), 169. Although the subject of the White House consistently looking the other way regarding the Dimona reactor is covered throughout, see especially chapters 11, 12, and 14.

50 See Douglas Little, "The Making of a Special Relationship: The United States and Israel, 1957–68," *International Journal of Middle East Studies*, 25, no. 4 (November 1993): 573.

51 Quoted in Spiegel, *The Other*, 123–4. See also Little, "Special Relationship," 574–5.

52 Tessler, *History*, 374.
53 Zeev Maoz, *Defending the Holy Land: A Critical Analysis of Israel's Security & Foreign Policy* (Ann Arbor, MI: University of Michigan Press, 2006), 104.
54 Quoted in ibid., 103. See also Tom Segev, *1967: Israel, the War, and the Year that Transformed the Middle East*, trans. Jessica Cohen (New York: Metropolitan Books/Henry Holt, 2007), 193.
55 See Green, *Taking Sides*, 192, and appendix document #12 (p. 343–9), which presents scans of the declassified consular telegram.
56 Norman G. Finkelstein, *Image and Reality of the Israel–Palestine Conflict*, 2nd ed. (London: Verso, 2003), 133. Finkelstein's is a realistic and well-documented evaluation of the Syrian border issue as well as the subsequent two points regarding Nasser; see also ch. 5, esp. 130–40.
57 Morris, *Righteous Victims*, 303.
58 Tessler, *History*, 378.
59 See Segev, *1967*, 151–4.
60 See Finkelstein, *Image and Reality*, 125.
61 See ibid., 134–40; Maoz, *Defending*, 83–99; and Segev, *1967*, 226–31.
62 Segev, *1967*, 300, 296, 380, 407.
63 The text of UN 242 can be found on the Avalon Project at Yale Law School, http://www.yale.edu/lawweb/avalon/un/un242.htm. See also Walter Laqueur and Barry Rubin, eds., *The Israel–Arab Reader: A Documentary History of the Middle East Conflict*, 7th ed. (New York: Penguin, 2008), 116.
64 Mansour, *Beyond Alliance*, 95.
65 Nixon reiterated the points made in Guam, where he originally issued the doctrine, in his November 3, 1969, address to the nation on Vietnam. See Michael Waldman, ed., *My Fellow Americans: The Most Important Speeches of America's Presidents, from George Washington to George W. Bush* (Naperville, IL: Sourcebooks, 2003), 219.
66 The December 9, 1969, statement by Secretary Rogers can be found on the Israel Ministry of Foreign Affairs site, http://www.mfa.gov.il.
67 See William B. Quandt, *Peace Process: American Diplomacy and the Arab–Israeli Conflict Since 1967*, 3rd ed. (Washington, DC: Brookings Institution, 2005), 66; and Spiegel, *The Other*, 185.
68 Nadav Safran, Israel: *The Embattled Ally* (Cambridge, MA: Belknap Press/Harvard University, 1978), 455.
69 Quandt, *Peace Process*, 85.
70 Quoted in ibid., 89. See also Shlaim, *Iron Wall*, 300.
71 Quoted in Morris, *Righteous Victims*, 389.
72 Sadat's complete February 4, 1971, speech can be found in the online archives at the Anwar Sadat Chair for Peace and Development at University of Maryland, College Park, http://www.sadat.umd.edu.
73 Shlaim, *Iron Wall*, 317. See also Smith, *Palestine*, 326–8.

74 Quoted in Thomas G. Paterson et al., *American Foreign Relations: A History*, vol. 2, *Since 1895*, 6th ed. (Boston, MA: Houghton Mifflin, 2005), 380.

75 For specific discussion of the "oil weapon," see Yergin, *The Prize*, chs. 29, 30 (esp. 606–9, 613–17).

76 Laqueur and Rubin, *Israel–Arab Reader*, 206.

77 Norman Finkelstein offers an informative analysis supporting the conclusion that Israel's interest in a Sinai-for-peace settlement was born of the credibility Egypt established during the 1973 war. As he states, "removing Egypt from the Arab front was the crucial precondition for the war plans now set in motion," regarding Tel Aviv's aims of dislocating the PLO in Lebanon, and therefore Palestinian nationalism as a whole. See Finkelstein, *Image and Reality*, 166–71.

78 Sadat is often characterized as looking to avoid a conference co-chaired by the USSR, e.g. see Sachar, *History*, 844. Though the Egyptian leader was perhaps not altogether positive on the idea (Shlaim, *Iron Wall*, 359), William Quandt (*Peace Process*, 189) emphasizes that "it was Carter's inability to stand up to Israeli pressure, coupled with evidence that Carter was tired of spending so much time on an apparently intractable problem, that seems to have convinced Sadat to strike out on his own." See also Chomsky, *Fateful Triangle*, 70. For interpretation of Israel's hesitancy in relation to the Soviets, see Smith, *Palestine*, 362.

79 Sadat's entire Knesset speech is printed in T. G. Fraser, *The Middle East, 1914–1979* (New York: St Martin's Press, 1980), 151–63; for the portion of the speech regarding Palestine, see 159–60. For a slightly abridged version of the speech, see Laqueur and Rubin, *Israel–Arab Reader*, 207–15.

80 Begin presented the plan to President Carter on December 16, 1977, and reiterated the proposal to the Knesset on the 28th. See Laqueur and Rubin, *Israel–Arab Reader*, 218–20, for the Knesset speech.

81 For the text of the Camp David frameworks and treaty, see ibid., 222–8.

82 See Kinzer, *Overthrow*, 70–1; and William Blum, *Killing Hope: U.S. Military and CIA Interventions since World War II*, rev. ed. (Monroe, ME: Common Courage Press, 2004), 351. John Cooley cites "over four million" refugees in his *Unholy Wars: Afghanistan, America and International Terrorism*, 3rd ed. (London: Pluto Press, 2002), xv.

83 For a brief but insightful examination of the events of 1979—mainly the Iranian Revolution, the Camp David Accords, and the Russian invasion of Afghanistan—see David W. Lesch, *1979: The Year That Shaped the Modern Middle East* (Boulder, CO: Westview Press, 2001).

84 John Lewis Gaddis, *Strategies of Containment: A Critical Appraisal of American National Security Policy during the Cold War*, rev. ed. (New York: Oxford University Press, 2005), 345.

85 Carter's 1980 State of the Union Address is available online at the Jimmy Carter Library, http://www.jimmycarterlibrary.org.
86 Paterson et al., *American Foreign Relations*, 2:428–9.
87 A scan of PD-59, though heavily excised, is available online at the Jimmy Carter Library.
88 Walter LaFeber, *The American Age: U.S. Foreign Policy at Home and Abroad, 1750 to the Present*, 2nd ed. (New York: W. W. Norton, 1994), 701.
89 Cohen, *Cambridge History*, 219. Such descriptions are commonplace among the standard scholarly and collegiate histories.
90 Quoted in Spiegel, *The Other*, 400.
91 Donald Neff, *Fallen Pillars: U.S. Policy towards Palestine and Israel since 1945*, 2nd ed. (Washington, DC: Institute for Palestine Studies, 2002), 180.
92 Quandt, *Peace Process,* 249.
93 Text of the Venice Declaration (June 13, 1980) is available on the UN Information System on the Question of Palestine (UNISPAL), http://domino.un.org/unispal.nsf. See also "Text of the Venice Declaration," *New York Times*, June 14, 1980.
94 Cf. Morris, *Righteous Victims*, 507; and Smith, *Palestine*, 378.
95 The November 1981 Memorandum of Understanding is available on the Avalon Project. See also "Text of American–Israeli Agreement," *New York Times*, December 1, 1981.
96 Quoted in Spiegel, *The Other,* 411.
97 Quoted in Mansour, *Beyond Alliance*, 153.
98 Henry Kissinger, *Years of Upheaval* (Boston: Little, Brown, 1982), 483–4; quoted in Mansour, *Beyond Alliance*, 119.
99 Ze'ev Schiff and Ehud Ya'ari, *Israel's Lebanon War*, ed. and trans. Ina Friedman (New York: Simon and Schuster, 1984), 43.
100 Quoted in Tessler, *History*, 569.
101 Ibid., 571.
102 Chomsky, *Fateful Triangle*, 195.
103 For a review of the US–Israeli communications, see Schiff and Ya'ari, *Israel's Lebanon War*, ch. 4 (esp. 72–7).
104 See Chomsky, *Fateful Triangle,* 221–3. Benny Morris (*Righteous Victims*, 558) asserts that the 20,000 (19,085) figure "seems a vast exaggeration." Morris cites the figure anyway, referencing Rashid Khalidi, *Under Siege: P.L.O. Decisionmaking during the 1982 War* (New York: Columbia University Press, 1986), 200n5.
105 Bernard Gwertzman, "Reagan Turns to Israel," *New York Times Magazine*, November 27, 1983.
106 Quoted in Jonathan Marshall, Peter Scott Dale, and Jane Hunter, *The Iran–Contra Connection: Secret Teams and Covert Operations in the Reagan Era* (Boston, MA: South End Press, 1987), 93.
107 Jane Hunter, *Israeli Foreign Policy: South Africa and Central America* (Boston, MA: South End Press, 1987), 98–102.

108 Quoted in Blum, *Killing Hope*, 352.
109 Quoted in Walter LaFeber, *Inevitable Revolutions: The United States in Central America*, 2nd ed. (New York: W. W. Norton, 1993), 271.
110 Quoted in Blum, *Killing Hope*, 300.
111 Weiner, *Legacy of Ashes*, 380.
112 John Prados, *Presidents' Secret Wars: CIA and Pentagon Covert Operations from World War II through the Persian Gulf*, rev. ed. (Chicago: Elephant/Ivan R. Dee, 1996), 397–8.
113 Quoted in Blum, *Killing Hope*, 295. See also pp. 295–6 and 363–5 for further discussion on this matter.
114 Quoted in Weiner, *Legacy of Ashes*, 383.
115 "The Gates Hearings, Text of Gates's 1984 Memo to Casey on 'Straight Talk' About Nicaragua," *New York Times*, September 20, 1991. See LaFeber, *Inevitable Revolutions*, 304.
116 Jeremy M. Sharp, "U.S. Foreign Assistance to the Middle East: Historical Background, Recent Trends, and the FY2008 Request" (RL32260), Congressional Research Service, July 3, 2007. See also Jeremy M. Sharp, "U.S. Foreign Aid to Israel" (RL33222), Congressional Research Service, January 2, 2008.
117 Carol Migdalovitz, "Israel: Background and Relations with the United States" (RL33476), Congressional Research Service, September 8, 2008.
118 Clyde R. Mark, "Israel: U.S. Foreign Assistance" (IB85066), Congressional Research Service, July 12, 2004.
119 Sharp, "U.S. Foreign Aid to Israel."
120 Migdalovitz, "Israel."
121 Donald Neff, "An Updated List of Vetoes Cast by the United States to Shield Israel from Criticism by the U.N. Security Council," *Washington Report on Middle East Affairs*, May/June 2005, http://www.wrmea.com/archives/May-June_2005/0505014.html.
122 Steven L. Spiegel, "U.S. Relations With Israel: The Military Benefits," *Orbis* (Fall 1986): 94.

CHAPTER 5

1 For information, see the UN Office for the Coordination of Humanitarian Affairs – Occupied Palestinian Territory (OCHA), http://www.ochaopt.org. See also the following human rights organizations: Amnesty International, http://www.amnesty.org; B'Tselem, http://www.btselem.org; Gisha, http://www.gisha.org; and Human Rights Watch, http://www.hrw.org.
2 Tovah Lazaroff, "Sharon: Occupation is 'Terrible' for Israel," *Jerusalem Post*, May 27, 2003.
3 Statistics published by B'Tselem, http://www.btselem.org/english/statistics.

4   Melvyn P. Leffler, *A Preponderance of Power: National Security, the Truman Administration, and the Cold War* (Stanford, CA: Stanford University Press, 1992), 99.

5   George C. Herring, *From Colony to Superpower: U.S. Foreign Relations since 1776* (New York: Oxford University Press, 2008), 134.

6   For a clear and informative analysis of this trend that readers might find thought provoking, see Immanuel Wallerstein, *The Decline of American Power: The U.S. in a Chaotic World* (New York: New Press, 2003).

7   The literature on the subject is extensive, though unfortunately it consists almost exclusively of academic and scholarly titles. For brief sketches of the main accords, see my and Todd Ferry's *The Palestine–Israel Conflict: A Basic Introduction*, 2nd ed. (London: Pluto Press, 2008), 112–16 (UN 242), 126–30 (Camp David I), 151–8 (Madrid-Oslo), 164–9 (Camp David II), 172 (Clinton Plan, Taba), 178–83 (Road Map, People's Voice, Geneva Accords), and 237–9 (suggested titles). For more detailed yet general discussion, see pertinent sections in Charles D. Smith, *Palestine and the Arab–Israeli Conflict*, 6th ed. (Boston, MA: Bedford/St. Martin's, 2007); and Ian J. Bickerton and Carla L. Klausner, *A History of the Arab–Israeli Conflict*, 5th ed. (Upper Saddle River, NJ: Pearson Prentice Hall, 2007). Three specific works on the peace process worth considering: William B. Quandt, *Peace Process: American Diplomacy and the Arab–Israeli Conflict since 1967*, 3rd ed. (Washington, DC: Brookings Institution, 2005), is a standard survey from 1967 to the 2003 Road Map; Shlomo Ben-Ami, *Scars of War, Wounds of Peace: The Israeli–Arab Tragedy* (New York: Oxford University Press, 2006), is a realistic account by an Israeli peace process participant, former foreign minister, and historian; and Yoram Meital, *Peace in Tatters: Israel, Palestine, and the Middle East* (Boulder, CO: Lynne Rienner, 2006), is a brief and informative analysis by an Israeli scholar. These and additional sources cited below.

8   See Tom Segev, *1967: Israel, the War, and the Year that Transformed the Middle East*, trans. Jessica Cohen (New York: Metropolitan Books/Henry Holt, 2007), 501; and Avi Shlaim, *The Iron Wall: Israel and the Arab World* (New York: W. W. Norton, 1999), 254.

9   Shlaim, *Iron Wall*, 254. For general discussion of the June 19 cabinet decision, see ibid., 253–5; Segev, *1967*, 501–5; and Zeev Maoz, *Defending the Holy Land: A Critical Analysis of Israel's Security & Foreign Policy* (Ann Arbor, MI: University of Michigan Press, 2006), 405–6. See also analysis and documentation in Norman G. Finkelstein, *Image and Reality of the Israel–Palestine Conflict*, 2nd ed. (London: Verso, 2003), 151–2, 260–1n4.

10   For text of UN 242, see Walter Laqueur and Barry Rubin, eds., *The Israel–Arab Reader: A Documentary History of the Middle East Conflict*, 7th ed. (New York: Penguin, 2008), 116. See also the UN

Information System on the Question of Palestine (hereafter UNISPAL) site, http://domino.un.org/unispal.nsf.

11 See Mark Tessler, *A History of the Israeli–Palestinian Conflict* (Bloomington, IN: Indiana University Press, 1994), 422; and Finkelstein, *Image and Reality*, 153.

12 Rogers A was contained in a speech given by the secretary; see "Text of Speech by Secretary Rogers on U.S. Policy in Middle East," *New York Times*, Dec. 10, 1969. The pertinent passages are also available in T. G. Fraser, *The Middle East, 1914–1979* (New York: St Martin's Press, 1980), 123–6. Rogers B was communicated in a letter, and is available on UNISPAL, entitled "The Ceasefire/Standstill Proposal," June 19, 1970.

13 For text of the Jarring aide-memoire, see Fraser, *Middle East*, 126–8.

14 Israel's response to Jarring available on the Israel Ministry of Foreign Affairs site, http://www.mfa.gov.il/mfa, under "The Jarring initiative and the response – 8 February 1971."

15 See Quandt, *Peace Process*, 87.

16 Nadav Safran, *Israel: The Embattled Ally* (Cambridge, MA: Belknap Press/Harvard University, 1978), 458–9.

17 Scans of Sadat's February 4, 1971, speech can be found online at the Sadat Archives, http://www.sadat.umd.edu, yet the source material is not identified and two pages (p. 250–1) are missing. A heavily abridged version containing the key passages is available in Raphael Israeli, ed., *The Public Diary of President Sadat*, vol. 1, *The Road to War, October 1970 – October 1973* (Leiden, NL: E.J. Brill, 1978), 30–2.

18 See Shlaim, *Iron Wall*, 306–7.

19 The text of UN 338 (October 22, 1973) is as follows:

> *The Security Council* (1) *Calls upon* all parties to the present fighting to cease all firing and terminate all military activity immediately, no later than 12 hours after the moment of the adoption of this decision, in the positions they now occupy; (2) Calls upon the parties concerned to start immediately after the cease-fire the implementation of Security Council resolution 242 (1967) in all of its parts; (3) Decides that, immediately and concurrently with the cease-fire, negotiations shall start between the parties concerned under appropriate auspices aimed at establishing a just and durable peace in the Middle East.
>
> (Source: UNISPAL)

20 The 1973 Geneva Conference was co-sponsored by the United States and the Soviet Union, chaired by the UN secretary-general, and attended by Egypt, Israel, and Jordan. Syria declined attendance, and the PLO were excluded as part of an American assurance to Israel. In turn, Israel's job was to be obstinate, but not too obstinate. According to William Quandt (*Peace Process*, 139), "Kissinger urged the Israelis not

to move too quickly in negotiations. Israel should not look weak. The Arabs should believe it was difficult for the United States to influence Israel; otherwise their expectations would soar." In Kissinger's words, "Our strategy depended on being the only country capable of eliciting Israeli concessions, but also on our doing it within a context where this was perceived to be a difficult task" (quoted in Steven L. Spiegel, *The Other Arab–Israeli Conflict: Making America's Middle East Policy, from Truman to Reagan* (Chicago: University of Chicago Press, 1985), 270). Nevertheless, the oil embargo remained a pressing issue, reflected in President Nixon's remarks to a group of governors: "The only way we're going to solve the crisis is to end the oil embargo, and the only way we're going to end the embargo is to get the Israelis to act reasonable. I hate to use the word blackmail, but we've got to do some things to get them to behave" (quoted in Quandt, *Peace Process,* 465n23). For general discussion, see Quandt, *Peace Process*, 138–41; Safran, *Israel*, 514–21; and Spiegel, *The Other*, 270–3.

21 For text of General Assembly resolutions 3236 and 3237, see UNISPAL. Resolution 3236 is printed in Fraser, *Middle East*, 143–4.

22 Quote from Security Council Resolution 381 (November 30, 1975), available on UNISPAL.

23 For text of draft resolution S/11940 (January 23, 1976), along with the entire council debate, see UNISPAL.

24 Consideration of the 1976 Arab proposal is rare in the general literature. Political analyst Noam Chomsky has correctly emphasized its existence and importance. See his *World Orders Old and New*, rev. ed. (New York: Columbia University Press, 1996), 218; and *Towards a New Cold War: U.S. Foreign Policy from Vietnam to Reagan* (1982; reprint, New York: New Press, 2003), 285, 330, 495n25.

25 Text of Likud platform in Laqueur and Rubin, *Israel–Arab Reader*, 206–7.

26 Helena Cobban, *The Palestinian Liberation Organization: People, Power and Politics* (Cambridge, UK: Cambridge University Press, 1984), 84; cited in Smith, *Palestine*, 360.

27 Text of the US–Soviet joint communiqué is available on the website that corresponds with Quandt's *Peace Process*: http://www.brookings.edu/press/appendix/peace_process.htm.

28 Sadat's November 9, 1977, speech is available on the Sadat Archives site.

29 For Sadat's November 19, 1977, Knesset speech, see Laqueur and Rubin, *Israel–Arab Reader*, 207–15.

30 Quoted in Shlaim, *Iron Wall*, 368.

31 Text of Camp David "Frameworks for Peace" in Laqueur and Rubin, *Israel–Arab Reader*, 222–7.

32 Quoted in Chomsky, *Fateful Triangle*, 77; for source, see Seth P. Tillman, *The United States in the Middle East: Interests and Obstacles* (Bloomington, IN: Indiana University Press, 1982), 218.

33 Tillman, *United States*, 222.
34 Quoted in Noam Chomsky, *Fateful Triangle*, 62.
35 Ben-Ami, *Scars of War*, 175–6.
36 Texts of the Fahd plan (August 7, 1981) and the Fez plan (September 9, 1982; contained in UN General Assembly annex S/15510, December 15, 1982) available on UNISPAL.
37 Text of the Shultz Plan in Laqueur and Rubin, *Israel–Arab Reader*, 321–2.
38 Quoted in Don Peretz, *Intifada: The Palestinian Uprising* (Boulder, CO: Westview Press, 1990), 169; see David K. Shipler, "Shultz Urges 'Historic' Israeli Step to End Impasse over Palestinians," *New York Times*, February 26, 1988. See also Shlaim, *Iron Wall*, 456–7.
39 See Kathleen Christison, *Perceptions of Palestine: Their Influence on U.S. Middle East Policy* (Berkeley, CA: University of California Press, 2001), 237.
40 The main 1988 items predating the Algiers summit are the "Fourteen Demands" (January), the "Sharif statement" (June), and the "Husseini document" (August). All three can be found in Peretz, *Intifada*, appendices 3–5 (p. 201–10). The first two are also printed in the *Journal of Palestine Studies*, 17, no. 3 (Spring 1988): 63–5; and 18, no. 1 (Autumn 1988): 272–5. The Fourteen Demands (or Points) are also available in Laqueur and Rubin, *Israel–Arab Reader*, 317–19. For the Algiers independence declaration and political communiqué, see ibid., 349–58; also reprinted in Peretz, *Intifada*, appendices 6 and 7 (p. 211–19); and *Journal of Palestine Studies*, 18, no. 2 (Winter 1988): 213–16, 216–23.
41 See Tessler, *History*, 722, 735.
42 Thomas L. Friedman, "U.S. to Seek Talks between Israelis and Local Arabs," *New York Times*, March 22, 1989; cited in Tessler, *History*, 723, 853n127.
43 Text of the Shamir Plan in Laqueur and Rubin, *Israel–Arab Reader*, 359–62.
44 Joel Brinkley, "Shamir Vote Plan: Closing the Palestinian Options," *New York Times*, April 24, 1989.
45 Text of Mubarak's ten-point plan in Laqueur and Rubin, *Israel–Arab Reader*, 362–3.
46 Text in ibid., 367–8.
47 "Excerpts From Iraqi Document on Meeting with U.S. Envoy," *New York Times*, September 23, 1990. See also Elaine Sciolino with Michael R. Gordon, "U.S. Gave Iraq Little Reason not to Mount Kuwait Assault," *New York Times*, September 23, 1990.
48 Quoted in Quandt, *Peace Process*, 309.
49 Meron Benvenisti, *Intimate Enemies: Jews and Arabs in a Shared Land* (Berkeley, CA: University of California Press, 1995), 151–2.
50 Donald Neff, *Fallen Pillars: U.S. Policy towards Palestine and Israel since 1945*, 2nd ed. (Washington, DC: Institute for Palestine Studies, 2002), 162.

51 Ibid.
52 David Hoffman, "Shamir Plan was to Stall Autonomy; Rabin Says He'll Cut Subsidies to Settlers," *Washington Post*, June 27, 1992. Cf. Clyde Haberman, "Shamir is Said to Admit Plan to Stall Talks 'or 10 Years,'" *New York Times*, June 27, 1992. A spokesman in the *NYT* article called into question the accuracy of the prime minister's remark. William Quandt (*Peace Process*, 491n47) comments: "Subsequently, Shamir claimed that he had been misinterpreted. But even his clarifications indicated that he envisaged the 'interim' agreement as lasting an indefinite time, during which Israel would continue to build settlements." See also Neff, *Fallen Pillars*, 162–3; and Shlaim, *Iron Wall*, 500.
53 Statistic reported by B'Tselem.
54 Clyde Haberman, "The Secret Peace/A Special Report; How Oslo Helped Mold the Mideast Pact," *New York Times*, September 5, 1993. Haberman's extended article sketches out how the Oslo talks came to be, how they were conducted, and who the main participants were.
55 Text of the "Declaration of Principles on Interim Self-Government Arrangements," including the Arafat–Rabin letters, is printed in Laqueur and Rubin, *Israel–Arab Reader*, 413–25; and is available online at the Israel Ministry of Foreign Affairs site.
56 For Darwish's letter of resignation, see Laqueur and Rubin, *Israel–Arab Reader*, 411–13. See also Youssef M. Ibrahim, "Palestinian Critics Accuse Arafat of Secret Concessions to Israelis," *New York Times*, August 25, 1993.
57 Edward W. Said, *Peace and Its Discontents: Essays on Palestine in the Middle East Peace Process* (New York: Vintage, 1996), x.
58 Ben-Ami, *Scars of War*, 211.
59 Benvenisti, *Intimate Enemies*, 214–15.
60 Text of the "Israeli–Palestinian Interim Agreement on the West Bank and the Gaza Strip" (hereafter "Interim Agreement") is available on the Israel Ministry of Foreign Affairs site.
61 "Interim Agreement," article XI, 3c.
62 Said, *Peace and Its Discontents*, 7.
63 Charles Enderlin, *Shattered Dreams: The Failure of the Peace Process in the Middle East, 1995–2002* (New York: Other Press, 2002), 148. See also Clayton E. Swisher, *The Truth about Camp David: The Untold Story about the Collapse of the Middle East Peace Process* (New York: Nation Books, 2004), 206–7. The Enderlin text is a standard account. Swisher, who cites Enderlin throughout his endnotes, added much to our knowledge about Camp David with his book, which is endorsed by Enderlin. Both are essential reading on the subject.
64 See Jeremy Pressman, "Visions in Collision: What Happened at Camp David and Taba?" *International Security,* 28, no. 2 (Fall 2003): 16–18. According to Pressman:

   [T]he 91 percent land offer was based on the Israeli definition of the

West Bank, but this differs by approximately 5 percentage points from the Palestinian definition. Palestinians use a total area of 5,854 square kilometers. Israel, however, omits the area known as No Man's Land (50 sq. km near Latrun), post-1967 East Jerusalem (71 sq. km), and the territorial waters of the Dead Sea (195 sq. km), which reduces the total to 5,538 sq. km. Thus, an Israeli offer of 91 percent (of 5,538 sq. km) of the West Bank translates into only 86 percent from the Palestinian perspective.

So the Israeli 91 percent offer was actually 86 percent for starters, not including further subtractions. See also Enderlin, *Shattered Dreams,* 206–8, 211–12, 213–14, 226–7, 242, 249–50; and Swisher, *The Truth,* 295, 310–19.

65   The epilogue in Swisher, *The Truth,* 335ff., contains informative discussion and numerous quotes on this point.

66   Hussein Agha and Robert Malley, "Camp David: The Tragedy of Errors," *New York Review of Books,* 48, no. 13 (August 9, 2001): section 4. For further comment on procedural matters, see Yoram Meital, *Peace in Tatters: Israel, Palestine, and the Middle East* (Boulder, CO: Lynne Rienner, 2006), 80–3.

67   Swisher, *The Truth,* 352.

68   Enderlin, *Shattered Dreams,* 242. See also Swisher, *The Truth,* 318.

69   Enderlin, *Shattered Dreams,* 202. Regarding Resolution 242, see also Swisher, *The Truth,* 262–3, 268–9. For comments on UN 242, Palestinian concessions, and the Palestinian map, see Pressman, "Visions in Collision," 22–3.

70   Palestinian negotiator Saeb Erakat's remarks to Clinton on this matter (quoted in Enderlin, *Shattered Dreams,* 254–5) provide a clear summary of the Palestinian perspective. See discussion of this perspective in Hussein and Agha, "Camp David," section 5.

71   Pressman, "Visions in Collision," 37.

72   Text of Clinton Plan in Enderlin, *Shattered Dreams,* 334–9; and Laqueur and Rubin, *Israel–Arab Reader,* 562–4.

73   The European Union envoy Miguel Moratinos, the only external observer at the event, compiled a report of the summit, after showing drafts to both delegations, which expressed their approval of the "Moratinos document." See Akiva Eldar, "'Moratinos Document': The peace that nearly was at Taba," *Haaretz,* February 14, 2002, http://www.haaretz. com; the article is also available on McGill University's site, http://www. arts.mcgill.ca/mepp/prrn/papers/moratinos.html. The Israeli–Palestinian joint statement, or Taba statement (January 27, 2001), is available on UNISPAL and the Israel Ministry of Foreign Affairs site.

74   Thomas L. Friedman, "An Intriguing Signal from the Saudi Crown Prince," *New York Times,* February 17, 2002.

75   Text of "Arab peace plan of 2002" on BBC News site, http://news.bbc. co.uk/2/hi/middle_east/1844214.stm.

76 See Aviv Lavie, "The peoples' choice," *Haaretz,* July 10, 2003.
77 For complete text of the Geneva Accord, see UNISPAL; see also Yossi Beilin, *The Path to Geneva: The Quest for a Permanent Agreement, 1996–2004* (New York: RDV Books, 2004), appendix 5.
78 The text of "A Performance-Based Roadmap to a Permanent Two-State Solution to the Israeli–Palestinian Conflict," is available on the UN's site, http://www.un.org/media/main/roadmap122002.html.
79 See Steven Lee Meyers and Helene Cooper, "Framework Set by Palestinians and Israelis for Peace Talks," *New York Times*, November 27, 2007.
80 "Text of Bush's Remarks at Annapolis Conference," *New York Times*, November 27, 2007.
81 See Donald Macintyre, "Angry start to Palestinian talks," *Independent*, December 13, 2007; and Ilene R. Prusher, "Mideast talks already tangled a month after Annapolis summit," *Christian Science Monitor*, December 27, 2007.
82 Michael Abramowitz, "Rice: Peace in Middle East is a Top Priority for Bush," *Washington Post*, October 15, 2007.
83 Resolution 63/29 (January 22, 2009) is available on UNISPAL. Voting records can be found on the UN Bibliographic Information System, or UNBISnet, http://unbisnet.un.org.
84 Glenn Kessler, "Clinton Pursues 'Comprehensive Peace' in Mideast," *Washington Post*, March 2, 2009.
85 Herring, *From Colony to Superpower,* 95.

CHAPTER 6

1 US Senate website, http://www.senate.gov.
2 A useful resource for lobbying information and data tracking is the OpenSecrets.org site, operated by the Center for Responsive Politics, http://www.opensecrets.org.
3 American Israel Public Affairs Committee (AIPAC), http://www.aipac.org.
4 OpenSecrets.org.
5 Glenn Frankel, "A Beautiful Friendship?" *Washington Post*, July 16, 2006.
6 Jeffrey H. Birnbaum, "Washington's Power 25," *Fortune*, December 8, 1997; and Jeffrey H. Birnbaum, "Fat & Happy in D.C." ("Washington Power 25"), *Fortune*, May 28, 2001.
7 Conference of Presidents of Major American Jewish Organizations, http://www.conferenceofpresidents.org.
8 See the United Jewish Communities report, "The National Jewish Population Survey, 2000–01," http://www.ujc.org. See also the Pew Forum on Religious and Public Life report, "U.S. Religious Landscape Survey," February 2008, http://www.pewforum.org.

9   Howard M. Sachar, *A History of the Jews in America* (New York: Alfred A. Knopf, 1992), 713.

10   Ibid.

11   Edward Tivnan, *The Lobby: Jewish Political Power and American Foreign Policy* (New York: Simon & Schuster, 1987), 54–5. See also Steven L. Spiegel, *The Other Arab–Israeli Conflict: Making America's Middle East Policy, from Truman to Reagan* (Chicago: University of Chicago Press, 1985), 6–7.

12   J. J. Goldberg, *Jewish Power: Inside the American Jewish Establishment* (New York: Basic Books, 1996), 137.

13   Paul Findley, *They Dare to Speak Out: People and Institutions Confront Israel's Lobby*, 3rd ed. (Chicago: Lawrence Hill, 2003), 28.

14   Cheryl A. Rubenberg, *Israel and the American National Interest: A Critical Examination* (Urbana, IL: University of Illinois Press, 1986), 375, 353, 345.

15   Tivnan, *The Lobby*, 168. See 166–80 passim.

16   George W. Ball and Douglas B. Ball, *The Passionate Attachment: America's Involvement with Israel, 1947 to the Present* (New York: W. W. Norton, 1992), 221; see also ch. 10.

17   See Goldberg, *Jewish Power*, 13, 199. Though a temperate and informative book, Goldberg includes Noam Chomsky's *Fateful Triangle* and Stephen Green's *Taking Sides* (see Bibliography) in his list of works asserting a "stranglehold" interpretation of the lobby's power—"a Jewish swaggering superpower ... in Washington"—which is a careless misreading of these texts. Chomsky's thoughts on the lobby debate are covered later in the chapter.

18   John J. Mearsheimer and Stephen M. Walt, "The Israel Lobby and U.S. Foreign Policy," *London Review of Books*, March 23, 2006, http://www.lrb.co.uk/v28/n06/mear01_.html. See also Harvard's KSG site for a downloadable version (Working Paper RWP06-011) with endnotes: http://ksgnotes1.harvard.edu/research/wpaper.nsf/rwp/RWP06-011. References and quotes throughout the chapter will correspond with the book, John J. Mearsheimer and Stephen M. Walt, *The Israel Lobby and U.S. Foreign Policy* (New York: Farrar, Straus & Giroux, 2007).

19   Mearsheimer and Walt, *Israel Lobby*, 5.

20   Ibid., 8.

21   Ibid., 8–9.

22   Ibid., 10.

23   Ibid., 14.

24   Ibid., 49.

25   Ibid., 58, 51.

26   Ibid., 52.

27   Ibid., 62, 74.

28   Ibid., 112–14.

29   Ibid., 168.

30   Ibid., 199.

31   Ibid.
32   Ibid., 202.
33   Ibid., 230.
34   The *Christian Science Monitor*, in a "special project" featured on
     its website, offers an adequate introduction to the neoconservative
     phenomenon and some of its key players. On the "roots of
     neoconservative beliefs":

> The original neocons were a small group of mostly Jewish liberal
> intellectuals who, in the 1960s and 70s, grew disenchanted with
> what they saw as the American left's social excesses and reluctance
> to spend adequately on defense. Many of these neocons worked
> in the 1970s for Democratic Senator Henry "Scoop" Jackson, a
> staunch anti-communist. By the 1980s, most neocons had become
> Republicans, finding in President Ronald Reagan an avenue for
> their aggressive approach of confronting the Soviet Union with
> bold rhetoric and steep hikes in military spending. After the Soviet
> Union's fall, the neocons decried what they saw as American
> complacency. In the 1990s, they warned of the dangers of reducing
> both America's defense spending and its role in the world.

See "Empire Builders: Neoconservatives and their blueprint for US
power," *Christian Science Monitor*, June 2005, http://www.csmonitor.
com/specials/neocon/index.html. The Bush II administration appointed
a number of neocons to influential positions, for example, Paul
Wolfowitz, Richard Perle, Lewis Libby, John Bolton, and Elliott
Abrams.

35   Mearsheimer and Walt, *Israel Lobby*, 233.
36   Ibid., 263.
37   Ibid., 282.
38   Ibid., 334, 333.
39   Jeffrey Goldberg, "The Usual Suspect," *New Republic*, October 8,
     2007.
40   Eliot A. Cohen, "Yes, it's Anti-Semitic," *Washington Post*, April 5,
     2006. For a longer, if agitated and puzzling, response to Mearsheimer
     and Walt along these and other lines, see Alan Dershowitz,
     "Debunking the Newest—and Oldest—Jewish Conspiracy: A Reply to
     the Mearsheimer–Walt 'Working Paper,'" Harvard University/John F.
     Kennedy School of Government, April 2006.
41   Abraham H. Foxman, *The Deadliest Lies: The Israel Lobby and the Myth
     of Jewish Control* (New York: Palgrave Macmillan, 2007), 48, 82.
42   Ibid., 227.
43   Benny Morris, "And Now for Some Facts," *New Republic*, May 8,
     2006. See also Goldberg, "The Usual Suspect."
44   Goldberg, "The Usual Suspect."
45   Walter Russell Mead, "Jerusalem Syndrome: Decoding the Israel
     Lobby," *Foreign Affairs*, November/December 2007.

46 Stephen Zunes, "The Israel Lobby: How Powerful is it Really?" *Foreign Policy in Focus*, May 16, 2006.
47 Noam Chomsky, "The Israel Lobby?" *ZNet*, March 28, 2006.
48 Mead, "Jerusalem Syndrome."
49 Zunes, "The Israel Lobby."
50 Michelle Goldberg, "Is the 'Israel Lobby' Distorting America's Mideast Policies?" *Salon*, April 18, 2006.
51 Joseph Massad, "Blaming the Lobby," *Al-Ahram*, March 23–29, 2006.
52 Zunes, "The Israel Lobby."
53 Norman G. Finkelstein, "The Israel Lobby: it's not Either/Or," *CounterPunch*, May 1, 2006.
54 Mead, "Jerusalem Syndrome."
55 Chomsky, "The Israel Lobby?"
56 Massad, "Blaming the Lobby"; Chomsky, "The Israel Lobby?"; Zunes, "The Israel Lobby."
57 See Mearsheimer and Walt, *Israel Lobby*, 274.
58 Ibid., 57.
59 Quoted in Israel Shahak, *Open Secrets: Israeli Nuclear and Foreign Policies* (London: Pluto Press, 1997), 41.
60 "Excerpts: Bin Laden video," BBC News, October 29, 2004, http://news.bbc.co.uk/2/hi/middle_east/3966817.stm.

CONCLUSION

1 Benjamin I. Page and Marshall M. Bouton, *The Foreign Policy Disconnect: What Americans Want from Our Leaders but Don't Get* (Chicago: University of Chicago Press, 2006).
2 Benedict Anderson, *Imagined Communities*, rev. ed. (London: Verso, 2006), 6–7.
3 Quoted in E. J. Hobsbawm, *Nations and Nationalism since 1780: Programme, Myth, Reality*, 2nd ed. (Cambridge, UK: Canto/Cambridge University Press, 1992), 44.
4 "Russian Leader Visits Venezuela in Show of Defiance," Agence France Press, November 26, 2008. Emphasis added. See Melvyn P. Leffler, *A Preponderance of Power: National Security, the Truman Administration, and the Cold War* (Stanford, CA: Stanford University Press, 1992), 18–19.

SELECT BIBLIOGRAPHY

Agha, Hussein, Shai Feldman, Ahmad Khalidi, and Ze'ev Schiff. *Track–II Diplomacy: Lessons from the Middle East*. Cambridge, MA: MIT Press, 2003.

Agha, Hussein, and Robert Malley. "Camp David: The Tragedy of Errors." *New York Review of Books*, 48, no. 13 (August 9, 2001).

Anderson, Benedict. *Imagined Communities*. Rev. ed. London: Verso, 2006.

Anderson, Perry. *Passages from Antiquity to Feudalism*. 1974. Reprint, London: Verso, 1996.

Antonius, George. *The Arab Awakening: The Story of the Arab National Movement*. 1938. Reprint, New York: Capricorn Books, 1965.

Aruri, Naseer H. *Dishonest Broker: The U.S. Role in Israel and Palestine*. Cambridge, MA: South End Press, 2003.

Ball, George W., and Douglas B. Ball. *The Passionate Attachment: America's Involvement with Israel, 1947 to the Present*. New York: W. W. Norton, 1992.

Beard, Charles A. *An Economic Interpretation of the Constitution of the United States*. 1913. Reprint, Mineola, NY: Dover, 2004.

Beilin, Yossi. *The Path to Geneva: The Quest for a Permanent Agreement, 1996–2004*. New York: RDV Books, 2004.

Ben-Ami, Shlomo. *Scars of War, Wounds of Peace: The Israeli–Arab Tragedy*. New York: Oxford University Press, 2006.

Ben-Zvi, Abraham. *Decade of Transition: Eisenhower, Kennedy, and the Origins of the American–Israeli Alliance*. New York: Columbia University Press, 1998.

Benvenisti, Meron. *Intimate Enemies: Jews and Arabs in a Shared Land*. Berkeley, CA: University of California Press, 1995.

Bialer, Uri. *Between East and West: Israel's Foreign Policy Orientation, 1948–1956*. Cambridge, UK: Cambridge University Press, 1990.

Bickerton, Ian J., and Carla L. Klausner. *A History of the Arab–Israeli Conflict*. 5th ed. Upper Saddle River, NJ: Pearson Prentice Hall, 2007.

Blum, William. *Killing Hope: U.S. Military and CIA Interventions since World War II*. Rev. ed. Monroe, ME: Common Courage Press, 2004.

Braudel, Fernand. *A History of Civilizations*. Trans. Richard Mayne. London: Penguin, 1993.

Bregman, Ahron. *Elusive Peace: How the Holy Land Defeated America*. London: Penguin, 2005.

Chomsky, Noam. *Fateful Triangle: The United States, Israel, and the Palestinians*. Rev. ed. Cambridge, MA: South End Press, 1999.

————. *World Orders Old and New*. Rev. ed. New York: Columbia University Press, 1996.

Christison, Kathleen. *Perceptions of Palestine: Their Influence on U.S. Middle East Policy*. Berkeley, CA: University of California Press, 2001.

Cleveland, William L. *A History of the Modern Middle East*. 3rd ed. Boulder, CO: Westview Press, 2004.

Cockburn, Andrew, and Leslie Cockburn. *Dangerous Liaison: The Inside Story of the U.S.–Israeli Covert Relationship*. New York: HarperCollins, 1991.

Cohen, Warren I. *The Cambridge History of American Foreign Relations*. Vol. 4, *America in the Age of Soviet Power, 1945–1991*. Cambridge, UK: Cambridge University Press, 1993.

Cooley, John. *Unholy Wars: Afghanistan, America and International Terrorism*. 3rd ed. London: Pluto Press, 2002.

Davies, Norman. *Europe: A History*. New York: HarperPerennial, 1996.

Enderlin, Charles. *Shattered Dreams: The Failure of the Peace Process in the Middle East, 1995–2002*. Trans. Susan Fairfield. New York: Other Press, 2002.

Findley, Paul. *They Dare to Speak Out: People and Institutions Confront Israel's Lobby*. 3rd ed. Chicago: Lawrence Hill Books, 2003.

Finkelstein, Norman G. *Image and Reality of the Israel–Palestine Conflict*. 2nd ed. London: Verso, 2003.

Flapan, Simha. *Zionism and the Palestinians*. London: Croom Helm, 1979.

Fraser, T. G. *The Middle East, 1914–1979*. New York: St. Martin's Press, 1980.

Gaddis, John Lewis. *Strategies of Containment: A Critical Appraisal of American National Security Policy During the Cold War*. Rev. ed. New York: Oxford University Press, 2005.

Ganshof, F. L. *Feudalism*. Trans. Philip Grierson. 3rd ed. New York: Harper & Row, 1964.

Gelvin, James L. *The Modern Middle East: A History*. New York: Oxford University Press, 2005.

Goldberg, J. J. *Jewish Power: Inside the American Jewish Establishment*. New York: Basic Books, 1996.

Goldschmidt, Arthur Jr., and Lawrence Davidson. *A Concise History of the Middle East*. 8th ed. Boulder, CO: Westview Press, 2006.

Green, Stephen. *Taking Sides: America's Secret Relations with a Militant Israel*. New York: William Morrow, 1984.

Greer, Thomas H., and Gavin Lewis. *A Brief History of the Western World*. 9th ed. Belmont, CA: Thomson Wadsworth, 2005.

Harms, Gregory, and Todd M. Ferry. *The Palestine–Israel Conflict: A Basic Introduction*. 2nd ed. London: Pluto Press, 2008.

Herring, George C. *From Colony to Superpower: U.S. Foreign Relations since 1776*. New York: Oxford University Press, 2008.

Hersh, Seymour M. *The Samson Option: Israel's Nuclear Arsenal and American Foreign Policy*. New York: Random House, 1991.

Hietala, Thomas R. *Manifest Design: American Exceptionalism and Empire*. Rev. ed. Ithaca, NY: Cornell University Press, 2003.

Hiro, Dilip. *Blood of the Earth: The Battle for the World's Vanishing Oil Resources*. New York: Nation Books, 2007.

Hobsbawm, E. J. *Nations and Nationalism since 1780: Programme, Myth, Reality*. 2nd ed. Cambridge, UK: Canto/Cambridge University Press, 1992.

Hofstadter, Richard. *The American Political Tradition: And the Men Who Made It*. 1948. Reprint, New York: Vintage, 1989.

Hourani, Albert. *A History of the Arab Peoples*. New York: Warner, 1991.

Hunt, Michael H. *Ideology and U.S. Foreign Policy*. New Haven, CT: Yale University Press, 1987.

Hunter, Jane. *Israeli Foreign Policy: South Africa and Central America*. Boston: South End Press, 1987.

Iriye, Akira. *The Cambridge History of American Foreign Relations*. Vol. 3, *The Globalizing of America, 1913–1945*. Cambridge, UK: Cambridge University Press, 1993.

Kamrava, Mehran. *The Modern Middle East: A Political History since the First World War*. Berkeley, CA: University of California Press, 2005.

Kasaba, Re at. *The Ottoman Empire and the World Economy: The Nineteenth Century*. Albany, NY: SUNY Press, 1988.

Keddie, Nikki R. *Modern Iran: Roots and Results of Revolution*. New Haven, CT: Yale University Press, 2003.

Khalidi, Rashid. *Resurrecting Empire: Western Footprints and America's Perilous Path in the Middle East*. Boston: Beacon Press, 2005.

———. *Sowing Crisis: The Cold War and American Dominance in the Middle East*. Boston: Beacon Press, 2009.

Kiernan, V. G. *America: The New Imperialism, from White Settlement to World Hegemony*. 1978. Reprint, London: Verso, 2005.

Kimmerling, Baruch, and Joel S. Migdal. *The Palestinian People: A History*. Cambridge, MA: Harvard University Press, 2003.

Kinzer, Stephen. *All the Shah's Men: An American Coup and the Roots of Middle East Terror*. Hoboken, NJ: John Wiley & Sons, 2003.

———. *Overthrow: America's Century of Regime Change from Hawaii to Iraq*. New York: Times Books/Henry Holt, 2006.

Koenigsberger, H. G. *Early Modern Europe, 1500–1789*. London: Longman, 1987.

Kolko, Gabriel. *Century of War: Politics, Conflicts, and Society since 1914*. New York: New Press, 1994.

———. *Confronting the Third World: United States Foreign Policy, 1945–1980*. New York: Pantheon, 1988.

Kolko, Joyce, and Gabriel Kolko. *The Limits of Power: The World and United States Foreign Policy, 1945–1954*. New York: Harper & Row, 1972.

LaFeber, Walter. *The American Age: U.S. Foreign Policy at Home and Abroad, 1750 to the Present*. 2nd ed. New York: W. W. Norton, 1994.

———. *America, Russia, and the Cold War, 1945–2006*. 10th ed. New York: McGraw Hill, 2008.

———. *Inevitable Revolutions: The United States in Central America*. 2nd ed. New York: W. W. Norton, 1993.

Laqueur, Walter, and Barry Rubin, eds. *The Israel–Arab Reader: A Documentary History of the Middle East Conflict*. 7th ed. New York: Penguin, 2008.

Leffler, Melvyn P. *A Preponderance of Power: National Security, the Truman Administration, and the Cold War*. Stanford, CA: Stanford University Press, 1992.

———. "The American Conception of National Security and the Beginnings of the Cold War, 1945–48." *American Historical Review*, 89, no. 2 (April 1984): 346–81.

Little, Douglas. "The Making of a Special Relationship: The United States and Israel, 1957–68." *International Journal of Middle East Studies*, 25, no. 4 (November 1993): 563–85.

Louis, Wm. Roger. *The British Empire in the Middle East, 1945–1951: Arab Nationalism, the United States, and Postwar Imperialism*. 1984. Reprint, Oxford: Clarendon/Oxford University Press, 2006.

Mahan, A. T. [Alfred Thayer]. "The United States Looking Outward." *Atlantic Monthly* (December 1890): 816–24.

Mansour, Camille. *Beyond Alliance: Israel in U.S. Foreign Policy*. Trans. James A. Cohen. New York: Columbia University Press, 1994.

Maoz, Zeev. *Defending the Holy Land: A Critical Analysis of Israel's Security & Foreign Policy*. Ann Arbor, MI: University of Michigan Press, 2006.

Marshall, Jonathan, Peter Scott Dale, and Jane Hunter. *The Iran–Contra Connection: Secret Teams and Covert Operations in the Reagan Era*. Boston: South End Press, 1987.

Masalha, Nur. *Expulsion of the Palestinians: The Concept of "Transfer" in Zionist Political Thought, 1882–1948*. Washington, DC: Institute for Palestine Studies, 1992.

McCarthy, Justin. *The Population of Palestine: Population Statistics of the Late Ottoman Period and the Mandate*. New York: Columbia University Press, 1990.

McNeill, William H. *A World History*. 4th ed. New York: Oxford University Press, 1999.

Mearsheimer, John J., and Stephen M. Walt. *The Israel Lobby and U.S. Foreign Policy*. New York: Farrar, Straus & Giroux, 2007.

Meital, Yoram. *Peace in Tatters: Israel, Palestine, and the Middle East*. Boulder, CO: Lynne Rienner, 2006.

Morris, Benny. *The Birth of the Palestinian Refugee Problem Revisited*. Cambridge, UK: Cambridge University Press, 2004.

———. *Righteous Victims: A History of the Zionist–Arab Conflict, 1881–2001*. New York: Vintage, 2001.

Neff, Donald. *Fallen Pillars: U.S. Policy Towards Palestine and Israel since 1945*. 2nd ed. Washington, DC: Institute for Palestine Studies, 2002.

———. *Warriors for Jerusalem: The Six Days that Changed the Middle East*. New York: Linden Press/Simon & Schuster, 1984.

Ninkovich, Frank. *Modernity and Power: A History of the Domino Theory in the Twentieth Century*. Chicago: University of Chicago Press, 1994.

Opello, Walter C., Jr., and Stephen J. Rosow. *The Nation-State and Global Order: A Historical Introduction to Contemporary Politics*. 2nd ed. Boulder, CO: Lynne Rienner, 2004.

Owen, Roger. *State, Power and Politics in the Making of the Modern Middle East*. 3rd ed. London: Routledge, 2004.

Painter, David S. *Oil and the American Century: The Political Economy of U.S. Foreign Oil Policy, 1941–1954*. Baltimore, MD: Johns Hopkins University Press, 1986.

Paterson, Thomas G., J. Garry Clifford, S. J. Maddock, D. Kisatsky, and K. J. Hagan. *American Foreign Relations: A History*. Vol. 1, *To 1920*. 6th ed. Boston: Houghton Mifflin, 2005.

———. *American Foreign Relations: A History*. Vol. 2, *Since 1895*. 6th ed. Boston: Houghton Mifflin, 2005.

Peretz, Don. *Intifada: The Palestinian Uprising*. Boulder, CO: Westview Press, 1990.

Perkins, Bradford. *The Cambridge History of American Foreign Relations*. Vol. 1, *The Creation of a Republican Empire, 1776–1865*. Cambridge, UK: Cambridge University Press, 1993.

Perkins, Dexter. *The Monroe Doctrine, 1823–1826*. 1927. Reprint, Gloucester, MA: Peter Smith, 1965.

Porter, Bruce D. *War and the Rise of the State: The Military Foundations of Modern Politics*. New York: Free Press, 1994.

Prados, John. *Presidents' Secret Wars: CIA and Pentagon Covert Operations from World War II through the Persian Gulf*. Rev. ed. Chicago: Elephant/Ivan R. Dee, 1996.

Pressman, Jeremy. "Visions in Collision: What Happened at Camp David and Taba?" *International Security*, 28, no. 2 (Fall 2003): 5–43.

Quandt, William B. *Peace Process: American Diplomacy and the Arab–Israeli Conflict since 1967*. 3rd ed. Washington, DC: Brookings Institution, 2005.

Quataert, Donald. *The Ottoman Empire, 1700–1922*. 2nd ed. Cambridge, UK: Cambridge University Press, 2005.

Reinhart, Tanya. *Israel/Palestine: How to End the War of 1948*. 2nd ed. New York: Seven Stories, 2005.

Roberts, J. M. *The New Penguin History of the World*. 4th ed. London: Penguin, 2002.

Rokach, Livia. *Israel's Sacred Terrorism*. 3rd ed. Belmont, MA: AAUG Press, 1986.

Roosevelt, Theodore. *The Winning of the West*. 4 vols. 1889, 1894, 1896. Reprint, New York: G. P. Putnam's Sons/Knickerbocker Press, 1928.

Rubenberg, Cheryl A. *Israel and the American National Interest: A Critical Examination*. Urbana, IL: University of Illinois Press, 1986.

Sachar, Howard M. *A History of Israel: From the Rise of Zionism to Our Time*. 3rd ed. New York: Alfred A. Knopf, 2007.

———. *A History of the Jews in America*. New York: Alfred A. Knopf, 1992.

Safran, Nadav. *Israel: The Embattled Ally*. Cambridge, MA: Belknap Press/Harvard University, 1978.

Said, Edward W. *Peace and Its Discontents: Essays on Palestine in the Middle East Peace Process*. New York: Vintage, 1996.

Schiff, Ze'ev, and Ehud Ya'ari. *Israel's Lebanon War*. Ed. and trans. Ina Friedman. New York: Simon & Schuster, 1984.

Schmitz, David F. *Thank God They're on Our Side: The United States and Right-Wing Dictatorships, 1921–1965*. Chapel Hill, NC: University of North Carolina Press, 1999.

Schoonover, Thomas. *Uncle Sam's War of 1898 and the Origins of Globalization*. Lexington, KY: University Press of Kentucky, 2003.

Segev, Tom. *1967: Israel, the War, and the Year that Transformed the Middle East*. Trans. Jessica Cohen. New York: Metropolitan Books/ Henry Holt, 2007.

Seton-Watson, Hugh. *Nations and States: An Enquiry into the Origins of Nations and the Politics of Nationalism*. Boulder, CO: Westview Press, 1977.

Shahak, Israel. *Open Secrets: Israeli Nuclear and Foreign Policies*. London: Pluto Press, 1997.

Shannon, Thomas Richard. *An Introduction to the World-System Perspective*. 2nd ed. Boulder, CO: Westview Press, 1996.

Shlaim, Avi. *The Iron Wall: Israel and the Arab World*. New York: W. W. Norton, 1999.

———. "The Oslo Accord." *Journal of Palestine Studies*, 23, no. 3 (Spring 1994): 24–40.

Smith, Charles D. *Palestine and the Arab–Israeli Conflict*. 6th ed. Boston: Bedford/St. Martin's, 2007.

Spiegel, Steven L. *The Other Arab–Israeli Conflict: Making America's Middle East Policy, from Truman to Reagan*. Chicago: University of Chicago Press, 1985.

Stephanson, Anders. *Manifest Destiny: American Expansionism and the Empire of Right*. New York: Hill & Wang, 1995.

Swisher, Clayton E. *The Truth About Camp David: The Untold Story about the Collapse of the Middle East Peace Process*. New York: Nation Books, 2004.

Tessler, Mark. *A History of the Israeli–Palestinian Conflict*. Bloomington, IN: Indiana University Press, 1994.

Tillman, Seth P. *The United States in the Middle East: Interests and Obstacles*. Bloomington, IN: Indiana University Press, 1982.

Tilly, Charles. *Coercion, Capital, and European States, AD 990–1992*. Rev. ed. Cambridge, MA: Blackwell, 1992.

Tivnan, Edward. *The Lobby: Jewish Political Power and American Foreign Policy*. New York: Simon & Schuster, 1987.

Todorov, Tzvetan. *The Conquest of America: The Question of the Other*. Trans. Richard Howard. 1984. Reprint, Norman, OK: Red River/ University of Oklahoma Press, 1999.

Turner, Frederick J. "The Problem of the West." *Atlantic Monthly* (September 1896): 289–97.

US Department of State (1948) *Foreign Relations of the United States 1948*, vol. 1, part 2: *General: The United Nations* (Washington, DC: GPO, 1976), 525.

Waldman, Michael, ed. *My Fellow Americans: The Most Important Speeches of America's Presidents, from George Washington to George W. Bush*. Naperville, IL: Sourcebooks, 2003.

Wallerstein, Immanuel. *World-Systems Analysis: An Introduction*. Durham, NC: Duke University Press, 2004.

Weiner, Tim. *Legacy of Ashes: The History of the CIA*. New York: Doubleday, 2007.

Williams, William Appleman. *The Tragedy of American Diplomacy*. Rev. ed. New York: W. W. Norton, 1972.

Wittes, Tamara Cofman, ed. *How Israelis and Palestinians Negotiate: A Cross-Cultural Analysis of the Oslo Peace Process*. Washington, DC: United States Institute of Peace, 2005.

Wolf, Eric R. *Europe and the People Without History*. 1982. Reprint, Berkeley, CA: University of California Press, 1997.

Woodward, Bob. *Veil: The Secret Wars of the CIA, 1981–1987*. 1987. Reprint, New York: Simon & Schuster, 2005.

Yaqub, Salim. *Containing Arab Nationalism: The Eisenhower Doctrine and the Middle East*. Chapel Hill, NC: University of North Carolina Press, 2004.

Yergin, Daniel. *The Prize: The Epic Quest for Oil, Money, and Power*. New York: Free Press, 1991.

Zertal, Idith, and Akiva Eldar. *Lords of the Land: The War Over Israel's Settlements in the Occupied Territories, 1967–2007*. Trans. Vivian Eden. New York: Nation Books, 2007.

Zinn, Howard. *A People's History of the United States: 1492–Present*. Rev. ed. New York: Harper Perennial, 2003.

INDEX